BUSINESS, TIME AND THOUGHT

Also by G. L. S. Shackle

EXPECTATION IN ECONOMICS
TIME IN ECONOMICS
EPISTEMICS AND ECONOMICS
IMAGINATION AND THE NATURE OF CHOICE
EXPECTATIONS, INVESTMENT AND INCOME
MATHEMATICS AT THE FIRESIDE
UNCERTAINTY IN ECONOMICS AND OTHER REFLECTIONS
DECISION, ORDER AND TIME IN HUMAN AFFAIRS
A SCHEME OF ECONOMIC THEORY
THE NATURE OF ECONOMIC THOUGHT
THE YEARS OF HIGH THEORY
EXPECTATION, ENTERPRISE AND PROFIT
AN ECONOMIC QUERIST
KEYNESIAN KALEIDICS

G. L. S. Shackle
by Oliver Thomas, 1983

Business, Time and Thought

Selected Papers of G. L. S. Shackle

Edited by
Stephen F. Frowen

M
MACMILLAN
PRESS

First published 1988

Published by
THE MACMILLAN PRESS LTD
Houndmills, Basingstoke, Hampshire RG21 2XS
and London
Companies and representatives
throughout the world

Typeset by Acorn Bookwork, Salisbury, Wiltshire

Printed in Hong Kong

British Library Cataloguing in Publication Data
Shackle, G. L. S.
Business, time and thought.
1. Economics—Philosophy
I. Title II. Frowen, Stephen F.
330.1 HB72
ISBN 0-333-39481-X

We, the author and the editor, dedicate this work to
Catherine Shackle

Contents

Acknowledgements

I wish to express my appreciation to all those editors of journals and books, and to their publishers, who gave me permission to reprint from published work the selections which are included in this volume. The details of first publication are given below.

1 'The Origination of Choice', in Kirzner, I. M. (ed.), *Subjectivism Intelligibility and Economic Understanding: Essays in Honour of Ludwig M. Lachmann on his Eightieth Birthday* (London: Macmillan, 1986) pp. 281–7.

2 'Means and Meaning in Economic Theory', *Scottish Journal of Political Economy*, vol. 29, no. 3, November 1982, pp. 223–34. Seventh Annual Lecture of the Scottish Economic Society delivered at the University of Stirling on 23 January 1982.

3 '*Treatise*, *Theory* and Time', in Rubio de Urquía, R. (ed.) *La Herencia de Keynes* (Madrid: Alianza Editorial, 1988). The Madrid volume contains the Spanish translation by Professor Lucas Beltrán of the original English version presented here.

4 'Cantillon Far Ahead of his Time', in *Homenaje a Lucas Beltrán* (Madrid: Editorial Moneda y Crédito, 1982) pp. 765–79.

5 'The Bounds of Unknowledge', in Wiseman, J. (ed.) *Beyond Positive Economics* (London: Macmillan, 1983) pp. 28–37.

6 'Harrod as Economist', in Spiegel, H. W. and Samuels, W. J. (eds) *Contemporary Economists in Perspective* (Greenwich, Connecticut: Jai Press Inc, 1984) pp. 85–92.

7 'Levels of Simplicity in Keynes's Theory of Money and Employment', *The South African Journal of Economics*, vol. 51, no 3, 1983 pp. 357–67.

8 'On Hicks's *Causality in Economics:* A Review Article', *Greek Economic Review*, vol 1, no 2, December 1979 pp. 43–55.

9 *On the Nature of Profit* The Finlay Lecture delivered on 24 May 1967 in University College, Dublin, *Woolwich Economic Papers* no 13, 1967 (London: Thames Polytechnic).

10 'The Romantic Mountain and the Classic Lake: Alan Coddington's *Keynesian Economics*', *Journal of Post-Keynesian Economics*, vol 6, no 2, Winter 1983–84 pp. 241–51.

11 'Marginalism: the Harvest', *The History of Political Economy*, vol 4, no 2, 1972 pp. 587–602.

12 'New Tracks for Economic Theory, 1926–1939', in Weintraub, S. (ed.) *Modern Economic Thought* (Oxford: Basil Blackwell and University of Pennsylvania Press, 1977) pp. 23–37.

13 'Hayek as Economist', in O'Brien, D. P. and Presley, J. R. (eds) *Pioneers of Modern Economics in Britain* (London: Macmillan, 1981) pp. 234–61.

14 'Keynes the Meeting-Point of History and Thought', in Poulon, F. and 13 economists *Les Écrits de Keynes* (Paris: Dunod, 1985) The paper included in the present volume is the first publication of the original English version of the French introduction to Part I 'Guerre et Paix' of *Les Écrits de Keynes* (pp. 19–23).

15 'Sir John Hicks' "IS–LM: an explanation": A Comment', *Journal of Post Keynesian Economics*, vol 4, no 3, Spring 1982 pp. 435–38.

16 'Controlling Industrial Economies: A Review Article', *Kyklos* vol 38, no 1, 1985 pp. 120–22.

17 'Markets, Entrepreneurs and Liberty: A Review Article', *History of Economic Thought Newsletter*, no. 36, Spring 1986.

18 This is an hitherto unpublished paper.

19 'News from Sweden', in Richards, H. (ed.) *Population, Factor Movements and Economic Development* Studies presented to Brinley Thomas (Cardiff: University of Wales Press, 1976) pp. 9–19.

20 'A Student's Pilgrimage', *Banca Nazionale del Lavoro Quarterly Review*, no 145, June 1983, pp. 107–16.

Preface

The idea to publish this volume of essays of G. L. S. Shackle was conceived during one of many memorable visits to George and Catherine Shackle at Alde House in Aldeburgh, enjoying their gracious hospitality and inspiring company. When I suggested the scheme to George Shackle, he at first hesitated about giving his consent, and it was the enthusiastic support of his wife which finally persuaded the author to allow me to go ahead with my endeavour. Moreover, without Catherine Shackle the present volume would never have seen the light for other reasons besides. In a deeper sense, she is the mentor of the papers included here, most of which might never have been written if George Shackle at his advanced age had not had the overwhelming good fortune of her encouragement and practical assistance of all kinds. She has given him the strength and energy through her all-embracing presence, intense interest, pertinent comments and endless care to write in his late seventies and early eighties more papers of outstanding quality than many scholars considerably younger would have been able to produce over the same number of years. In fact fifteen out of the twenty papers included in this volume were published between 1981 and 1987 when George Shackle ranged in age between 78 and 84 years.

For the unlimited help and advice from both George and Catherine Shackle in my editorial tasks, I am immensely grateful. Any remaining inaccuracies are entirely my own responsibility.

In spite of the fact that this book is entirely the product of the extraordinary talents of George Shackle at his time of life, both the author and the editor wish to acknowledge that it would never have been achieved without Catherine's wholehearted support, and it is for this reason that we wish to dedicate the volume to her.

March 1988 STEPHEN F. FROWEN

Introduction

This collection is, in effect, a sequel to G. L. S. Shackle's earlier collections of essays *Uncertainty in Economics and Other Reflections* (1955) and *The Nature of Economic Thought: Selected Papers 1955–1964* (1966).

There is a distinct principle which links the papers presented here, and the suggestion for the book title came into our heads without much searching. We felt from the beginning that a title for the collection as a whole should be invented on its own, not borrowing that of any essay. The title finally chosen, *Business, Time and Thought*, stood out because of its brevity and reference to the central ideas running through the essays. The expression 'business, time and thought' encapsulates exactly what this diverse but highly consistent body of pieces has as its theme from beginning to end.

Business requires imagination and nerve, it is able to yield brilliant successes because it can also yield failures and misfortune. The essence of all this is that the businessman embarks his hopes on time-to-come. No one can surpass you yourself in real and exigent direct knowledge of your business, and the words 'business' and 'time' are almost extensions of each other's meaning. The business of the businessman is thought.

The title *Business, Time and Thought* is meant to suggest philosophy and to bring the philosophical problems of business right into the market-place. George Shackle has always felt that 'business' describes the field of economists better than 'economics', a word fadged up from two Greek ones. In fact, the suggestion of philosophy in the title was deliberate, for these essays *are* concerned with philosophy. It is the philosophical aspect of economics which has always chiefly interested George Shackle. His books are concerned with philosophical problems: with 'epistemics', especially with the inescapable need to make decisions in the face of *un*knowledge. Economics is as wholly entangled with time as is history itself.

The word 'decision' was deliberately omitted from the title because, although 'decide' or 'decision' belong in the context of the book title, there is quite a danger of their becoming hackneyed. We further rejected the expression 'theory of business' as a title, as it would have suggested a rather detailed technical concern. George

Shackle does not claim in these essays to discuss as wide and complex a field as that – only the 'business of business-decisions'. Nor do these essays concern themselves with cut-and-dried simplified 'models'. Instead they are about the mutual forming of thought and event, linked by the middle term of action: enterprise. This is indeed what has always been George Shackle's slant on economics, and it is recognised as such. Perhaps readers should also be warned not to think of these essays as conventional economics. Nothing could have been further from the author's mind than this.

The general principle throughout the book has been to make successive essays as different from each other as possible. The inherent danger of grouping the essays by similarity of subject might have been to invite anyone who picked up the book to omit whole groups.

The essay on 'The Origination of Choice' was placed first as it is meant by the author to be a readable, condensed account of his oft-repeated theme. The second essay 'Means and Meaning in Economic Theory' might well stand as a sample of Shackle's kind of writing at its most characteristic, especially the last section of the paper entitled 'The unquiet market'. The third essay '*Treatise, Theory* and Time' is a long lecture on Keynes given in Madrid in 1984, which may be appreciated even by those readers with sated palates for that subject. That lecture sprang originally from a suggestion of Lucas Beltrán, for whose *Festschrift* Professor Shackle wrote the fourth essay on 'Cantillon Far Ahead of his Time'. The fifth essay entitled 'The Bounds of Unknowledge' is a true classic and, I think, the best statement yet of his decision-theory Shackle has produced to date.

The essay on Sir Roy Harrod (Chapter 6), whom Shackle describes as 'an innovator of the topmost rank', and on F. A. Hayek (Chapter 13), who 'on any reckoning . . . must be accorded by friend or foe his unquestioned place amongst the giants', are penetrating appraisals of two of the most outstanding economists of the twentieth century.

Business, Time and Thought includes further critical and illuminating essays on Keynes and Keynesianism, on the Swedish School, on Hicksean economics, on the nature of profit and on Shackle's views on marginalism. Those interested in the history of economic thought will be interested in the paper 'New Tracks for Economic Theory, 1926–1939' (Chapter 12), which is a brilliant assessment of the great spasms of creative effort in economic theory in the late 1920s and 1930s. It required an insider like Shackle to produce such a work.

Also included in this collection are the reviews of some books which provided the author with stimulus and scope for relating his thoughts to the views of others. Thus, these pieces also reveal much of George Shackle's train of thought.

Lastly, it seems fitting that this collection of essays should end on a personal note through the inclusion of George Shackle's absolutely charming autobiographical paper 'A Student's Pilgrimage'. This essay clearly shows the great advantages of growing up in a scholarly environment but also the adversities the author had to overcome during the precarious 1930s in pursuing his studies. Present-day students would do well to peruse this paper carefully.

As a whole, this collection serves well to illustrate not only the recent development of George Shackle's theoretical work but also the striking originality of his thought.

March 1988 STEPHEN F. FROWEN

1 The Origination of Choice

THOUGHT AND TIME

With Cantillon economic theory came suddenly to full flower in one great work, as a description of business. Business depends on numerical comparisons, and thus economic theory took on at the outset the air of a quantitative science. Many of the notions involved were measurements of natural or technical processes to whose relations the principles of nature gave repetitive constancy. But Cantillon incisively made plain that these relations provided only the rules of the game, within which the play and its results were the work of thought, of knowledge and irremediable lack of knowledge, and of the powers of mind which exploit that lack. Business appears as technics, but behind this lies psychics. Imagination, the power of conceiving the unprecedented, the alchemy of thought, are liberated and ignited by mankind's elemental predicament, human imprisonment in *present time*.

Present time is the transience of thought. Each moment of thought exists by its passage into another. It is succeeded by another. This succession is experienced, but it can also be imagined. The imagined unceasing succession of moments is time-to-come. Imagined time must itself be filled by work of imagination drawing suggestions from the present. The chooser amongst rival actions open to him, rival deployments of his resources, asks himself: What will the sequel be, if I do this, or if I do this? What can be the form of his answer?

Can this answer describe a singular, unequivocal path which, given his commitment to some specific action, the chooser supposes his affairs will follow? This would imply that he can know, when he makes his decision, just how the course of his affairs will be affected by choices of action made by others in time-to-come. Such knowledge of choices-to-come could only exist in the present, if each such choice was entirely determined by present circumstances and takings-place. To suppose that choices-to-come are thus predetermined destroys the meaning of choice, robbing human choices of all power of their own. The notion of choice would be empty and the act of choice sterile. A non-determinist view of history requires us to suppose that a choice can be in some respects exempt from governance by antecedent thought or contemporary circumstance, that a choice can be in some respects an *uncaused cause*. If so, the question that the chooser can validly ask himself, concerning a particular envisaged action, is: What, at best and at worst, can the sequel be? If, as my theme assumes, there is an essential, irreducible, pervasive non-determinacy in human affairs, no single supposed sequel can be deemed certain to prove true, no *list* of such hypotheses can be deemed certain to contain among its members the one that will prove true. The valid concept is a skein of imagined, invented sequels, a list *endlessly variant and augmentable*, subject only to the constraint of adjudged *possibleness*.

THE SKEIN OF POSSIBLES EPITOMISED BY BEST AND WORST

What the chooser should seek, for each of the rival actions he envisages, is a conception of the best and of the worst outcome he can deem possible for it. Then, how must he interpret 'best' and 'worst', and how must he interpret 'possible'? How, amongst rival envisaged actions, must he conceive the degree to which, in each, the best outcome deemed possible outweighs the worst for his purpose of choice? 'Best' and 'worst' refer of course to the desiredness or counter-desiredness of the outcomes according to his own psychics and circumstances and to the character of the imagined outcomes in any degree of their complexity. It seems evident that such a business of weighing good and bad and comparing the results of such weighing cannot in general be explicitly dissected. What splendour resides for the individual in some formal result, and what exposure to possible crippling misfortune he will accept for its sake, are matters surely unsearchable. There is little to be gained, I think, by searching for a scalar proxy for desiredness and counter-desiredness when these judgements apply to a complex or a vague result. It is only when they apply to an imagined sequel which is itself inherently numerical that the chooser between two available actions can make explicit the grounds of his choice. But in business it is just such cases that are pervasively typical. They arise momentously in the investment-decision, where large resources committed to an enterprise will bring their return only in the course of many years. All these suggestions, however, refer to sequels imagined for specific courses of action, and deemed *possible*. How is *possible* to be understood?

POSSIBLENESS

In order to bear upon choice of action, a hypothesis of the outcome must be deemed possible, that is to say, it must seem, after critical scrutiny, to be compatible with the chooser's entire body of suppositions about the nature of things and their existing posture, and about their orientation, the place assigned to them in the plans of others. I shall call this body of suppositions the chooser's subjective knowledge. We can suppose the chooser to ask himself, concerning each hypothesis he forms of the sequel of some action, whether it is entirely compatible with his body of knowledge, and if it is not, to dismiss it. This is to treat possibleness as a category. This view would simplify my theme, for it reduces the rivalry amongst imagined sequels of some action to the matter of their desiredness or counter-desiredness. Their possibleness is a matter of yes or no, not of degree. When, in this rivalry of content, the sequels which, up to the deadline-moment for decision, the chooser has had time to conceive are arranged in order from most desired to most counter-desired, it is evident, I think, that all others will be *eclipsed* by one or other of these two extremes. It is these two extremes amongst the sequels all equally deemed possible which will constitute for the chooser the power of his action to benefit or harm him. He cannot know what his action *will* do for him. The two extremes are what, at best and worst, he supposes that it *can* do.

The conception and procedure of the business of choice amongst actions, to which my suggestions lead, on the one hand, and those derived from the calculus of probabilities, on the other, stand in absolute contrast. Probabilities can be assigned only to the members of a list of kinds (a list of classes of result) taken to be exhaustive and therefore certain to include the true kind or class. The probability-table is a sharing of certainty and thus consists, in meaning if not in realisable practice, of proper fractions summing to unity. Probabilities in such a table are additive, and when multiplied respectively into the utilities of the items of the list, are in fact additively used, even when each choosable action will be, if adopted, a once-for-all, singular, crucial and self-destructive experiment. When the table of probabilities refers to a once-for-all experiment it implies the meaningless adding-together of mutual exclusives. Its irrelevance in such a case is made explicit when it is called a *frequency*-table. By contrast with these contradictions, possibleness is adjudged to a hypothesis or imagined sequel of specific action in its own right, regardless of the number of its rivals.

When the grounds of desiredness and counter-desiredness are themselves numerical, and when possibleness is for the chooser a yes-or-no category and not a matter of degree, the business of choice between two courses of action can be formalised explicitly. I shall refer to the best and the worst sequel deemed possible for some action respectively as its focus-gain and focus-loss. We may suppose the chooser to compare the numerical excess of the focus-gain of course *Z* over that of course *Y*, with the numerical excess of the focus-loss of course *Z* over that of course *Y*. According to his tastes and circumstances, the former of these differences may outweight the latter. If so, his choice will fall on course *Z*. Let it be noticed that the ultimate comparison is not a numerical one. It is subjective, and its decision could be different for a different individual, or for the same individual in different circumstances. It will be evident also that we have here a decision-problem simplified in two respects. Desiredness is scalar, and possibleness is a category.

THE EPISTEMIC INTERVAL

Possibleness need not be a category. Sometimes the chooser will feel, as his decision-date approaches, that he has not had time to examine fully the congruity of some hypothesis with his subjective knowledge. Sometimes that knowledge will seem plainly insufficient in relevant respects. For his business of choice amongst actions he still needs to decide what is the best and what is the worst that a specified course would expose him to, but now the location of those extremes may depend on the degree of doubt he feels about the possibility of this or that hypothesis. If so, he is treating possibleness as a variable. Its range of definition will lie between entire possibility and non-possibility, and these two are the natural bounds of what we may call the *epistemic interval*. His judgements of possibleness, as of desiredness, will be the product of grounds and intuitions peculiar to himself and his experience. If, from that experience, he can select instances where typical assemblages of evidence led him to adjudge degrees of possibleness roughly or vaguely fixable in memory, some approach to a stable graduation of the epistemic interval may be within reach. At best, however, this would be a matter of private thought scarcely communicable to others. Even in private thought the fixing of degrees of possibleness raises a further question. Possibleness is not objective. It is, in itself, an abstraction. In order to make it in any sense fixable or graduable, it needs to find reflection in some emotion whose intensities lend themselves to comparison. Such an emotion, responding directly to epistemic circumstance, is to hand in the feeling of *surprise*.

To envisage a specific sequel of some course of action and to find this thought engendering the thought that such a sequel would be surprising is a direct reflection of doubt concerning its possibility. The intensity of that potential surprise will surely reflect the impressiveness of the doubt. Degrees of potential surprise may provide the chooser with a means of expressing to himself his judgements of comparative possibleness. However, such a frame of thought need not be supposed to provide a permanent scale. The act of decision is a fusing of judgements of different kinds, and these judgements in effect are made all at once in that moment and have their mutually relevant existence in that moment. The chooser of action wishes to fix upon the best and the worst imagined outcome of each action that are *possible enough*: the best that is possible enough to be worth hoping for, and the worst that is too possible to be dismissed.

REFINEMENTS

There is a temptation to think in terms of continuous functions. Their manipulations are elegantly incisive, and lend to any argument which can be forced into their mould an air of conclusive truth. But decision is an act not only of deliberative thought but of moral commitment. It is an action taken in face of unknowledge of its sequel. The decision-maker's knowledge allows him to imagine that sequel in many widely variant forms. His choice of one action rather than another is not a matter of small exact differences but of a quantum-shift. Decision is discrete. Yet these admissions need not deny us the suggestiveness of continuity. If the epistemic interval can be vaguely graduated, let us suppose it to be precisely graduable. Then we shall be able to say that for some specified action, the desiredness of outcomes imagined for it, and the degrees of potential surprise respectively assigned to them will, over some ranges, be functions of each other. Let us allow ourselves a third variable, that of ascendancy or the attention-arresting power of some degree of desiredness or counter-desiredness, and its assigned degree of potential surprise. Ascendancy will assuredly be an increasing function of desiredness, and a decreasing function of potential surprise. There will be within some range of greater or less desiredness, a constrained maximum of ascendancy; and again within some range of greater or less counter-desiredness, another such constrained maximum. When we treat possibleness as a variable, and represent it by potential surprise, the two constrained maxima of ascendancy can serve as the focus-gain and focus-loss of the action. One further refinement will exploit continuity to the utmost in aid of formal elegance. The constrained maxima of ascendancy can be thought of as maxima of a 'twisted curve' (in American, a 'space-curve') that is to say, a path traced on an implicit surface in which every point will correspond to some pair of values of desiredness and potential surprise conceived in abstraction from any specific action. On this surface, equal-ascendancy lines will enable us to find the 'entirely possible' equivalent of any particular pair of associated values of desiredness and potential surprise.

EPISTEMIC STANDING: THE INVERTED MEASURE

In the foregoing I have defined the epistemic interval as the range from entire adjudged possibility through entangled possibility to eliminated possibility. However, it is better to relate the term epistemic interval to the notion of epistemic standing, that is to say, the seriousness with which the chooser of action treats a hypothesis of the sequel, regardless of its desiredness or the opposite. Epistemic standing is traditionally represented by probability, somehow defined, somehow determined or adjudged. I have argued that probability, as a sharing of certainty, is illicit in the case of an essentially ever-extensible list of hypotheses, since this can at no stage be treated as necessarily including what will prove to be the truth. *Disbelief*, in any particular degree that may be fixable, can be accorded to mutually *rival* hypotheses without limit of number. It can be so accorded in zero degree and will then correspond to adjudged entire possibility. Disbelief, or potential surprise, is thus an inverted expression of epistemic standing. By this inversion of measurement we rid ourselves of the crippling additive character of probability, inherited from its origin in games of chance.

At the root of my theme lies the supposition that thought can be an uncaused cause, what I would call a beginning. This notion involves a leap of thought that many will find senseless. Yet how else can we claim to be (as plenipotentiaries, if you will) the authors of our history? Certainly the scrambled writing of many hands in the book reads differently from what any individual intended. But if we can suppose that not all of these writings were dictated, that gives meaning to the idea of originative choice. My theme repudiates the possibility of a calculable dynamics of history. In seeking to express it I am handicapped by the lack of a word for *ex nihilo* origination. It is this meaning that I intend in calling this brief paper the Origination of Choice.

2 Means and Meaning in Economic Theory

PREFACE

It is plainly imperative that the notation of mathematics or symbolic logic should be uniform with all users. The terms used in natural science can also be standardised, since they are operational, they refer to the results of practical and describable procedures. Some may think that economics should follow the same rule. But, despite the intense endeavours of half-a-century to mathematise economics, and all the work of the accountancy profession, Leontief's great invention of input-output analysis and despite the computer revolution, economic theory cannot be deemed operational and it cannot be thought of as a unity. The most admired of its constructs in the eyes of the profession, the one appealed to with more unquestioning assurance than any other is, if we insist on a strict validation, one which describes a timeless system. General equilibrium wipes out the experience with which consciousness itself can be identified, the transience of thought, the necessity to reckon with a succession of moments, to acknowledge time-to-come and to exploit it. This repudiation of the process of history has taken place despite the plainest warnings of one of the Founding Fathers of British economics, Alfred Marshall. Its ascendancy has survived the turmoil of the twentieth century and the ever-faster spread throughout all societies and institutions, of the character of a vast casino. The market, on which the liberal society so centrally relies, is now unmistakably a speculative market. But the market is essentially, elementally the seat of the eternal business of exploiting humanity's irremediable, built-in unknowledge of time-to-come. We were told so, insistently and repeatedly, by another of the greatest economists, and the first of them, Richard Cantillon. Cantillon has suddenly become as modern as the hour.

THE TIME-EXEMPT IDEAL

In the last decade of the Victorian age, economic theory attained an ideal. It had a coherent unity, a simplicity and self-sufficiency which could answer all questions about what seemed to be the economic organism of those days. Its elemental assumptions were few, but of tremendous effect. The ascendancy over men's thought which this conception exercised was that of beauty. General pre-reconciliation of choices of action, in a universal equality of freedom constrained only by the freedom of others and by the psychic and circumstantial endowments of individuals, seemed an ultimate good. This pre-reconciliation ensured rationality to every choice, by enabling it to be made in knowledge, actual or virtual, of every other person's choice. The means of pre-reconciliation was the perfect market, the language of agreement was price. Diminishing marginal utility enabled every individual, by adjusting his quantities bought and sold, to bring his marginal rates of substitution into equality with the relevant prices of goods in terms of each other. Thus all prices were universally agreed prices, prices were thus given the authority of public facts, like those of Nature herself, and could, if anyone desired it, be used in aggregation, for the reckoning of national income.

It is small wonder that a lamp which seemed to show the whole scene of men's business lives as an orderly ritual pageant, the marvellous combination of individual freedom with perfect social co-ordination, and which in short seemed almost to fuse science, divinity and art into one superb validation of human dignity, should have gained over the minds of scholars an influence and command which to this day it still exerts. It may seem to scholars and even to practical administrators that if this rational ideal is kept, in spite of all, before our eyes, it will be gradually approached and virtually in the end attained. It has other claims. It is a work of logic. It is an axiom-system, the geometry of business. It offers the intense intellectual satisfaction of demonstrative proof. Given its pre-suppositions, its march of reason is irresistible. What, then, are those pre-suppositions?

Pre-reconciliation of choices means the making of choices in knowledge of each other. No choice can be made in knowledge of a choice whose making lies in time-to-come, if the making of a choice is in the extreme sense an *absolute origination*, an *autonomous* act, something which is a law unto itself. For a choice in this sense, the sense which gives to the human individual the dignity of responsibility, cannot be foreknown. It is exempt from entire governance by antecedents, and knowledge of such influential antecedents as it has thus cannot be sufficient to give knowledge of a choice-to-come. Then, there can be no foreknowing how choices-to-come will affect the sequel of today's action. It follows that an all-encompassing pre-reconciliation of choices requires the universal simultaneity of all choices. That is to say, the entire system of choices must belong to one-and-the same moment, they must compose, by themselves alone, the whole of a system encompassed within a single moment, a *timeless* system.

We could suppose all choices to be pre-reconciled by the sending-in by each individual of a list of mutually rival conditionally-promised actions, the condition for each being some set of actions, one by each person, promised by others. It is conceivable, though far from logically guaranteed, that a solution could be found prescribing for each person the particular action from his own list that he would prefer, given the particular actions prescribed for the other persons. However, when the conditionally promised actions involved are all of them the giving or receiving, in mutual exchange, of particular quantities of goods, a knowledge of individual choices by others is not needed by each chooser. He needs only to know the various rival prices at which he can buy or sell various quantities of some one good. A solution, if one exists, will then consist in a set of prices which will equalise for each good the aggregate quantity of it offered and demanded; a set of prices which will 'clear the market'. The question which this construction seeks to answer is one of logical consistency, not of practical procedure. This question is: Could all choices conceptually be made in knowledge of each other?

All theory is abstraction. To reject some conception on the ground that it is abstract is to reject theory itself. The question which allows us to go forward is whether the abstract system of ideas, the theory, makes illuminating suggestions about our perceived world. It is only when we have searchingly examined a theory to be as sure as we can that, for the time being, it has no more to tell us, that we can put it aside in favour of new proposals. To abstract is to *leave out*, to exclude from study everything except the abstracted ideas. The need to abandon a theory will grow more pressing, the more acutely we are made aware of the extent, the influence and the momentousness of what the theory leaves out. What, then, does the theory of perfect general pre-reconciliation leave out?

It leaves out time. Some may feel that all it essentially does is to *squeeze* time. We have used the word 'action'. What we thus name ought no doubt to have a claim to unity in some degree, to coherence, to singleness of purpose. But we need not mean by *an action* something that occupies only a moment, a vanishingly small segment of the calendar. That would rob the term of nearly all its intuitive content.

The expressions an *action*, a *course of action*, a *plan*, an *enterprise*, a *policy*, are all in varying degrees synonymous. Some of them distinctly and obviously imply the occupation of a stretch of the calendar. But it is the unity or coherence, the organicity of the action or the plan that matters. Need we be concerned at having to suppose the 'successive' parts of the action or the plan to be telescoped? Does the dimension of lapse of time matter? The timeless system of choices must ignore the need for lapse of time. Is there something about the time-squeezed economy that need worry us?

Or let us put this question otherwise. If we accept the timeless world of universal pre-reconciliation of choices, what do we renounce? We transform the supposable nature of humans and their place, their standing, in the Scheme of Things. For we deny them the power of *absolute origination*. We rule a line under the sum of human knowledge, the total human inventive accomplishment. The world of universal co-ordinated choice is a sterile world. In it, men know all that there is to know. In it, men have created all that is in their power to create. Strictly, in every sense, the totally pre-reconciled world is a world without hope. We can conceive of the telescoping of actions and even of plans, but not of hope.

TIME AND UNCAUSE

To say that I hope for some defined taking-place is to say two things: that I desire it, and that I deem it possible. The possibleness which can be an element in my business of choice of action is a character of my own thought, it exists in my thought. Possibleness adjudged by others, unless it convinces me, or possibleness which might be asserted as an objective feature of the world outside my thoughts, but is not acknowledged by them, is no concern of mine. What, then, is possibleness? It is the absence from my thought, after a careful scanning and scrutiny of things, of any discernible obstacle to the coming-true of the supposed course of things. Can such freedom from obstruction be the case in my thoughts, unless the supposed course of things is implicit in, and therefore guaranteed by, the nature of things and their posture in my present moment? Either of two conditions, if satisfied, could enable me to answer yes.

The one which presents itself most readily is that of my failing to discern obstacles which I should acknowledge if they were disclosed to me. Evidently, I can be blind to principles or postures which forbid some hypothetical course of affairs. This would be a contingent circumstance giving the appearance of possibleness where it did not belong. However, there is something else which, if we elect to assume it, would, in any present posture of things, entail the possibleness of an infinity of rival imagined courses of affairs. It would be left, then, to the individual whose thoughts we are concerned with to engage in the business of imagining these rival courses of affairs. This other, non-contingent but essential, character of the scheme of things would be the existence of thoughts not entirely governed by antecedent thoughts or circumstances.

If every thought can in every respect be completely accounted for as the necessary and only possible successor of what has just preceded it in the individual's mind, we must regard all choices as passive, inert, infertile and determinate links in a history to which they add nothing new, that is, nothing that was not implicit in their own antecedents. The contrary of this idea of the nature of choice eludes expression in any brief phrase. English has no term (except perhaps 'source' in physics) which means *coming into being at a point of the calendar out of nothing*. To mean a thought which in some respects conforms to this definition I shall use the phrase *autonomous*, or *absolute*, *origination*. A choice of action which is in some respects an absolute origination is in those respects uncaused. It will itself, however, be followed by a history of affairs differing in some respects from what would have followed a different choice. Thus we may say that it is a cause. A choice of action which is an autonomous or absolute origination I will call a *beginning*. A beginning is an *uncaused cause*. If we elect to suppose that choices can be beginnings, we are saying that the chooser of present action cannot assign to each available action a sole and unique sequel, for the sequel of any action will be affected by choices-to-come which, being beginnings, cannot be foreknown. Since such a choice-to-come is partly exempt from governance by antecedents, no inspection of present antecedents can give foreknowledge of it.

The assumption that choices can be beginnings has consequences for our conception of the business of choice. The sequels which the action-chooser can invent for any course of present action available to him are not limited in number by anything in their own nature, but since each will take some span of time to invent, a deadline for the making of a choice will bring the proliferation of sequels to a stop. The characters of the sequels invented for any action will, however, be constrained by their need for possibleness. No sequel deemed impossible can, we may say, have any bearing on choice.

In this frame of ideas, what effect will the action-chooser bring about by choosing one rather than another of the courses of action which he sees open to him? Given the skein of sequels he has had time to invent, to *imagine*, for this course and for that, a choice of one action will expose him to some sequels which a different choice would have excluded.

What authenticity have such imagined sequels of defined actions, defined uses or orientations of an array of resources, as elements in a business of choice amongst such actions or orientations? The chooser has critically examined each to find it free from discernible obstruction in his thought, or else to exclude it. The imagined sequels have a definite *epistemic standing*, that of adjudged unobstructed possibility, each subject to a condition, that the chooser commits himself to that action which does not exclude it. The chooser's freedom, in principle, to proliferate *rival* hypothetical sequels of any action rests in my thesis on the supposition that choices-to-come of other individuals can be *beginnings*. This freedom entails that any such skein of the imagined sequels of some one action must be deemed always incomplete and uncompleteable. The mutual rivalry alone of the members of any skein would obscure the meaning of an assignment of degrees of positive confidence or belief in the members. Their liability in principle to an indefinite extension of their numbers seems to destroy any such meaning. Possibleness by contrast, that is freedom from conceptual obstruction, can be accorded to any number of imagined sequels and will not be rendered a less valid judgement by the recognition that the number of rivals can be indefinitely increased.

Possibleness can be looked on as a yes or no condition. We can adopt merely the two categories, 'possible' or 'not possible'. Then the expression or recognition of unknowledge of the sequels of actions will consist in the plurality of rival hypotheses of those sequels, in their degrees of mutual unlikeness or range of diversity, and in their liability to indefinite proliferation. It will reside in this, as it were, horizontal compass of diversity rather than in assigned degrees of epistemic standing or of positive belief.

It may be asked whether economists need or ought to concern themselves with the ultimate enigmas, the riddle of time, the nature of the seeming historic transience, whether it is illusory or the product of human absolute originative power. But our practice directly and intimately depends on our elected view of these questions. The election to be made is between the basing of action on supposed objective knowledge of its sequel, or on the supposition that the nature of things and their posture in the present moment imply constraints but not determination of the sequels of action, that the content of time-to-come is not, as it were, densely packed by the implications of the present, but waits for those implications to be used by invented human enterprise, the creation of the presently non-existent by work of imagination. In the foregoing, and in many places for a long time, I have tried to show the practical implications of this elective challenge. If there is objective knowledge to be had, positive belief may in itself make sense (though what becomes of the meaning of choice is not clear). Between the horns of the dilemma, the assumed existence of determinate history-to-come but the lack of time to discover it, we can perhaps suspend a structure of probabilities. These would be based, somehow, on the visible evidence before our eyes in our present moment. Objective probability rests on the counting of cases. In the last sixteen years the concept of probability-distributions has been embedded in a more general body of ideas, the theory of fuzzy sets. Fuzzy sets are a seed from which a vast proliferation of ingenuity is proceeding. I have to express the conviction that this great arabesque of brilliant intellectual endeavour has still the same essential purpose: to eliminate the true unknowledge which gives us imaginative freedom. The choice of a membership-function for fuzzy sets is the prescription of objective shape to our basis of action. To prescribe objective knowledge, however ingeniously disguised, as the conditioning frame for the genuine origination of history, is a contradiction in terms.

ALFRED MARSHALL AND A META-SCIENCE

It is perhaps inevitable that a work of profound inspiration should sometimes baffle the reader by its shifting use of terms in pursuit of novel and elusive ideas. Alfred Marshall invented his own tools of thought and gave them names of capacious meaning. The *Principles* is the expression of an idea which few seem to recognise. The opening sentence of the Preface to the first edition gives a hint of what is to come:

> Economic conditions are constantly changing and each generation looks at its own problems in its own way.

Afterwards his warnings are repeated and emphatic:

> The main concern of economics is thus with human beings who are impelled, for good and evil, to change and progress. The central

> idea of economics, even when its Foundations alone are under discussion, must be that of living force and movement (Preface to the eighth edition).

Marshall's aim was to find principles of change which should themselves be unchanging. He was convinced of the vital need for economists to study in particularity and detail the world they could observe, yet he saw that in organisation, scale of operations, technology and the regulating frame of laws the business world was constantly evolving, and he believed that even human nature was 'pliable'. What the student of economic society had before his eyes for study was the historic transience itself. The object of study was the economic history of the observer's own lifetime, a story of unceasing change in which he might yet discern eternal principles. These were the true final objects of the economist's search. For this task of intense difficulty Marshall invented a new mode of discourse, involving a new vocabulary and in some sense and degree a new suggestive employment of words. The task of understanding Marshall calls for the reader's utmost quickness and sensitiveness of response. He must follow a gossamer thread, or must respond as a dancer does to a partner's lead.

We have more to learn from Marshall than his formal apparatus and results. The whole of the *Principles* illustrates a particular texture of thought and style of its presentation, the lines of which converge on his use of certain terms in a designedly suggestive, variable and imprecise way, which in effect invites the reader's collaborative effort in interpreting them and filling out their meaning. Language, after all, is *essentially*, *irremediably* imprecise, its words and phrases capacious for richly various meanings, a medium immeasurably more powerful in suggestion than in mere assertion. These are its qualities from careless conversation to the poet's imaginative glory. Why should the economist be censured for exploiting the basic nature and aptitudes of language?

In the six pages of the Preface to the first edition of the *Principles*, the word 'continuous' or 'continuity' occurs some eleven times rather evenly spread throughout, and including, three times, the phrase 'the Principle of Continuity'. Yet within this Preface those words are given two essentially unrelated meanings. One of them is thus introduced:

> Our observations of nature in the moral as in the physical world, relate not so much to aggregate quantities as to increments of quantities. In particular the demand for a thing is a continuous

function, of which, in stable equilibrium, the marginal increment is balanced against the corresponding increment of its cost of production.

Here, *continuity* means that when we suppose some measurable thing to be able to receive increments which are related in some regular way to those received by another measurable thing, the ratio of mutually related increments remains defined and determinate as we deem the increments to approach but not attain zero through infinitely many stages.

If a rule can be discerned according to which the members of some class of measurements, actual or potential, can be paired one-for-one with those of another class, so that by selecting a member of one class we indicate a member of the other, we can speak of each class of measurements as a variable quantity and of either variable as a function of the other. The class from which we propose to select a member, or value of the variable, is then the *argument* and the other is the dependent variable. This conception, which I describe, despite its familiarity, for the sake of explicitness in my subsequent theme, is of course central and essential to the whole business of economic analysis and explanation. The study of such a relation by 'the method of small increments' or the differential calculus has provided economists not only with a technical method of the utmost readiness, conclusiveness, versatility and suggestive fertility, but even with a basic philosophy and a faith. For if two conditions are fulfilled, it immediately puts into our hands a formal prescription by which the businessman or the individual consumer can tell whether some mode of using his resources gets out of them the most satisfaction they can yield. If a number of different numerical values of the argument are considered, differing from each other by small increments, and if we find one such difference to which there corresponds a zero difference of the dependent function, we have located in terms of the argument a locally extreme (greatest or least) value of the function. But this is a bait which surely the economist cannot forbear to swallow. By a reasonable conceptual injection of wisdom into the businessman or the householder, the economist can easily persuade himself that maximising output or minimising cost are trivial manipulations which will be universally applied, because they subserve what is surely the economic counterpart of the force of gravity, namely, self-interest. What, then, are the two necessary conditions?

They are, that the functions involved should be exactly known, and that they should be continuous in the mathematical sense. The first of these is one more aspect of economics' blinkered vision, its neglect of the questions, what knowledge can in abstract principle exist, what part of this is attainable by the chooser of action, and to what process of mind he must resort to cope with elementally or practically irremediable unknowledge.

In the ever-changing world which Marshall pointed to, the representation of a firm's market by a demand-curve is no more than an aid to thought. It has invaluable suggestions to make. If such a curve slopes steeply down, the rectangles portraying sales-proceeds at two different prices bring home most visibly the meaning of *inelastic demand* or a *limited market*, or yet again they show why the farmer in Macbeth 'hanged himself in the expectation of plenty'. But how can the shape of such a curve be known in practice? That shape is at the mercy of rival firms' pricing, advertising and innovative encroachments, it is a mere thread floating wildly in the gale. The supply-curve is in still worse case. It cannot co-exist with a demand-curve, for any movement along the demand-curve will require the re-drawing of the supply-curve, except under the fantasy of perfect competition. Many of these considerations could, no doubt, be represented by a sufficiently complex algebraic statement. Even that would be wholly artificial, representing the impossible supposition of complete relevant knowledge.

Cartesian diagrams are brilliantly, excitingly suggestive. Indifference-curves and contract curve (it would have been well in the centenary year of 1981 to celebrate *Mathematical Physics*), subtleties of shape and intersection of offer-curves, the backward-rising supply-curve of labour, the curves of present value of deferred receipts, the diagrams of combined revenue and cost curves of a firm: all these have in their time set thought afire. All these, however, are analytic. They illustrate the implications, the fulfilled conditions, of a solution to some problem, or the logical impasse presented by some problem, when the pressures and constraints, capacities, endowments and desires, of all the participants have been assembled in each other's presence and a pattern has been contrived from them. They have suggestions for us about the paths and methods, or trial-and-error gropings, by which a solution can be approached. But though self-interest plays the part of gravity in its universal operation (we should remember that self-interest includes the satisfying of conscience and compassion) there is one vital difference. Gravity does not have to seek for the massive objects, from a planet to a particle, on which it operates. Self-interest must start by an intensive search. The curves or functions embody the *results* of that search. And all the while the searches of the various parties are proceeding, ineluctable needs are compelling action which has not found its optimum.

The curves that the theorist can draw *in abstracto* show how the businessman, the man he employs, or his customer could instantly infer his best action, if he had all relevant knowledge of unchanging conditions. They do not tell him how to get this knowledge. The knowledge itself would refer only to the conditions of a single historical moment. To suppose the curves continuous has two justifications. It pictures an elegant mode of calculation, and it broadly conforms to natural conduct. We do balance available small differences against each other. But this is the mere surface of the business of choice. We pick our way carefully over the stony ground of life, but only after we have made the momentous, hopeful and hazardous decision, what line of country to explore.

Marshall was unhampered by niceties of conventional procedure. The *long-period supply curve* serves both to illustrate the reduction of unit costs which a firm might look to achieve in the course of years through economies of scale, and also to exhibit a relation between scale and unit costs which might be deemed to prevail in the abstract at some one date.

Marshall's other meaning for *continuity* is expressed in his tag *Natura non facit saltum*. He insisted that despite the wide range over which individuals or firms differ from each other in the attention and skill they bring to their affairs, this range is composed of imperceptible gradations, so that, for example, in any industry at a given epoch a Representative Firm can be described whose history and prospects will suggest those of the industry as a whole. In the language of Nicholas Georgescu-Roegen's magisterial survey,[1] economic society is not *arithmo-morphic*, but resembles the colour-spectrum where the 'law of excluded middle' does not apply, and a tint can be at once orange and yellow, or indigo and violet. The Representative Firm enables Marshall to epitomise the process of industrial evolution.

Marshall regarded 'statical assumptions' as mere stepping-stones towards an understanding of the historic process. They could not lead to a science of economics, still less themselves constitute or even compose one. The ultimate goal, the only one constant enough to lead us anywhere, was that of an insight into principles of evolution, of change. In this search his use of language was itself variable and imprecise, well adapted to the essential imprecision of its subject matter.

There is in the received economics of our day a central paradox. 'The market' serves the theoretician as the supposed means of pre-reconciliation of choices. The markets whose real performance is daily and hourly reported show a volatility, a seeming senselessness which mocks the notion of pervasive harmony of purpose.

THE UNQUIET MARKET

The market for any good which can, however briefly, and by whatever means, endure between the market's present moment and a moment still to come is *speculative*. To buy it now is to put oneself in the way of selling it later at a higher price, to sell it now is to put on the cards that one may buy it later at a lower price. Whichever he does, the dealer 'hopes for gain'. To hope is to desire a specified event and to think it possible. Can a dealer calculate what will take place? To think he can is wildly to deceive himself. He has some impressions. He may even call them data. There can be no knowing what other data are in the pack waiting to be dealt, or can yet be put into it by human ingenious ploys. The dealer cannot know that the problem he is set to solve has been completely set, all experience, all reason tells him that the statement of its conditions, that he has in mind, are bound to be mere fragments. His impressions give him only *suggestions*. Different dealers will receive different impressions from different sources, will interpret them against a different background of memories and records, will wrap them in different colours of the mind, and will do different things in the market.

Why do people deal in a speculative market? Because there is, except for goods utterly ephemeral, no other kind of market. Because the speculative market enables a man to expose himself to the possibility of gain (at the price of exposing himself to the possibility of loss).

What like is a speculative market? It is *inherently restless*, it is the *unquiet* market. All dealers want it to move. They want it to move in opposite ways, but they cannot make a worthwhile gain unless it moves. Any impact which has suggestive power enough to stir the excitement of dealers will be greedily exploited to make the market move. Wild horses will be eagerly harnessed. If the suggestion appeals to many dealers their combination will send the price up, or down, and this movement will confirm the suggestion, and be thus self-reinforcing. Where or when will the movement stop? Only when it has gone far enough to seem 'unrealistic', to seem to ask: What justification is there for so low, or so high, a price? Only when some dealers feel unsafe and decide to take their profit.

There is an extreme ironic contrast between the part played by 'the market' in the supposed pursuit and attainment of general equilibrium, and the part it plays increasingly in a world whose thirst for the thrills of gambling has led to the enormous proliferation of futures markets in every quarter of the financial scene, with what ultimate consequences, who dare imagine?

Where can the market stand still, and for how long? Only where the two camps, the Bulls and the Bears, are filled with opposite convictions at equal strength, or where they have no convictions and are waiting on events. How long will they wait? A speculative market that is standing still is like a train in a station. It will not stay there for ever. The longer it stays, the more pressingly it is 'due out'.

What are the fixed points of the business landscape, on which a speculative market can take its bearings? Ultimately, there are none. What brakes or limits are there on its movements, what can absorb its momentum? Are there objective factors which will restrain it? Human decisions spring from the pictures of the world that humans paint for themselves, their decisions leap out in pursuit of things imagined, and imagination is no more governed or held prisoner by 'objective' factors than the autumn gale is governed by the leaves it sweeps along. The incentive of action, the product of judgement however painstaking, is figment, for 'fact' itself is figment, a free mosaic of the impressions of which it seeks to make coherent elements of thought. The brakes that bring speculative movements to a halt are the memories of former turning-points. 'Price has never gone lower than this' some dealers will say. They will cease to sell, begin to buy, and the face of the market is changed.

In such a market, profit is not something anomalous, enigmatic, hard to explain. It belongs to the very essence and fundamental nature of such a market. Hope of gain is the incentive, the propelling force of action, fear of loss is the demon of practical conscience, the instinct of self-preservation, which causes hesitation, the urge to get out of the market (whether a participant has been a Bear or a Bull) and so brings about the halt and reversal of movement. *Movement* of prices in such a market is its heart-beat, unknowledge and the freedom which unknowledge gives to hopes and fears, to *figment*, is its breath of life. Restless and incalculable, the speculative market reflects the wild ambitions, the reckless imagination, the haunted mind and ever-mutable outlook of the human business world and of humanity at large.

Profit hoped for, profit deemed possible, drives the market. Profit or loss *emerging*, realised and recorded, is a prime source of suggestion for dealers' fresh decisions. In speaking of a market and conceiving its fundamental nature and operations, we need not and in logic cannot confine ourselves to the buying and selling of things which exist already in usable form. *Investment* in long-lasting and complex equipment is also in essence an operation decided on under market influences, under the hope of profit. Here evidently many distinct particular markets may bear upon the decisions, and the general market, embracing them all, will during many years give interim judgements on the felicity or failure of the enterprise. In the long course of the delivery of this judgement the enterprise-investor, the businessman, will have many successive opportunities, or necessities, to assess the further prospects of his plant on the basis of its history up to date. The assessment will surely give most weight to the most recent operational experience of the plant, its trading profit for the most recent year or quarter. I suppose the businessman to have in mind for this operating profit, at the threshold of the interval concerned, two numerical values for this profit, the best and the worst he judges to be possible. If, at the end of the interval, realised trading profit exceeds the best that was thought possible, the excess according to its size may be supposed to stimulate a re-assessment of the total discounted value of the trading profits still to come, that is, a re-assessment of the value of the plant at the date in question. Any such re-valuation of an existing plant in its mid-career will surely be reflected in decisions concerning further investments of related kinds. In several publications[2] I sought to give these suggestions concerning the investment-influence of *ex post* on *ex ante* a formal embodiment as a class of elasticities which I called *elasticities of surprise*. They relate the proportionate effect, on valuations and decisions for investment-spending, to the proportionate excess of realised over best-hoped-for trading profit which is the source of this effect, an excess which must by its nature be supposed to engender surprise, the degree of which will help to determine the effect of the episode on the businessman's judgements and decisions.

Profit gambled for and deemed possible, profit realised and recorded, the one linked with the other by the individual's process of thought, a process shaped by his personal history and taking place in the light of what Keynes called 'the news', seems to be inherent in the nature of the business world, an element as essential to it, we might almost say, as consciousness to the nature of man. Profit springs from the human response to the human predicament, to the human imprisonment in 'the present', our inescapable station on the edge of the void of time-to-come. I would say that the *unquiet market*, if I may propose this phrase, is the business aspect of the kaleidic world we are born to.

3 *Treatise, Theory* and Time

THE TIME ENIGMA

Time is experienced, time is imagined: the one is formed by the other, the other is formed by the one. This is the enigma that Keynes unwittingly sought twice by different means to solve. In the solitary present moment, in the individual mind, both themes proceed as one. But in order to formalise them and so understand the effects they can produce, we must envisage them separately. The *Treatise on Money* did not in its central apparatus make explicit the idea of expectation, the idea of imagined time. The *General Theory* spoke of equilibrium instead of the suggestive and impelling power of the divergence of result from expectation. The *Treatise* used implicitly, unwittingly, the distinction of what is conceived *ex ante* from what is perceived *ex post*, Gunnar Myrdal's momentous formulation which in the *Treatise* year he had just published in a Swedish thesis, and which compelled economists to recognise that time-to-come is different in nature from time past. This distinction is latent in the Fundamental Equations of *Treatise* chapter 10.

PRICE LEVEL NON-DISTURBANCE

The Fundamental Equations of the *Treatise* describe implicitly a temporal sequence of takings-place, a number of phases following each other naturally, organically, in a process which implies a lapse of time. The thoughts and actions of a human individual take place in a solitary present moment which exists by its transience into a different moment. The Fundamental Equations must be deemed to describe the passage of the present moment of a society through the phases of a process. At the outset, the entrepreneurs, being able to engage supplies of means of production at certain rates of pay, and each having in mind some supposition of the sale proceeds he would get from this or that size of output of his product, decide upon their respective quantities of product for the immediately coming unit interval of time. The output as a whole thus decided on will consist partly of goods ready for consumption, and partly of things suitable for augmenting and improving productive facilities. That is to say, the general output will consist partly of consumption goods and partly of investment goods. The society's income, out of which expenditure on consumption goods during the time interval can be made, will seem at the outset of the interval to consist of the payments promised to the suppliers of productive means, and of the excess, over these payments, of the sale proceeds on the supposition of which the entrepreneurs have decided on their outputs. If, in the event, just that part of the society's income which derives from the production of consumption goods, is spent on these goods, everyone will be satisfied, apart from variations of individual fortune amongst the entrepreneurs. Prices in the market for consumption goods will have turned out to be what answers the suppositions on which outputs were decided. It will be natural for Keynes's reader to suppose that these prices are those which prevailed in the recent past. If so, prices during the interval in which the entrepreneurs carry out their production and selling decisions will be unchanged from the immediate past. The condition which is necessary for this price stability is that the proportion of consumption expenditure to income shall be the same as the proportion of consumption output to output as a whole, when these outputs are measured in terms of the expense for the means of their production.

INVESTMENT, SAVING AND PROFIT

A prime concern of a theory of money is to show how *changes* of price levels come about. If output decisions are taken in the way we have supposed, it follows that if in some interval the society spends a larger part of its income on consumption goods than it derives from their production, the price level of consumption goods will in that interval turn out to be higher than in the preceding interval. The excess of sale proceeds of consumption goods over the entrepreneurs' outlay for the means of their production will be greater than the entrepreneurs were counting on when they decided on their outputs. What they counted on, Keynes treats as a part of the society's *income*. What they receive above this he calls *profit*.

The difference between the society's income in some proper-named unit calendar interval (the money then earned by production, including the remuneration that the entrepreneurs count on at the outset of the interval) on one hand, and the society's expenditure on consumption in that interval, on the other hand, is *saving*. That part of its income which is not earned in producing consumption goods is earned in producing investment goods. If, then, its consumption expenditure is greater than its consumption earnings, its saving will be less than its investment goods earnings. Thus the 'excess' consumption expenditure, which raises the prices of consumption goods, can be alternatively expressed as the difference between investment goods earnings, say I, and saving, say S. If consumers have reserves of money, they can even spend more than their income on consumption, and saving will then be negative.

Keynes does not in these chapters go fully into the case where consumption expenditure emerges as less than consumption earnings; the case, that is, where the consumption goods as a whole are sold for less than what is earned in their production. We have here, I think, to take *output decision* to mean the decision to produce certain goods and sell them at once *for what they will fetch*. Then $I - S$ can be negative, and if it so turns out, the consumer price level will fall.

TIME-LAPSE IMPLICIT IN THE EQUATION

In the foregoing I have sought to reform Keynes's argument by giving it an explicit frame of time ideas. I have taken his First Fundamental Equation to be an account of what takes place in the passage of the society's present moment from the opening to the close of a time interval. That *present*, at every point of its transit, is *solitary*. It cannot be *both* at the outset and the end of the interval. It is first at one and later at the other. When it is at the outset of the interval, the interval is *imagined* time. When it reaches the end of the interval, the interval has become *experienced* or *recorded* time. The takings-place in the interval will spring from the inter-play of actions of the individuals who compose the society, and each such action will have been shaped or suggested by what its author *imagined and deemed possible* for the interval. Experienced time is formed by imagined time. But when the individuals in their moving solitary present have traversed the interval, the takings-place, often different from anything they had envisaged, which they have experienced will suggest and shape the imagined content of an interval to come.

THE SEQUEL OF ACTION NOT FOREKNOWABLE

It seems to me conceivable that thoughts can be in part *uncaused*, exempt from governance by antecedent thoughts or perceptions. If those thoughts which are decisions, choices of action, can be thus in some respects anomalous; can be absolute originations; then there can be no foreknowledge of such decisions either by inspection or by inference. Without breaking so sharply as this with unquestioned habits of thought, we can still appeal to the evident practical impossibility of pre-reconciling even synchronous decisions. Action must be chosen in unknowledge of its sequel, and we cannot suppose the entrepreneur to use a knowledge of his sale proceeds when he decides how much to make of the goods he means to sell. (Cantillon, who made this the insistent theme of several pages of his *Essai*, perished just two centuries and a half ago.) Keynes for some reason eschewed an explicit temporal dissection of the business process. He implicitly supposes the entrepreneurs to assume that the outputs they decide on will give them particular incomes. He says nothing about their reliance on these assumptions, or recognition of their fallibility.

KEYNES'S *PROFIT* NOT SPENDABLE UNTIL EARNED

Keynes would have scorned such an attempt as mine to display the time-syntax of his thought. Action springs from thought. But what kinematic formalism can overtake and grasp the fleeting elusive something that is conscious thought? He sought instead to manipulate suggestions. The actuality of takings-place, the simultaneity of the recording of experience and the imagining of its sequel he wrapped up in the word 'current', just as he made 'sentiment' stand for the genesis of motive in a combination of thought and feeling. Yet at one point his sleight-of-hand with time ideas seems to mislead him. The profit, in his meaning of the word, which may be engendered in the interval during which entrepreneurial decisions take effect can in his view be built up without constraint by the spending of it by the entrepreneurs on consumption. But this profit, by definition, is unforeseen, or unreckoned on, until the end of the profit-engendering process. Cannot the time lapse of this process be long enough to allow of such spending? If it is, we are in a different, subsequent interval.

THE ARGUMENT OF THE *TREATISE*

The *Treatise on Money* is concerned with the questions: How does a change come about in the purchasing power of money? and What are the effects of such a change? Using ingenious, incisive, drastically simplified aggregations, the Fundamental Equations showed the economic process in terms of elemental classes of decisions: the decisions of the entrepreneurs to make goods of all sorts in certain quantities in an immediate unit interval of time; to divide this output on one hand into consumption goods which they would put on the market within the interval for whatever they would fetch, and on the other hand into investment goods for augmenting and improving productive facilities; the decisions of the members of the society as a whole, namely the suppliers of means of production and also the entrepreneurs is this other capacity, to spend some part of their income from all this production on the consumption goods and leave some part of it unspent. In speaking of *decisions* we are taking our stand with the members of the society at the outset of the interval. All the decisions we have spoken of can be, and we suppose that they will be, carried out. But there is nothing in our suppositions to guarantee that the actual outturn from the executing of these decisions will be what was assumed when the decisions were formed. The outturn that results can be different from the imagined outturn on which the decisions were based. If we could suppose that the entrepreneurs as such, and the members of the society in general, were able to pre-reconcile their respective sets of decisions, so that the society's income was divided in the same proportions between consumption and saving, as those in which it was derived from producing consumption goods and investment goods, the entrepreneurs' assumptions would be fulfilled. If, when they made their output decisions, they had assumed that they would realise the same prices as in the immediate past, prices would in fact remain unchanged. But such pre-reconciliation is inconceivable. Output decisions must first be taken, and only then executed and their soundness tested. Already at the outset of the interval, the entrepreneurs could together write the first term of the first Fundamental Equation. But they could not write the second term until the end of the interval. The first term is something they, taken together, see *ex ante facto*. The second term, and the profit, zero, positive or negative that it expresses, is something they can only see *ex post facto*.

KEYNES'S CONSTRUCTION IN SOME RESPECTS ARBITRARY

The means by which the Fundamental Equations achieve their incisive simplicity of argument and result are in several respects arbitrary.

Products are divided into two classes. Consumption goods are those which provide the immediate support of life. Investment goods are those whose value in the present depends on ideas concerning time-to-come. It is obvious that in fact goods fall *more or less* into one and the other of these classes. However, the distinction can be sharpened by saying that consumption goods are bought for use and not for resale, while investment goods are bought with a view to subsequent sale of themselves or their services or products. Because their concern is with time-to-come, the value of investment goods in any present time is influenced by two factors which do not bear on the value of consumption goods. One factor is our unknowledge today of what prices will be paid at deferred dates for investment goods produced today, or for their services. The other factor is the percentage per annum at which today's bond market discounts such deferred values to the present. This second factor gives the banking system, and through it the monetary authority, some power to influence the size of output of investment goods which entrepreneurs decide on in the present. The bond market however, through which this influence is exerted, is a *speculative* market with whose nature Keynes in later chapters is deeply concerned.

An arbitrary feature of greater moment is Keynes's definition of the society's income. This is designed to make possible a concept of equilibrium of the price level of consumption goods or its inverse, the purchasing power of money. Equilibrium means here a state of things where consumption goods prices as a whole can remain unchanging. Equilibrium will prevail in some brief interval if the expenditure on consumption goods in that interval is equal to the expense of producing them, when this expense includes the necessary rewards of all factors of production. Amongst the factors are the entrepreneurs themselves.

If we are to speak of equality between the society's expenditure on goods for consumption, and the income received by the factors for producing these goods, we must suppose the reward of the entrepreneurs to be some definite amount. Keynes in chapter 9 supposes the entrepreneurs to decide on the sizes of their outputs in view of specific assumed rewards. If their actual remuneration, the excess of their sale proceeds of consumption goods over their payments to the other factors of production, exceeds the aggregate of their assumed rewards, this excess Keynes calls *profit*. He then elaborates the paradox that if they spend this realised profit on consumption goods, their profit will be increased by the amount of this spending, and is thus inexhaustible. This argument is fallacious in so far as it assumes that profit, which by definition only comes into existence in a known amount when output and spending decisions have had time to take effect, can have its disposal decided at the time when those output and spending decisions are made. The paradox would be resolved (though in a manner leading to an indeterminate explosion of profit and prices) if output and spending decisions could be fully co-ordinated at the outset of the interval of action. Such co-ordination is inconceivable in its practical and perhaps in its essential aspects.

INDETERMINACY OF REAL-INCOME DISTRIBUTION

However, Keynes's paradox suggests a more essential weakness in his argument. There is a true and not merely a phantasmal indeterminacy in his construction. For since the entrepreneurs are free to determine the size of the income they will count on, and are free to decide how much of this assumed income they will spend on consumption goods, it follows that any assumption of their income, however large, may be capable of being validated if they spend enough of it. The effect, however, of their assuming a very large income and deciding to spend on consumption goods a very large part of it in the face of given output decisions will be to raise the prices of consumption goods without increasing profit under Keynes's definition. This would mean a transfer of *real* income (quantities of goods obtained in a unit of time) away from the non-entrepreneurial factors to the entrepreneurs. To what degree can such a transfer be deemed actually to occur? The question would require us to define a price-level equilibrium on some principle other than Keynes's, which is indeterminate.

FORMALISM AND NARRATIVE IN THE *TREATISE*

Keynes's treatment of the genesis and effects of price level changes proceeds in two modes. The Fundamental Equations are a formal scaffolding of relations amongst quantities. They contain implicit time relations, but nothing is said of these in the chapters, 9 and 10, which define and relate the quantities. In chapter 11 these quantities take part in the sequential phases of events, they are attributed to deliberative action which could by no means certainly foresee them, but was based on expectations, themselves suggested by immediately past experience. In this chapter 11, section IV is headed 'The causal direction of change' and section V is called 'The behaviour of entrepreneurs'. This latter section begins as follows:

> We have spoken so far as if entrepreneurs were influenced in their prospective arrangements entirely by reference to whether they are making a profit or loss on their current output as they market it. In so far, however, as production takes time . . . and in so far as entrepreneurs are able at the beginning of a production period to forecast the relationship between saving and investment in its effect on the demand for their product at the end of this production period, it is obviously the anticipated profit or loss on new business, rather than the actual profit or loss on business just concluded, which influences them in deciding the scale on which to produce. . . . Strictly, therefore, we should say that it is the *anticipated* profit or loss [Keynes's italic] which is the mainspring of change.

In this passage we can see Keynes's thought evolving. The time enigma, half seen (and later lost), has suggested the need for distinguishing expected from recorded time, the nearest, perhaps, that we can get to seizing the live moment when actual experience ferments into imagination and imagination is distilled into decision.

Here, Keynes himself contrasts his earlier language with an explicit time sequence of the action phases and the thoughts of those engaged. The entrepreneurs make 'prospective' arrangements; 'at the beginning of a production period' they . . . 'forecast . . . the demand for their product at the end of this period'. 'New business' is contrasted with 'business just concluded'. 'Anticipated profit' is twice spoken of, the second time with Keynes's italic emphasis.

INVESTMENT AND THE INTEREST RATE

The title of chapter 13, 'The General Theory of the Rate of Interest', gives little hint of the rich brilliance of its content. Here is the nerve centre of Keynes's theme. In order that the price level of consumption goods may remain equal to their cost of production it is required that the cost of production of investment goods be equal to saving, and in order that the price level of all output may remain equal to its cost of production, it is required that the value of the output of investment goods be equal to its cost of production. What action by the banking system can ensure these equalities, $I' = S$ and $I = I' = S$, or favour their attainment?

Investment goods are valued in the present in view of the productive services they may yield in time-to-come. One question, therefore, is how much, at each future date, the services of such a good will at that date bring in. A second question is what sum of present cash is to be reckoned the equivalent of those supposed deferred earnings. The first question, concerning some content of imagined time, can be given endless variant answers. How such a skein of answers can be formed and how made use of is something on which neither the *Treatise* nor the *General Theory* has anything to say. They are *rival* answers, mutually denying each other's truth. But so far as any one answer is paid attention to, its equivalent in present cash is determined by the market rate of interest prevailing in that present moment when the businessman is deciding what plant or system he will build. Whatever stream of future earnings he may ascribe, in the course of his deliberations, to his projected investment good, it is the sum of the present cash equivalents, the discounted values, of the instalments of that stream which is to be compared with the construction cost, the 'first cost', of the investment good, in approaching a decision whether to invest in it or not.

The 'present value' of a specified deferred sum of money is that sum of present cash which, if allowed to accumulate at compound interest at today's market rate until the due date of the deferred sum, would by then amount to equality with it. The 'present value' of a supposed stream of earnings taken to represent the performance of a projected investment good will thus be a function of the interest rate, and will be higher, the lower the rate. If the banking system can bring about a lowering of long-term interest rates, it will thus increase the 'present value' of any supposed stream of positive earnings which, in the mind of some businessman, represents the potential of an investment good whose construction he is debating, and may lift that value above the construction cost of this good. The *Treatise* as a whole is largely concerned with the nature and effectiveness of the banking system's influence on rates of interest. It takes little notice of the elusive, conjectural and entirely uncertain nature of the businessman's suppositions about the earnings of projected investment goods. In the *General Theory* the conception of the marginal efficiency of capital is recognised to be permeated by the phenomenon of 'confidence' or its absence, but what makes for 'confidence' is not discussed.

THE MARGINAL EFFICIENCY OF CAPITAL

The central thread of thought in this chapter is the formal entity which we can call a rate of discount. But two different meanings can inform such a rate. It can be the percentage per unit interval of time at which money can be borrowed or lent today in exchange for some one or more stated sums payable at stated deferred dates. Or it can be the rate, similar in arithmetical form, at which the imagined, hoped-for or assumed services of specific tools or plant would have to be discounted in order that the sum of the discounted values might be equal to the cost of production of these tools in the decision makers' present. The former meaning is that of the market rate of interest. The second meaning is what, in the *General Theory*, Keynes called the marginal efficiency of capital. These two meanings correspond in some respects to what Knut Wicksell called the natural rate and the market rate of interest. But whereas Wicksell thinks of the natural rate as a datum to which the market rate must be adjusted, if businessmen are not to have an incentive to make investment exceed saving, Keynes in the *General Theory* supposes that the marginal efficiency will become adjusted, by variation of the output of investment goods, to the market rate of interest. In the *Treatise* Keynes has all the elements of the question: How can bank policy affect the inducement to invest (that is, the inducement to produce goods of types designed for augmenting or improving durable productive facilities)? but his ranking of them in relative importance is the reverse of what he later came to express in the *General Theory* and in the article of 1937 in the *Quarterly Journal of Economics*. In these latter writings we are told that it is through the marginal efficiency of capital that the conjectural future looms over the present. In the *Treatise* this factor is treated as too vague and indeterminate to be worthy of attention, while the effect of interest rate changes is obvious and direct. But it is this very uncertainty and vagueness of the rewards of investment which make the inducement to invest, as it works in the minds of businessmen, so variable and vulnerable.

DECISIONS TO INVEST AND TO SAVE ARE NOT LINKED

Between Book III and Book IV of the *Treatise* there is a change in the style of thought. Book III is concerned with the setting of the stage, and Book IV with what can take place upon it. In Book III the anatomy of economic society in its organic relations is set out, with an implicit hint of its mode of life. The Fundamental Equations with their constituent concepts defined in chapter 9 are, as Keynes says, identical equalities. But they can be given either of two meanings. They show the range of variant results that could follow such-and-such a set of decisions, *or* such-and-such another set, taken at the outset of some interval. Or, they show what, at the end of the interval, has actually resulted because of the decisions taken at its beginning. The members of the society, the entrepreneurs and the other earners and spenders of income, must be conceived to pass through this interval from its beginning to its end, their thoughts at each standpoint being of quite different nature. Keynes gives no hint of such interpretation. The heart of the matter, in the Fundamental Equations, is that different sets of individuals, or the same individuals in different capacities, can take decisions independently of each other leading to discordant results. *Intended* investment can differ in amount from *intended* saving. Quite beside the point, in this regard, is the logical necessity for what has, *in the event*, been produced but not bought to have cost exactly what has been earned but not spent. Had Keynes understood this irrelevance he need not have been persuaded, in the *General Theory*, into abandoning his implicit distinction between *ex ante* and *ex post*. Keynes had an instinct, sometimes fruitful and suggestive, for telescoping ideas into each other to produce an illusion of simplicity. But in supposing, as he did in the *General Theory*, that he could, and that he must, telescope the future into the past he was deluded.

THE NARRATIVE MODE

What we find in chapter 15 is narrative in the garb of argument. There are those economists who believe we can discover and broadly say what *must* happen. There are those who think that at most we can suggest what sort of thing *can* happen. On this latter view, many variant things can happen, and in describing them our account cannot be a rigid logical structure. Inevitably, as a writer follows up one out of many branching possibilities, sometimes returning on his tracks and making a fresh excursion, the method turns to narrative. Narrative, a chain of choices and events, is the form we give to the recorded past. The economist must often be content with it.

THE SECURITIES MARKET *INHERENTLY RESTLESS*

In chapter 15, we see the double feedback process of imagined and experienced time at a pitch of intensity which Keynes attempts but hardly manages to describe. The market in securities, in stocks and shares, like every market in long-lasting things, is *speculative*. In such a market, prices asked or offered today rest largely on ideas of what prices will be tomorrow, next week or next year, on prices in imagined time. Such ideas can change at any piece of news, and at any actual movement of prices paid today. They are not governed or steadied, as in a market for commodities, by the quantities per unit of time which can be supplied or can be used, for the yearly volume of trading in existing assets is overwhelmingly greater than any quantity that a year may see added to the mass. Such trading feeds continually on its own effects. Any movement of prices is suggestive, sometimes of continuance, sometimes of reversal. Prices can stay at rest only so long as the pressure of 'Bears' to sell is matched by the pressure of 'Bulls' to buy. This picture itself encloses two notions. Price steadiness can result from an exchange of money for securities between Bears and Bulls, or from each camp being for the moment satisfied, in view of its conjectures or its doubts, with its present holding of its respective kinds of asset. The subtleties of inference and influences are innumerable and unseizable. Even at rest, prices are generating forces for movement, for when prices are at rest, Bears are losing potential interest rates they could be earning, and both camps are frustrated, for no profit can be made while the market is inert. It was Keynes in the *Treatise* who brought the securities market into focus as an influence on entrepreneurs' incentive to produce or to buy investment goods, tangible productive facilities, and thus affect price levels and the volume of output and the giving of employment. But he by no means pictured the seething eddies of a speculative market, he did not touch on its *inherent restlessness*. Even in the remarkable pages of chapter 15, Keynes inclines to speak, for example, of 'a level of security prices which, on the average of opinion just balances the bullishness'. We may gloss this a little. At each successively higher level of prices, some of those who have been Bulls will desert the Bull camp, until at some level, Bull and Bear pressures are in balance. Keynes's language does not here well suggest the volatile dependence of expectation on event and circumstance.

WICKSELL–KEYNES–MYRDAL

The theme of the *Treatise* as a whole is a transformed and improved conception of the Quantity Theory of Money as an explanation of the governance of the price levels of goods. The transformation is Wicksellian. Wicksell's condition for price-level stability was the equality of the rate of earnings of proposed investment goods in excess of their expense of operation, on one hand, with the rate of interest charged by the banks to finance their purchase, on the other. In speaking of *proposed* investment goods I am taking advantage of Myrdal's momentous recasting of Wicksell's thought in *ex ante facto* terms. Keynes added his own equally vital improvement, when he laid special stress, in many places of the *General Theory*, on the necessity of looking, in some manner, to the whole prospective life of a tool or plant in judging its earning power. His concept of the Marginal Efficiency of Capital is that rate of time discount of supposed future net earnings, which will bring the total of their discounted values to equality with the initial cost of construction of the plant. The word *marginal* refers to his assumption that the rate of earnings of proposed equipment will be a decreasing function of the size of flow of intended investment in equipment of the kind in question.

Wicksell described his condition as equality of the money rate of interest with the *natural* rate of interest. The natural rate was for him perhaps a technologically determined thing to which it was desirable that the banks should adjust their money rate. Keynes in the *General Theory*, in its chapter eleven, thought rather of the businessmen adjusting the size of their investment flow so as to bring the marginal efficiency of capital to equality with a money rate of interest determined by the bond market, under the influence of the banking system. In the *Treatise*, he thought the aim of banking policy should be to bring about equality of the (intended) investment flow with the (intended) saving flow. This latter condition was a separate condition enunciated by Wicksell for price level stability. He perhaps regarded his two conditions as equivalent.

Keynes in the *Treatise*, then, uses Wicksell to improve the Quantity Theory. Using the vital Myrdalian improvement of Wicksell, the explicit adoption of the *ex ante* temporal viewpoint, which is implicit in Keynes's Fundamental Equations, we can say that the heart of the Wicksell–Keynes account of price-level changes is the relation between intended investment and intended saving. There is no reason why these two should not differ, and, except through superlative foresight and restraint on the part of the banking system, every possibility that they will. If the banking system contrives so to administer that lending rate of interest which is under its direct control (what Keynes, with full warnings, decides to call bank rate) in such a way that the market rate of interest is high enough not to induce businessmen to plan a larger output of investment goods than the society's intended saving can just match, prices will as a whole be undisturbed. In a society whose affairs are undistorted by monopolistic action, either by the suppliers of productive means or the entrepreneurs, I think Keynes's account with its Wicksellian inspiration and his own ingenious brevities, brilliantly illuminates the problem of price levels, the question of the purchasing power of money.

What, then, can disturb the equality of the income from production and the expenditure on the products? If, with this equality prevailing, the banks at some time find themselves able to lend more than they have been doing, they may think that by reducing the rate of interest by a small proportion, they can increase the amount they are lending by a larger proportion, and thus increase their revenue. If this action lowers the money rate of interest below the natural rate, businessmen will be tempted to borrow so as to increase their output and their acquisition of investment goods. Keynes thinks also that saving will be discouraged. Thus the output of investment goods, in terms of what it costs to produce and of its sale proceeds, will come to exceed the flow of saving, and there will be 'windfall' profits for the entrepreneurs. From such a start, the story can be developed in countless different ways. Will the profit induce an increase of general output, requiring a larger supply of factors of production, to attract which the rates of pay must be increased with the effect of increasing the flow of income in money terms and the prices of goods? Or which of a thousand other courses will things take? Keynes at this point has shown how equilibrium can be destroyed. What kind of account can he offer of the sequel of its destruction?

MULTIPLE SCENARIOS

Keynes's method in Book IV of the *Treatise* is what today would be called that of multiple scenarios. Departure from equilibrium is described in plural narratives, classified according to the kinds of event which respectively start them, or by which they afterwards develop in one way or another. Evidently there is no question here of proving that affairs must follow such and such a course. Business is not in this treatment a closed and determinate system where all is subject to fully-specified endogenous causes. What we have is narrative claiming only to be a natural outcome of easily supposable circumstance. Part of such circumstance may consist in policy decisions of the monetary authority or the banking system. Plainly these institutions can influence affairs. Can they know what effect, in direction and degree, their influence will have? In the fifty years and more since the *Treatise* was written, the institutional frame and the sophistication of society have greatly evolved. But was it ever realistic to speak of banks as adjusting their lending interest rate to equality with a *natural rate* of earnings of investment goods, a natural rate which they would somehow have had to define and determine for themselves? Even Keynes, in the *Treatise*, was treating most cavalierly the question of what knowledge action choosers can gain, how and when they can come by it, and how meagre and elusive it must be when they make their decisions, even if it is such knowledge as the Scheme of Things does not eternally deny us, knowledge of time-to-come.

TREATISE AND *THEORY*: COMPLEMENTARITY IN UNITY

Between the writing of the *Treatise* and the writing of the *General Theory*, the world economic scene had drastically, dramatically changed. This is even reflected in the manner and mental frame of the two books. The *Treatise* is genial and gently didactic, relaxed and assured. It describes a world which responds to the policy measures of those in charge, a world where policy can be formed on lines of clear reason, where it can be given rather precise criteria, and where its effects can be foreseen and counted on. This orderly world, so far as it ever existed, came down in ruins in the years when the *Treatise* was about to appear. The question to be answered had changed. In the *Treatise* the question was: How do changes come about in the purchasing power of money over consumption goods? In the *General Theory* it was: How does the demand for productive services come to be what it is, what factors bear upon businessmen's decisions on how large an output of goods in general they shall produce? Yet the two books are one book. In each, the heart of the matter is the genesis and scale of decisions to invest, to augment and improve productive facilities; and this theme includes the question what can discourage and inhibit such decisions. But if the *Treatise* and the *General Theory* are two versions of the same theme, how has this theme evolved between the earlier and the later books, what does the *Theory* do that the *Treatise* fell short of doing, what does the *Theory* itself leave muted or unsaid, that needed the gathered and impatient force of the *Quarterly Journal* article to make plain at last?

LIQUIDITY; LIQUIDITY-PREFERENCE; MONEY

Investment commits resources to imagined time. What is imagined floats on suggestions of all degrees of authenticity and robustness, of mutual conflict and incoherence. It is fragile, mutable and anxious. The *Treatise* often refers to expectation, but says little of its nature and quality. This was something left unsaid, not something wrongly said. The *Theory* insists that the marginal efficiency of capital is an expression of ideas about the entire series of years-to-come in the practicable life of plant and systems. But it says nothing of how these ideas are formed or changed. Their mutable anxious uncertainty is given immense importance, but only by implication. It is the source and basis of the *General Theory*'s greatest stroke of originality, the making central and essential of the idea of liquidity preference. To make liquidity, namely the quality which stands at the opposite pole to specialisation, the heart of the argument is to make *money* the heart of it. Did not the whole theme start with money, with a *Treatise on Money*? Money is something that policy can influence, manipulate and in some degree control. The winds of technological, political and social change, by contrast, are entirely out of hand. Liquidity is a refuge from uncertainty. But to take refuge from uncertainty is to take refuge from enterprise, from the giving of employment. The title of Keynes's tormented book encapsulates his theme: *The General Theory of Employment, Interest and Money* shows how, in a money-using economy, a failure of nerve on the part of entrepreneurs, a failure whose occasional genesis is inherent in the Scheme of Things, can produce unemployment. Keynes's theory of money and employment is not a crude hydraulic Quantity Theory. It is a Wicksellian theory where the influence of money is exerted through the interest rate, and it is a Keynesian theory where the interest rate results from the interplay of the public's and the business world's demand for liquidity, and the banking system's policy in supplying liquidity.

WINDFALL, SURPRISE AND NEW DECISION

The *Treatise* was like a young tree, complete with roots, trunk and branches, but some of these members far from full development. Instead of considering how they might grow, Keynes decided that the tree was misshapen, and cut it down. A passage in the preface of the *General Theory* shows Keynes, as I think, deluding himself in two respects. He says: 'what now seems to me to be the outstanding fault of . . . that work [the *Treatise*] [is] that I failed to deal thoroughly with the effects of *changes* in the level of output. My so-called "fundamental equations" were an instantaneous picture taken on the assumption of a given output.' But in fact he refers in several places to the effect of profit, or loss, in his *Treatise* sense, as leading the entrepreneurs to decide on a larger, or a smaller, output than hitherto. In the *Treatise*, profit is something *not counted on*, something in some degree surprising, which accordingly induces an evolution if not a sharp re-study of production plans. Such a change of output decisions requires an increase or decrease in the quantities of productive factors which must be hired and this, Keynes says, will require a change in their rates of pay; that is, in the unit cost of production of goods. All this in the *Treatise* is carefully spelled out. As for the Fundamental Equations, their nature is more subtle than Keynes of the *Theory* understood. In each, the two terms present respectively an earlier and a later state of mind of the entrepreneurs. The first term shows the unit costs of output of both kinds, which the entrepreneurs intend to pay out and expect to recoup from their sales. The second term shows how far, in the event, their sale proceeds of consumption goods turn out to be different from what their output decision had implicitly assumed. The first term of each Fundamental Equation summarises the entrepreneurs' view of things before the goods have been made and sold, it is their view *ex ante facto*. The second term shows, *ex post facto*, the actual and recorded combined effect of the two sets of decisions, taken independently and in mutual ignorance by the entrepreneurs regarding outputs and by the income receivers (including the entrepreneurs) regarding their use of income to spend on consumption or to save. If this spending on consumption exceeds the cost of what it is spent on, the difference is received by the entrepreneurs as a *windfall*, a profit not reckoned on when output decisions were taken. There is here, I think, a field of enquiry of intense interest and importance, which Keynes leaves unnoticed and untouched. It would seem from the *Treatise* that output decisions are taken in view of expected sale proceeds which, for any specific output that an entrepreneur contemplates, are a single definite amount, treated for practical purposes as certain. If so, any windfall profit or loss must be in some degree *surprising*. It must be in some sense counter-expected. But if so, it must call in question the fabric of ideas on which the entrepreneur's output decision was based. Keynes in the *Treatise* does most explicitly assume that a windfall profit or loss can, or will, lead an entrepreneur to decide, when he is next free to do so, on a larger or smaller output than he has been producing. The very fact, however, that a former judgement has proved fallible in some degree must make the entrepreneur wary of treating such judgements, when they are singular and name one figure, as if they were a virtual or practical certainty. Keynes in the *Treatise* gives very little place to uncertainty.

LOST BEARINGS IN THE *GENERAL THEORY*

In the *General Theory* the Fundamental Equations were abandoned; the notion of profit as something uncovenanted, surprising and such as ought to spur a re-examining of plans and even a re-thinking of policy, was lost; investment and saving were treated as equal by definition. The all-important gap, $I' - S$, or $I - S$, the dynamic heart of change, was obliterated. These steps were taken despite an extraordinary passage, which stands out in brilliant contrast to the tedium of chapter 2 (of the *Theory*) as a whole:

> They are fallaciously supposing that there is a nexus which unites decisions to abstain from present consumption with decisions to provide for future consumption; whereas the motives which determine the latter are not linked in any simple way with the motives which determine the former.

All that is produced in some month must either be sold to consumers in that month or remain unsold to them at its end. If we mean by investment the income paid out for production of goods not sold to consumers, and by saving, the income earned by production in the month but not spent in it on consumption, investment and saving mean the same thing and are identically equal. This identity has *nothing to say* about the relation of what, at the beginning of the month, entrepreneurs decide in terms of cost (that is, of income paid out) to produce but not sell to consumers during the month, and what consumers decide to leave unspent on consumption out of their productive earnings during the month. These two sets of decisions, as Keynes says in the passage quoted above, are made quite independently of each other, and there is no reason at all to suppose that they will be equal. How can the inequality of those two sets of *ex ante* quantities resolve itself into an *ex post* identity? It can come about either by quantity or price, or both. If the intended quantity of consumption goods is put on the market to fetch what it can, and saving is greater (consumption spending is less) than businessmen expected, prices of consumption goods realised and recorded *ex post* will be lower than the businessmen expected. If saving is less than expected, prices will be higher than had been expected. If we suppose that businessmen can change their decisions in the course of the month, they may reduce or increase the quantity of consumption goods put on the market. They may allow goods they had intended to sell, to remain unsold. All this is allowed for and discussed in some sense within the apparatus of the *Treatise*. In the *General Theory*, except in such rare passages as I have quoted, it is lost in the mute *ex post* identity.

THE *THEORY*'S THWARTED INSPIRATION

At the moment of completion of the *Treatise on Money*, Keynes's work of creating his theory of money and output-as-a-whole came under both a fruitful and a damaging influence. The fruitful influence was the catastrophic business depression, which opened a field altogether more dramatic, full of greater moment and menace, for the application of his novel, Wicksell-inspired theory. The heart of that theory was the rate of interest, and in the *Treatise* we already see the rate of interest as the upshot of a speculative market, a price subject to expectation and all this implies, rather than the equilibrator of two potential flows, of saving and investment. Speculation is made possible by uncertainty. In the early nineteen-thirties uncertainty spread blackly over the whole economic sky. In defining the marginal efficiency of capital Keynes had already moved outside the Wicksellian orbit by making the marginal efficiency depend, not on a market figure derived from the visible present (that is, the immediate past) but on the whole imagined, conjectured, profoundly uncertain life of the capital goods, the plant or systems, in which investment was about to be made. Thus far he went in chapter eleven. In chapter twelve he seems suddenly to perceive the full force of what he was doing. How can the vague, elusive and precarious marginal efficiency of capital be used as an exact criterion for adjusting the investment flow as a whole to just that level where the gain from it will be seen to be maximised by a zero difference between the marginal efficiency and the rate of interest? Such a criterion can be no more than symbolic. It was, indeed, the re-asserted ascendancy over Keynes's mind exerted by notions of precise and stable functions whose maxima could be located by the vanishing of a derivative, that robbed the theory of its life and realism. This was the damaging influence that undid the *General Theory*.

INTEREST NOT THE EQUILIBRATOR OF INTENDED INVESTMENT AND INTENDED SAVING

The *General Theory*, nonetheless, had immense tasks and went some way to perform them. If investment is the lever that can lift or lower employment and general output, what can move this lever? Inspired inventiveness and surging competitive ambition are hardly to be summoned by authority. But there is another blade of the Marshallian scissors. If, as Keynes incautiously supposed, the marginal efficiency of capital is a decreasing function of the size of the investment flow, and there is for businessmen an incentive to push the size of the latter up to a level where the marginal efficiency is no higher than the interest rate, then by lowering the latter we can induce an increase of the investment flow, and of employment. But, *can* we lower the interest rate? Is not the interest rate the equilibrator of saving and investment? If interest is constrained by a general equilibrium, how can it be manipulated? It was this theory of the interest rate that Keynes had to do away with and replace by another. He was the theoretician of money, and he showed the interest rate to depend on a property of money, namely, its *liquidity*.

LIQUIDITY AND LIQUIDITY-PREFERENCE: KEYNES'S TRANSFORMING INSIGHT

The notion of liquidity belongs to a different world from that of the theory of value which suddenly took root and blossomed in the last third of the nineteenth century. (Cantillon, Cournot and Gossen did not labour in vain, but, like Archimedes the mathematician, they were too solitary in their brilliant penetrations to launch a movement of thought.) The theory of pre-reconciled exact maximisation of the fruits of given endowments of resources was a theory tacitly based on the assumption of universal perfect relevant knowledge. It *assumed away* the problem of how each individual can know what his resources can do for him, what the sequel will be of this use or that use which he might alternatively make of them, what the effect on that sequel will be of the unknowable choices which others will make in time-to-come. There is, in this world of the late-Victorian theory of value, no ignorance, doubt or uncertainty. In the world we live in, choice is made amongst thoughts of our own invention, and those thoughts can be formed only on suggestions whose representation of what we must cope with may be insufficient or misleading to an unknown degree. A liquid resource is one that can be used to achieve *something* in any of a vast range of different circumstances.

Liquidity has no place nor use in a world of adequate and certain knowledge. In such a world we can decide now what to accept in exchange for what we can offer. It is only in a world where knowledge seems sometimes more and sometimes less sufficient and well-attested, that it can seem desirable, or imperative, to *defer decision* by accepting and retaining money instead of using it at once. When knowledge seems especially elusive, we desire money rather than specialised, vulnerable assets. We sell the assets, their prices fall, and it becomes no longer worthwhile to produce them, no longer worthwhile to invest, to give employment. Had Keynes attended to Cantillon, he could have freed himself from the proposition that an employer will always offer a wage equal to the marginal product of value of his body of employed people. For since he must employ people first and sell their product later, he cannot know for sure what their marginal product is going to be. Keynes solved the problem of the occurrence of massive general unemployment by pointing to two ideas: unknowledge of time-to-come (the elemental human predicament itself) and the presence, in all assets in varying degrees, of the quality of liquidity, present in the purest form in money itself.

Even by the end of the *General Theory* itself, Keynes had not distilled his vision to its ultimate simplicity. He had overthrown the economics of perfect knowledge, but he had not installed in its place the recognition that investment is launched upon imagined time.

4 Cantillon Far Ahead of his Time

PREFACE

In writing this chapter I have been moved by the charisma of two men. No one who has come under the spell of Professor Lucas Beltrán can wonder at my joy in being asked to write in his honour. In choosing Richard Cantillon as my subject, I look back to the man who first perceived the need and possibility of our discipline as a distinct, coherent whole, and who saw its theme as the history-making operation of human nature. In years long after his, economics put on a very different mask. It saw itself as the science of a calculable, determinate world, and later still as a manipulable world. In this vision of itself, its Narcissism has denied the nature of man. At the end of the nineteenth century, only a very few, such as Philip Wicksteed, saw business as essentially conditioned by uncertainty, a lesson so long since taught by Cantillon.

I have used as my source the edition produced with devoted labour by Henry Higgs and published by Macmillan and Co. Ltd. in 1933. Higgs says of his edition 'It follows the French text of 1755 with all faults of grammar, spelling, accent and punctuation'. I do not know how far it is justifiable to refer to Cantillon's divergencies from modern French as faults, but certainly his accentuation is chaotically inconsistent. In quoting from the French text, I have endeavoured faithfully to preserve what Cantillon and Higgs put in print.

A few weeks before completing this chapter, I had the pleasure of listening to a lecture on Cantillon by Professor Orbert Hébert of Auburn University, Alabama. I have not read the script of this lecture, but I gained the impression that his high esteem of Cantillon was based on reasons much like those which have caused my own.

CANTILLON

The first great economist bore a name of Spanish origin. Richard Cantillon's *Essai sur la Nature du Commerce en Général*, written between 1730 and 1734, had to wait nearly a century and a half to gain the attention of a reader able to grasp and proclaim its genius, able to see in it a combination of intimate and practical knowledge of the world of business, a deep understanding of human nature, and a capacity for imaginative synthesis and clear descriptive simplification. William Stanley Jevons contributed to the *Contemporary Review* of January 1881 an article called 'Richard Cantillon and the nationality of political economy', where he says: 'The name of course is an essentially Spanish one, and it is well known that many Spanish merchants settled on the west coast of Ireland. Their houses of distinctly Spanish architecture may be seen in Galway to the present day.' In 1931 the *Essai* was printed in its French form, with an English translation on facing pages, in the admirable edition by Henry Higgs, who included with it Jevons's article and a 28-page chapter of his own on the 'Life and Work of Richard Cantillon'. The reader who is not a devoted antiquary will doubtless tire of the intricate, confusing and perforce self-contradictory details given by Jevons and more elaborately by Higgs of the family connections and the career of Richard Cantillon. On the last page of this chapter Higgs says that Cantillon 'brushed ethics and politics aside'. This is surely a superficial view. Cantillon's description of business life treats it as a reflection of human nature, and as the interaction of acquisitive endeavours by people of many kinds and many different stations in life. Economic society is an organism where each part depends upon the whole and the whole depends upon each part, yet the parts are in some sense and degree in rivalry with each other. The rivalry of different classes and professions, and of the State itself with the citizens, is the stuff of politics, and this aspect of things is not neglected by Cantillon. As to ethics, the attitude conveyed by his book is touching and fastidious. When he is about to describe activities of doubtful morality, he often begins by calling them 'raffinements', but then his distaste appears in the word 'fourberies' and in his explicit repudiation of any scholarly concern with dishonest practices. The impression thus given may be difficult to reconcile with the career of a speculative banker who made a great fortune, but men of great gifts are subject to great temptations.

The gifts which produced the *Essai* were in their combination unparalleled, even for centuries. Men who could imagine an utterly new theoretical discipline had appeared in other fields. Mathematics in especial had exemplified this transcendental power. But even this power needs the fuel of suggestion. There must be experiences which articulate questions which unrelentingly engage the mind. For the astronomer and the chemist, even the anatomist, these experiences were impersonal, they did not essentially involve human emotions, ambitions, rivalries and material interests. Purely contemplative minds could be touched by them. But the world of business is precisely the arena of acquisitive battle. To understand what happens there, a man must descend into the dusty tumult and take part. Can a man with a taste for this, a man indeed superlatively good at it, yet be possessed also by the scholar's manic drive to think, originate and write? The task calls for a Keynes, or a Cantillon.

INCERTITUDE

Those names are not here juxtaposed by chance. Cantillon and Keynes made fortunes by speculation, that is, by an activity the very possibility of which depends on men's *unknowledge* of the sequels of their deeds. The speculator makes his gain, if he makes one, by the act of now investing money whose amount he knows, for the sake of getting money back in time-to-come of an amount that now he cannot know. But this is not only what Cantillon did and Keynes, and every speculator else, it is the essential and constituting act of the merchant, the entrepreneur and the lender, whose respective ostensibly various but fundamentally like operations it is the *Essai*'s business to explain. Business, the exchanging of things in the most encompassing sense, productive means and efforts for products and products for each other, is performed at every phase in uncertainty of its result. This is the most insistent, pervasive and unifying theme of the *Essai*, and in all three of its parts such words as *incertitude*, *hasard* and *crainte* are used repeatedly. This theme indeed reflects the elemental predicament of men. Was it, then, a central strand in all subsequent economic thought? For two centuries it almost disappeared. Marshall indeed saw business as an aspect of the process of history. Frank Knight in 1921 published *Risk, Uncertainty and Profit*. And in 1930 Keynes's *Treatise on Money* showed the rate of interest to be a price determined on a speculative market. In the span between Cantillon in the early eighteenth century and Knight and Keynes in the early twentieth, and especially in the half-century to 1914, economic theory aspired to become an exact science like celestial mechanics. Such a science cannot accommodate as part of itself the most uniquely human of all gifts, the power to originate ideas and pursue them in action. Such enterprise can have no place in it. Yet General

Equilibrium remains to this day the core of theoretical orthodoxy. Keynes's suggestions in Chapter 12 of the *General Theory*, his downright words in the *Quarterly Journal of Economics* for 1937, have been little attended to until the late seventies of this century. Most interpreters of the *General Theory* have rejected what Dr. Alan Coddington in a classic paper[1] has called 'Chapter 12 Keynesianism'. In its recognition of the essentially speculative nature of all business, Cantillon's *Essai* waited two centuries and a half for ideas to come full circle.

The theme of *incertitude*, the fact that all classes and occupations in society, save only the landed proprietors, do their work and conduct their affairs in unknowledge of the gain or loss their activities may bring them, is almost the whole content of Chapter XIII of Part I. The title of this chapter is 'La circulation et le troc des denrées et des marchandises, de même que leur production, se conduisent en Europe par des Entrepreneurs, et au hazard'. The idea and the word *incertitude* are repeated and repeated:

> Le Fermier est un Entrepreneur qui promet de païer au Propriétaire, pour sa Ferme ou Terre, une somme fixe d'argent, sans avoir de certitude de l'avantage qui'il tirera de cette entreprise. Il emploie une partie de cette Terre à nourrir des Troupeaux, à produire du grain, du vin, des foins, et cetera, . . . sans pouvoir prévoir laquelle des especes de ces denrées rapportera le meilleur prix. Ce prix des denrées dépendra en partie des Saisons et en partie de la consommation. . . . Qui est celui qui peut prévoir le nombre des naissances et morts des Habitans de l'État, dans le courant de l'année? Qui peut prévoir l'augmentation ou la diminution de dépense qui peut survenir dans les Familles? Cependant, le prix des denrées du Fermier dépend naturellement de ces événements qu'il ne sauroit prévoir, et par conséquent il conduit l'entreprise de sa Ferme avec incertitude [pp. 46, 48].
>
> . . . quelques-uns s'érigent en Entrepreneurs . . . Ceux-ci s'obligent de païer au Fermier un prix certain de ses denrées, qui est celui du Marché du jour, pour en tirer dans la Ville un prix incertain, qui doit néan-moins les défraïer des frais de la voiture, et leur laisser un profit pour leur entreprise; cependant la variation journalière du prix des denrées dans la Ville, quoiqu'elle ne soit pas considérable, rend leur profit incertain [p. 48].

In these pages the merchant or the entrepreneur are characterised again and again as men whose function it is to buy at a known price with a view to selling later at a price which, when they buy, they cannot know. These instances are too many to be all quoted. One or two more must suffice:

> Ces Entrepreneurs ne peuvent jamais savoir la quantité de la consommation dans leur Ville, ni même combien de tems leurs Chalans acheteront d'eux, vu que leurs Rivaux tacheront par toutes sortes de voies de s'en attirer les Pratiques: tout cela cause tant d'incertitude parmi tous ces Entrepreneurs, qu'on en voit qui font journellement banqueroute [p. 50].

Oligopoly, it seems from this passage, added its hazards to enterprise even in pre-industrial Europe.

> Le Drapier est un Entrepreneur qui achetent des draps et des étoffes du Manufacturier à un prix certain, pour les revendre à un prix incertain, parcequ'il ne peut pas preévoir la quantité de la consommation; il est vrai qu'il peut fixer un prix et s'obstiner à ne pas vendre à moins qu'il ne l'obtienne, mais si ses Pratiques le quittent pour acheter à meilleur marché de quelqu'autre, il se consumera en frais en attendant de vendre au prix qu'il se propose, et cela le ruinera autant ou plus que s'il vendoit sans profit.

Might not Keynes himself have consulted these pages with advantage, when he felt himself awkwardly compelled, in seeking to account for involuntary unemployment, to accept the proposition that an employer will always engage such a number of workers as brings down their marginal product to equality with their wage? For how can he *know what is* their marginal product, when he cannot know at what price he will be able to sell what they produce? The whole of the *General Theory* can be distilled into the word *incertitude*, if the implications of that word are fully seized. Did Cantillon write in vain?

PRICE

A price is the amount of money which is required on some occasion in exchange for one unit of some good. Regarding the circumstances which govern price or lead to its changes, two distinct questions have been asked and have been given respective answers on quite different lines. One question refers to the price of some one good, the other to the level of prices of goods in general. Since goods differ from each other in their qualities and the conditions of their production, it is natural to look for the source of a general change of prices to the other member of the exchange, money. Thus there arose in economics side-by-side a Theory of Value and a Theory of Money, and these were usually segregated in separate chapters or books. The Theory of Value, indeed, eschewed all discussion of money, and expressed the price of a good in terms of some other good, both goods being commodities or services wanted for the sake of their technological or aesthetic qualities. Moreover, in its form of climactic elegance and self-sufficiency, namely, the conception General Equilibrium, the theory of value rested on the attainment of a general pre-reconciliation of choices, which can perhaps apply only to a single moment when all choices are made. Money is acceptable in exchange for goods only in view of a further exchange into goods in time-to-come. In the nineteenth century under the influence of Ricardo, value came to be thought of as bestowed on a good by virtue of the conditions of its production. In the 'labour theory of value', the measure of value was the quantity of labour (number of man hours of work) devoted to its production. Value, in this view, was in some sense *intrinsic* to the good. Cantillon introduced the term *valeur intrinseque* to the economist's vocabulary, but his conception of it was much more firmly grounded than a mere labour theory. The 'valeur intrinseque' of a staple commodity, grain, wool, wine or timber, was measured by the acreage of land required, not only to grow the disposable crop itself, but to grow in addition enough necessaries to support the workers who cultivated and harvested the whole produce of the acreage.

In this proposal, Cantillon is fully aware of complications. The *valeur intrinseque* of a crop of given quantity, measured by the acreage necessary to grow the disposable crop and support the workers, would vary with the fertility of the soil and its aptness for a particular product, and with the strength and skill of the workers. These are difficulties of measurement which do not invalidate the essence. These difficulties, moreover, are no worse than those which confront economic theory at countless other points. Economics is a discipline in which imprecision is not a tiresome accident but a characteristic of its fibre and nature. The notion of the general level of prices can itself be embodied in as many different formulae of calculation as we care to invent. The gift that most of all distinguishes the great writers, Keynes in especial, is that of encapsulating an elusive and complex idea in a suggestive word or phrase which, by its associations in ordinary usage, conveys the plurality of strands of thought that are relevant yet too difficult to disentangle in the midst of an argument. Such words are 'current', in reference to a notion of time, and 'sentiment' in the sense of a combination of thought and feeling. I do not think that 'valeur intrinseque' is to be rejected on the ground of vagueness or non-uniformity of meaning. The valid question is what is the proper use of it. Is it to be regarded as the sole determinant of price? Cantillon has no truck with such a suggestion. He declares that prices are settled by the 'altercations du marché', and makes perfectly clear and explicit the two-sidedness of price, its governance by the confrontation and comparative strengths of demand and supply:

> Il est constant que la quantité des denrées ou des marchandises mises en vente, proportionnée à la demande ou à la quantité des Acheteurs, est la base sur laquelle on fixe, ou sur laquelle on croit toujours fixer, les prix actuels des Marchés; et qu'en général, ces prix ne s'écartent pas beaucoup de la valeur intrinseque [p. 118].

If we here interpret 'valeur intrinseque' as cost of production we have an epitome of the theory of market price which emerged from the work of the subjective value theorists of the 1870s and after. On page 162 we read:

> Les altercations du Marché, ou la demande pour la viande, le vin, la laine, et cetera, étant plus forte qu'à l'ordinaire, ne manquent pas d'en hausser le prix.

This passage not only rests price upon demand (as well as supply) but hints at the distinction between a difference in the quantity bought on one occasion and another, on one hand, and on the other hand, a *strengthening* of demand, that is, an increase in the quantities that would be bought at various given prices, or as would nowadays be said, a bodily shift of the demand curve. In Part III of the *Essai*, where Cantillon is concerned with the relative values of gold and silver, the subjective nature of value is again incisively expressed:

> Pour juger donc de la proportion de l'or à l'argent, il n'y a que le prix du Marché qui puisse décider: le nombre de ceux qui ont besoin d'un metal en echange de l'autre, et de ceux qui veulent

faire cet echange, en détermine le prix. La proportion dépend souvent de la fantaisie des Hommes: les altercations se font grossièrement et non géometriquement. Cependant je ne crois pas qu'on puisse imaginer aucune règle pour y parvenir que celle-là: au moins nous savons dans la pratique, que c'est celle-là qui décide, de même que dans le prix et la valeur de toute autre chose [p. 278].

Cantillon here anticipates not only the 1870s but even the 1970s, where 'Austrian' and 'Subjectivist' economics is assailing the neoclassical position.

Cantillon did not arrive at the full subjective-marginalist theory of individual prices, nor at the conception of a general equilibrium in which the quantities and prices in all exchanges of goods mutually determine each other. Marginalism, which is in effect the finding of that (algebraic) value of an argument (independent variable) which gives a local maximum of a dependent function, by setting the derivative of the function equal to zero, was left for Cournot to demonstrate a century after Cantillon. The idea of general equilibrium was the achievement of Léon Walras in 1874.

MONEY

Having from the outset treated price as something expressed in money, and as governed on one hand by the amount of money brought to market by would-be buyers, Cantillon needed no conscious change of method when he turned to the question of prices in general. When we speak of the amount of money brought to market, we mean of course the amount brought on a particular occasion or within some time interval of specified length. This is a measurement of the kind called a flow. Flows of money, its movements from one holder to another, are in the main the separate events composing a circulation, a system in which individuals are all the time receiving as well as parting with money, so that if the only existing money consists of uniform metallic coins, the flows can continue indefinitely by means of a set of coins of unchanging number and identity. In such a system, the daily number of events each consisting of the transfer of a coin from one holder to another would be greater if every coin in the particular collection changed hands more frequently, or if, instead, the collection became more numerous. The collection of coins is a *stock*, measured simply as so many coins. The daily total value of payments made by means of the coins is a *flow*, measured as so many money units per day. If we divide the total daily number of transfers, each of one coin, by the number of coins composing the stock, we get the *velocity of circulation* of the stock. The flow of money can be increased by an increase either in the quantity of money or in its velocity. These terms, of *quantité* and *vitesse*, are those in which Cantillon describes the power of a monetary circulation, and by which he explains how prices in general are raised or lowered. Thus he anticipates by a century and a half Irving Fisher's famous formula $MV = PT$, in which M is the quantity of money, V its velocity, T is the number of items bought and sold in the unit interval of time and P is the price per item reckoned by adding up the prices of all items and dividing by their number.

Cantillon is an expositor of utmost thoroughness and patience, believing in concrete examples most carefully spelled out. This obliges the commentator to quote at length. On velocity of circulation of money we have the following among many references:

> Supposons maintenant que l'argent qui conduit toute la circulation d'un petit État, est égal a dix mille onces d'argent, et que toutes les paiements qu'on fait de cet argent, de la Campagne a la Ville et de la Ville a la Campagne, se font une fois l'an; . . . Les rentes des Proprietaires correspondront à cinq mille onces, et toute la circulation d'argent, qui restera entre les gens de la Campagne et ceux de la Ville, et qui doit se faire par paiements annuels, correspondra aussi à cinq mille onces. Mais si les Proprietaires stipulent avec leurs Fermiers les paiements par quartier, . . . et si tous les autres paiements se font par quartiers, il ne faudra que deux mille cinq cens onces pour la même circulation qui aurait été conduite par dix mille onces en paiements annuels.

Irving Fisher's equation is an identity. Given the meanings of its four symbols, it is necessarily and always true. If one of these symbols takes a different numerical value, one or more of the others must also change, and the identity shows what kinds of change can compensate each other. The Fisher identity has no place for any reference to human taste, judgement or decision. Anything which affects its numerical values must happen, as it were, off-stage. It is on these lines, however, that part of Cantillon's account of general changes of price proceeds:

> Tout le monde est d'accord que l'abondance de l'argent ou son augmentation dans le troc enchérit le prix de toute chose. La

quantité d'argent qu'on a apportée de l'Amérique en Europe depuis deux siècles, justifie par expérience cette verité [p. 160].

[Monsieur Locke] a bien senti que l'abondance de l'argent enchérit toute chose, mais il n'a pas recherché comment cela se fait. La grande difficulté de cette recherche consiste à savoir par quelle voie et dans quelle proportion l'augmentation de l'argent hausse le prix des choses [p. 160].

J'ai déja remarqué qu'une accélération, ou une plus grande vitesse, dans la circulation de l'argent du troc, vaut autant qu'une augmentation de l'argent effectif [p. 160].

Cantillon examines the *process* of general price rise, and considers successive and various repercussions:

J'estime en général qu'une augmentation d'argent effectif cause dans un État une augmentation proportionée de consommation, qui produit par degrées l'augmentation des prix [p. 162].

Have we not here the upward-sloping supply curve and the recognition that outputs as well as prices are likely to be increased by an influx of money to the State? A little later we have cost-push inflation:

Si l'augmentation de l'argent effectif vient des Mines d'or ou d'argent, le Proprietaire de ces Mines, les Entrepreneurs, les Fondeurs, les Affineurs, et généralement tous ceux qui y travaillent, ne manqueront pas d'augmenter leurs dépenses à proportion de leurs gains. Ils consommeront dans leurs ménages plus de viande et plus de vin . . . Par conséquent, ils donneront de l'emploi à plusieurs Artisans qui n'avaient pas auparavant tant d'ouvrages, et qui par la même raison augmenteront aussi leur dépense. La demande pour la viande, le vin, la laine, et cetera étant plus forte qu'à l'ordinaire, ne manquera pas d'en hausser les prix. Ceux donc qui souffriront de cette cherté seront d'abord les Proprietaires des terres, pendant le terme de leurs Baux, puis tous les ouvriers et gens à gages fixes. Les Proprietaires en congédieront plusieurs, et il arrivera que les autres demanderont une augmentation de gages pour pouvoir subsistir à leur ordinaire.

There is one price of a peculiar and special kind, which like other prices is affected by the size of the stock of money in the State, but unlike others is affected rather on the supply than the demand side. This is the interest rate, the price for borrowing money. In the two editions of his great work, the *Treatise on Money* and the *General Theory*, Keynes produced two great original ideas. One, in the *Treatise*, was the *ex ante–ex post* distinction, which is implicit in the Fundamental Equations, and in which Myrdal had anticipated him in Swedish, and therefore without his knowledge, by a few years. The other, beginning in the *Treatise* but made more explicit in the *General Theory*, is the liquidity preference theory of the interest rate. Cantillon, too, understood that money can be desired for holding as well as for passing on in purchases. For Cantillon's *Essai*, unencumbered by neo-classical preconceptions that life in general, and therefore business life, is tidy, rational and harmonious, and seeing it instead as the field where men play unendingly the game of out-guessing each other in markets essentially *speculative*, shows us the very vision which Keynes presents in the *Treatise on Money*, of interest rates determined by the operations of Bulls and Bears on a Stock Exchange, with the government joining in by inducing the creation of bank money to buy securities:

> Si un Ministre d'État an Angleterre, cherchant à diminuer le prix de l'intérêt de l'argent, ou par d'autres vues, fait augmenter le prix des fonds publics à Londres, et s'il a assez de crédit sur les Directeurs de la Banque, pour les engager (sous obligation de les dedommager en cas de parte) à fabriquer plusieurs billets de banque, dont ils n'ont reçu aucune valeur, en les priant de se servir de ces billets eux-mêmes pour acheter plusieurs parties et capitaux des fonds publics; ces fonds ne manqueront pas de hausser de prix, par ces opérations: et ceux qui les ont vendus, voïant ce haut prix continuer, se détermineront peut-être, pour ne point laisser leurs billets de banque inutiles et croïant par les bruits qu'on seme que le prix de l'intérêt va diminuer et que ces fonds hausseront encore, de les acheter à un plus haut prix qui'ils ne les avoient vendus. Que si plusieurs particuliers, voiant les Agens de la Banque acheter ces fonds, se mêlent d'en faire autant croïant profiter comme eux, les fonds publics augmenteront de prix, au point que le Ministre souhaitera; et il se pourra faire que la Banque revendra adroitement à plus haut prix tous les fonds qu'elle avoit achetés [pp. 320, 322].

Money held by such speculators between their sale and purchase of stock is evidently being held for one of the three Keynesian reasons for liquidity preference, that one which in the *General Theory* is in fact called the speculative motive. But Cantillon hints also at the one which Sir John Hicks explained in his 'A Suggestion for Simplifying the Theory of Money',[2] and which Keynes included, without discussion, in his list as the transactions motive; and Cantillon refers plainly also to the precautionary motive:

> Tous les ordres d'un État, qui ont de l'économie, épargnent, et tiennent hors de la circulation, de petites sommes d'argent comptant, jusqu'à ce qu'ils en aient suffisamment pour les mettres à intérêts ou a profit. Plusieurs gens avares et craintifs enterrent et reservent toujours de l'argent effectif pendant des intervalles de tems assez considerables. Plusieurs Proprietaires, Entrepreneurs, et autres, gardent toujours quel qu'argent comptant dans leurs poches ou dans leurs caisses, contre les cas imprévus, et pour n'être point a sec.

Cantillon exhibits interest rates as a price arrived at on the market by bargaining between would-be borrowers and potential lenders, finding its level higher or lower according to the relative numbers and urgency of the two parties:

> Comme les prix des choses se fixent dans les altercations des marchés par les quantités des chose exposées en vente proportionnellement à la quantité d'argent qu'on en offre, ou ce qui est la même chose, par la proportion numérique des Vendeurs et des Acheteurs; de même l'intérêt de l'argent dans un État se fixe par la proportion numérique des Prêteurs et des Emprunteurs [p. 198].

Such a market is subjective, influenced and governed by the thoughts and feelings of individuals:

> Un homme qui prête son argent sur de bons gages ou sur l'hypotheque de terres, court au moins le hasard de l'inimitié de l'Emprunteur, ou celui des frais, des procès et des pertes; mais lorsqu'il prête sans sureté, il court risque de tout perdre. Par rapport à ces raisons, les Hommes nécessiteux doivent avoir tenté les Prêteurs par l'appas d'un profit; et ce profit doit avoir été proportionné aux nécessités des Emprunteurs et à la crainte et l'avarice des Prêteurs [p. 198].

> Le prix de l'intérêt hausse et baisse tous les jours sur de simples bruits, qui tendent à diminuer ou à augmenter la sureté des Prêteurs [p. 214].

Cantillon perfectly understood the universal connectedness of economic quantities, values and takings-place. He judged that the prevailing interest rate would serve as the guide or standard in other contexts for the ratio of a stream of income to the capital asset from which it was drawn, and that prices paid for land would be settled in this way:

> Les prix courans de l'intérêt dans un État semblent servir de base et de règle pour les prix de l'achat des terres. Si l'intérêt courant est à cinq pour cent, qui répond au denier vingt, le prix des terres devroit être de même [pp. 220, 222].

This conception of business as a world of all-pervasive mutual influences included a recognition that price by affecting the quantities demanded of goods also affected the amount of employment given to their producers. A special aspect of this arises in foreign trade:

> Maintenant si l'augmentation d'argent dans l'État provient d'une balance de commerce avec les Étrangers (c'est à dire, en envoiant chez eux des ouvrages et des Manufactures en plus grande valeur et quantité que ce qu'on en tire, et par conséquent en recevant le surplus en argent) cette augmentation annuelle d'argent enrichira un grand nombre de Marchands . . . et donnera de l'emploi à quantité d'Artisans et Ouvriers qui fournissent les ouvrages qu'on envoie chez l'Étranger d'où l'on tire l'argent [p. 166].

Cantillon thus anticipates by two centuries Keynes's advocacy of an export surplus as a cure for unemployment. The goods composing the surplus (whichever they are deemed to be) have to be produced in the home country, but are not available there to satisfy and soak up demand. And it is not only the direct effect of foreigners' demand for the goods exported to them which will increase employment at home. The influx of hard money to the home country, to pay for the goods sent abroad in excess of those bought from abroad will tend to lower the interest rate at home and encourage investment and enterprise:

> Ces façons d'augmenter l'argent dans l'État y rendent réellement l'argent plus abondant, et diminiuent le prix de l'intérêt. Par le

> moïen de cet argent, les Entrepreneurs de l'État trouvent moïen d'emprunter plus facilement, de faire faire des ouvrages et d'établir des Manufactures, dans l'espérance d'y gagner; les Artisans et tous ceux par les mains de qui cet argent passe, ne manquent pas de consommer plus qu'ils n'eussent fait, s'ils n'avoient été empoïés au moïen de cet argent [p. 190].

In this brief passage a glimpse is given of a theory of enterprise investment, making it to depend on the hope and expectation of profit and to be susceptible of encouragement by low interest rates; making it the source of extra employment and by that means, the source of extra consumption. There is here, indeed, a glimpse of the Multiplier. All this is given in plain, suggestive language with no tangled knots of theory or impalpable subtleties of thought. The real world of business is described by a master practitioner in terms as vivid as the sunlight.

CURRENCY EXCHANGE AND BANKING

Cantillon's quality as an expositor, depending as it always must on the writer's demand upon himself for the utmost prior clarity of dissection, on patience and stamina in step-by-step spelling out of detail, and on a mastery of language, is well illustrated by his explanations of the technical procedures of foreign trade and of banking, closely related aspects of business in which he was expert. He had at all points a keen sense of business as interaction and process, of the history of today influencing the history of tomorrow:

> L'augmentation de la quantité d'argent qui circule dans un État, lui donne de grands avantages dans le commerce avec l'Étranger, tant que cette abondance d'argent y continue. L'État échange toujours par là une petite quantité de produit et de travail, contre une plus grande . . . Il est vrai que la continuation de l'augmentation de l'argent causera dans la suite par son abondance une cherté de terre et de travail dans l'État. Les ouvrages et les Manufactures coûteront tant à la longue, que l'Étranger cessera peu-à-peu de les acheter, et s'accoutumera à les prendre ailleurs a meilleurs marché.

Here we have terms of trade ingeniously explained by means of Cantillon's dual theory of value. If money prices are high in the home country compared with those abroad, any trade that is done will consist in the giving by the home country of the product of a small acreage in exchange for the product of a large acreage, since these respective products will correspond to equal money values.

The business of bankers in facilitating foreign trade brings into especial prominence the pervasively speculative character of all business:

> Si la Hollande envoie en Angleterre pendant le mois de Janvier des marchandises pour la valeur de cent mille onces d'argent, et l'Angleterre n'en envoie en Hollande dans le même mois que pour la valeur de cinquante mille onces (je suppose la vente et le paiement faits dans le même mois de Janvier de part et d'autre), il reviendra à la Hollande dans ce mois une balance de commerce de cinquante mille onces, et le change d'Amsterdam sera à Londres au mois de Janvier à deux ou trois pour cent au dessus du pair. Mais si un Banquier Anglois prévoit en Janvier que la Hollande lors des paiemens et ventes en Mars redevra considérablement à l'Angleterre, il pourra dès le mois de Janvier, au lieu d'envoier les cinquante mille onces qu'on y doit ce mois-là à la Hollande, fournir ses lettres de change sur son Correspondant à Amsterdam, païables à deux usances ou deux mois pour en païer la valeur à l'échéance: et par ce moïen gagner doublement sans envoier un sol en Hollande. Voilà ce que les Banquiers appellent des spéculations qui causent souvent des variations dans les changes pour un peu de tems indépendamment de la balance du commerce [pp. 256, 258].

Chapter VI of Part III is concerned with the banker as lender:

> Si cent Seigneurs économes qui amassent annuellement de l'argent par leurs épargnes déposent chacun dix mille onces d'argent entre les mains d'un Orfèvre ou Banquier de Londres . . . souvent ils le laisseront là long-tems. Dans ces circonstances le Banquier pourra prêter souvent quatre vingt dix mille onces d'argent (des cent mille qu'il doit) pendant toute l'année, et n'aura pas besoin de garder en caisse plus de dix mille onces pour faire face à tout ce qu'on pourra lui redemander. Voilà premièrement l'idée qu'on peut former de l'utilité de ces sortes de banques; les Banquiers ou Orfèvres contribuent à accélérer la circulation de l'argent, ils le mettent a intérêt à leurs risques et périls, et cependant ils sont ou doivent être toujours prêts à païer leurs billets à volonté et à la présentation [pp. 298, 300].

It is not only in his having composed a new landscape of understanding, where the great lines of structure of a country hitherto undescribed can be discerned, but in his unerring instinct for the critical dangers which the explorer of this landscape must avoid and the effortless ease of his coping with them, that evokes the reader's astonished admiration. In his dissection of the world of business, the tools he uses with sure touch are the modern tools:

> Le fond des Terres appartient aux Proprietaires, mais ce fond deviendroit inutile si on ne le cultivoit pas, et plus on y travaille, toutes autres choses étant égales, plus il rend de denrées; et plus on travaille ces denrées, toutes autres choses étant égales, lorsqu'on en fait des marchandises, plus elles ont de valeur [p. 46].

Ceteris paribus twice made explicit, as again on pages 148 and 186.

Alfred Marshall referred to 'the element of Time, which is the centre of the chief difficulty of almost every economic problem'.

I have quoted a passage on the speculative role of bankers, where Cantillon assigns the different phases of the banker's operations to particular, 'proper-named' months, and thus makes explicit the distinguishing mark of economic dynamics, which Sir John Hicks in our day has identified as the presence of *dated* quantities.

As the baffling and disorderly 1970s and 1980s turn into the 1990s, we are perhaps becoming receptive to the spirit of Cantillon's economics, and able, like Jevons, to see in the *Essai* an imperishable masterpiece.

5 The Bounds of Unknowledge

A question faces everyone at almost every hour: what will the sequel be, if I do this, or if I do this? Whence can the answer to that question come, what form will it take, what force will it have, how will the questioner make use of it? The question admits of no escape, for even to sit silent and motionless is to take a course of action. What resources are at hand to help answer it? The individual has a conception of the technology of nature and of the capacities and propensities of human nature. Thus he has notions of the sort of thing that can take place. But when he sets himself to choose a course of action out of many which seem open to him, he may implicitly assume himself to be making history, on however small a scale, in some sense other than mere passive obedience to the play of all-pervasive causes. He may assume that his act of choice is in some respects an ***absolute origination***, something not wholly implicit in antecedents, he may deem his thoughts to be not entirely determinate, but able to come in part *ex nihilo*. If choice can be of this kind, I shall call such an act of choice a *beginning*. It is a taking-place in some respects uncaused, yet it can help to shape its sequel. It is then an *uncaused cause*. A beginning in this sense is out of reach of foreknowledge. We cannot know in our present whether or when a beginning, a choice in part uncaused, may occur in time-to-come, or what may be its character. We cannot know these things by inspection, for there is no inspecting time-to-come. We cannot know them by inference from causal circumstances operating in the present, for the power to do this would contradict the essential nature of a beginning. Then, if choices can be beginnings in our sense, the question what will the sequel be of some specified action cannot legitimately be given only one single, solitary, self-consistent and unified answer. For the sequel will be partly the work of many people's choices-to-come whose character, if they can be beginnings, the chooser of present action cannot know. He is free to invent answers concerning the sequel in numbers unlimited by anything in their nature, in a business of invention only to be halted by his arrival at a deadline for decision. That deadline will find him with a list of answers incomplete and essentially uncompletable. Are we then saying that, for all the chooser can tell, any choice whatever of present action can have any sequel whatever? If this were so the choosing of action would be wholly without effect, powerless and pointless. If in the chooser's thought choice is to be effective, if a choice is to be a cause, each choosable course of action must be linked with some imagined sequels, or some combination of imagined sequels, which belong to this course alone. What can effect such a discriminated linkage? The means of action, which give the chooser the power to do this, *or* to do this, or this, will be an array of material things and of human employable capacities each able to be used in any one of many different ways in endless different combinations of uses. The choosing of action will consist in the chooser's committing himself to set his array of means in motion in some exclusive way. By excluding all other ways that were open to him, the chooser excludes some sequels that he could have *imagined and deemed possible*. They are excluded because materials, tools and brains that were essential to them have been denied them by the chooser's mode of inception of his enterprise, by their pre-emption for processes incompatible with those sequels. The excluded sequels may comprise some which are desired and some which are counter-desired. Choice of action is effective by *what it does not exclude*. For what does the act of choice do for the chooser? It gives to some, by denying to others, of his works of imagination a seriousness, an epistemic standing of a particular kind and quality, it gives them *possibility*, freedom from known obstruction. Imagination may be said to have two levels, two intensities. At one level, it is merely pictorial, a cloudscape. At the other it has the power to enter the counsels of the mind, to present itself as something weighable, judgeable, pursuable. Choice of action decides which works of the chooser's imagination shall be lifted to this second level. If in the chooser's thought this freedom is complete, if possibility is perfect, this is the best that can be done to give the imagined sequels validity in their bearing on his business of choice. If, as my argument suggests, present action is at the mercy of choices-to-come which can be beginnings, the highest epistemic standing that is logically attainable by its envisaged sequels is that of perfect possibility.

We said that effective choice depends on each choosable course of action having some imagined sequels, or some combination of sequels, which belong to it exclusively (others it may share with other courses). This requirement could be satisfied in the abstract by sequels distributed over a limitless range of diversity, so that the mutual unlikeness of sequels envisaged for one-and-the-same course were subject to no constraint. But this would present the chooser with a picture of a daunting degree of complexity. Sequels envisaged for a variety of courses would perhaps be mutually interspersed. To hold lucidly in thought the selective linkage of sequels of wide-ranging mutual unlikeness with the various courses open to him would be excessively difficult. But such a conception is unreal. The sequels suggested to imagination by any one inceptive use of his resources will have at least this origin in common. They start the race from the same mark. But it is not only what, given this common start, the chooser can deem possible, but also what he desires and will by his subsequent actions seek to bring about, and what his practical conscience insists that he shall prepare his mind for, that makes the sequels imagined and deemed possible for any one inceptive course of action to be in some respects kith and kin, and entitles us to think of them as a skein, the mutual unlikeness of whose members is ***bounded***.

The chooser's array of means of action can be compared to the collection of chessmen which are on the board at some stage of the game. For each of them the player knows its powers in general and the scope given to those powers by its position on the board in relation to other pieces. From most states of the game the course of play can take any one of a very great number of different paths. But there are also a very great number of configurations of the chessmen which, within some specified number of moves, are unattainable from the existing configuration. The chess game provides in some respects a suggestive analogy for the predicament of the action-chooser in the general field.

We have reached the notion of a skein of sequels imagined and deemed possible for some course of action and not all of them possible for any other. Any one sequel will require for its description many statements of physical quantities, money values and human performances and utterances. This we may call a technological account. It presents the character of the sequel in all those respects which can bear on the chooser's task of deciding on one course out of many which are open to him. But comparisons of one sequel with another in the performance of this task cannot be made directly by means of such a technological description, for when two sequels are compared, one may be more desired than the other in one respect but less desired in another. The two respects must then be relatively weighted in order to see with which sequel the balance of advantage lies. Such a procedure of assigning weights, when carried through the whole gamut of respects in which the two sequels are to be compared, provides a measure of the desiredness of each sequel as a whole. It is a product of relative valuation. When every sequel in every skein has been assigned a degree of desiredness, we can conceive each sequel to be represented by a point on an axis measuring, or ranking, degrees of desiredness or counter-desiredness. A skein of sequels will thus be represented by a set of points on this axis. Each such point represents something deemed possible on condition of an appropriate choice of action, and desired or counter-desired in greater or less degree. How can the set of such points representing one skein of sequels and thus one available course of action be compared with the set representing another skein? The solution flows from the nature of *possibility* as we are conceiving it. When each of the choosable courses of action, the different ways the chooser can envisage of setting in motion his array of resources, has been supplied by him, by way of plural rival sequels, with products of imagination exempt, in his thought, from fatal obstacles to their being realised, and when each of the choosables thus conceived has been assigned a set of points on the axis of valuation or desiredness, each imagined sequel will have been given two characteristics: some degree of desiredness or counter-desiredness, and the quality of unobstructedness in the chooser's thought. Unobstructedness is here, for us, a characteristic which can be possessed or not possessed by some creation of thought, but which we do not yet regard as varying in degree. An imagined history-to-come is, for our immediate argument, either possible or not possible. This means that we do not discriminate amongst imagined sequels on grounds of possibility: all those that are possible are *equally possible*.

Possibility means for us a character of the individual's thought, the absence from it, when he considers some imagined taking-place in time-to-come, of any obstacle that he can discern to its coming true. If he can discern no obstacle at all, possibility is *perfect*, his degree of *disbelief* in the hypothetical taking-place is zero. The two expressions here used, perfect possibility, zero disbelief, are two expressions of a degree of *epistemic standing*, that is, of the claim of the hypothesis in question to an audience in his self-counsels of decision, its claim to exert upon him without qualification or diminution such influence as its desiredness or counter-desiredness merits. When he finds upon examination that the possibility, given his present knowledge, is perfect, he is conceding the highest degree of epistemic standing, the degree which represents the upper bound of the range of assignable degrees. Can we attach any meaning to an intensifying or reinforcement of this state of thought? Suppose that the eventuality in question can be the upshot of any one of several paths of history-to-come. What bearing has this? If a building can be entered by any one of several doors, entry into it is assured by the openness of one sole door, and access is not made more real by the openness of several doors. The absence of obstacles from one route does not need, and does not allow of or afford meaning to, reinforcement by the absence of obstacles from other routes. Perfect possibility is not a matter of the piling up of 'evidence' or of suggestions, but of the existence in thought of one unobstructed path. It follows that when an available course of action is linked by the action-chooser with a skein of rival imagined sequels all deemed perfectly, and therefore equally, possible, and when these sequels are represented by a set of points on an axis of desiredness or valuation, the sequels whose points are in the interior of the range of the points as a whole have no claim to the action-chooser's attention, for they are *eclipsed* by sequels equally possible but more desired or counter-desired. This we can express otherwise by saying that since no point on the desiredness or valuation axis has any advantage of epistemic standing over any other, it follows that the best result which the *skein as a whole* can suggest is that one suggested by the most desired individual sequel, while the threat posed by the most counter-desired sequel is the threat posed by the skein as a whole, since interior sequels *offer no defence* against this worst one. Our conclusion is that the whole force and effect of the set of points belonging to the skein as a whole resides in the two extreme points. When we divide all hypotheses into possible and not-possible, it is only the valuation-extremes of the 'possible' set which count.

In the frame of thought that I have outlined, the business of choice of action is conceived to proceed in three phases. The first is imaginative, the origination of various inceptive modes of use of the chooser's array of means of action, and the conceiving, for each such mode, a skein of rival imagined sequels. The second phase is that of critical examination. The sequels which, in such time as his deadline or some exterior signal allows him, the chooser has invented for any one mode, must be *tested for possibility*. The path of each must be scanned for obstacles. Those sequels which emerge unscathed are the basis of the claim of the particular course of action or mode of inceptive use of resources to be the chosen one. The third phase is that of valuation. Each sequel imagined and deemed possible for some course of action must be assigned a representative point on an axis of desiredness–counter-desiredness. The two extreme members of any such set of points are the final specification of the course of action in question. Such pairs of *focus-points* (as I have habitually called them) may stand in any one of three kinds of relation to each other. The chooser may settle on a greatest tolerable degree of undesiredness (if his valuations are in money terms, the greatest tolerable loss) and out of those courses whose worst outcomes do not exceed this limit, choose the one whose 'desired' outcome is the best. A more general method will first exclude from consideration all those pairs of focus-points whose best outcome is less good, and whose worst outcome is worse, than those of some other available course. This will leave him with the task of deciding what degree of extra badness of its 'bad' outcome can be outweighed, for some course, by the extra goodness of its good outcome.

If thoughts can be absolute originations in some part of their character, if choices can be in some respects absolved and exempt from entire governance by cause, the content of time-to-come is not merely unknown but non-existent, and the notion of foreknowledge of human affairs is vacuous. Then the effort to gather enough data to establish an unique path of history-to-come can be renounced in favour of the discipline of possibility. We ask, not what will take place but what can take place on condition of our acting thus or thus. This is an essentially different posture of thought from that which regards unknowledge as a deficiency, a falling-short, a failure of search and study. This latter attitude leads us to say that one hypothesis of the sequel of specified action must be right *ex ante facto* and not merely *ex post facto*. If that were so, we could legitimately seek to determine and specify, perhaps numerically, the claim to rightness of any hypothesis, we could seek to put a figure on that claim, we could try to calculate its probability. The claim of an unique supposed path of history-to-come to be right is an *exclusive* claim. If one answer to the question, what will the sequel be if I do this, is right *ex ante*, and not merely *ex post*, answers which disagree with it are wrong. The more probable are some answers to the question, the less probable must some others be. Probability is *distributed* over hypotheses. By contrast, possibility is non-exclusive, is not distributive, is not limited in the number of rival, mutually exclusive ideas, answers, imagined sequels to which, in highest degree, or any stated degree, it can be accorded. The possibility, in itself, of one sequel does not, for example, by any means, in any degree, defend the chooser from acknowledging the possibility of a less-desired or counter-desired sequel of his contemplated action.

When we take possibility to be assignable to each of many rival answers or hypotheses, regardless of its being also assigned to others, we are ascribing to it an essential nature quite different from that of probability. The possibility of some hypothesis does not by its pure acceptance diminish that of others. The chooser having invented some answers to his question concerning the sequel of specified action, and having assigned them possibility, is by no means thereby precluded from inventing others and yet others, and assigning possibility to them. Any thought of 'adding together' the possibility of one answer and that of another and so on is wholly vacuous and meaningless. Possibility as I am using this term is primarily qualitative and not essentially quantitative. It represents the absence of something, the absence of discernible obstruction, and thus, of the natural product of recognised obstruction, *disbelief*. Possibility is absence of disbelief, and we can make explicit the non-additive nature of the possibility of this and of that rival hypothesis, by using as a synonym for possibility the expression zero disbelief. The adding together of zeros will not attract us.

At this point I could declare my theme complete. If I am allowed the premisses or the policies of thought that I have asked for, I think the structure can stand by itself. But if, as it were, we take our stand upon it and look outwards, there is ground to be explored, the structural elements when tapped sometimes ring out a question. The last such element we put in place especially does so. To speak of *zero* disbelief prompts the question whether it may not be meaningful, and even obligatory, to consider other degrees of disbelief. Yet, in what terms, by reference to what direct sentiments, to what self-subsisting means of comparison, or to what metrical scale, can we define and locate degrees of disbelief? Disbelief is an intellection, something which has, in itself, form rather than intensity. What psychic experience can we find, that will reflect these forms as intensities? There is one emotion which directly springs from the combination of some formal kind or source of disbelief, and an actual taking-place which belies that disbelief. This is the feeling of *surprise*. The individual may be supposed to ask himself: How much or little should I be surprised if, with no relevant change in my present knowledge, such-and-such occurred? Potential surprise seems to me a practical link between formal and emotional disbelief.

We can approach the same question from a different starting-point. In my core-argument I proposed to treat the question: Is such-and-such a taking-place possible? as a Yes or No question. We had the two categories of 'possible' and 'not possible'. Could we treat these two notions as the bounds of an interval? To do so would of course be to step outside our core-argument. The epistemic interval so defined would be necessary to the notion of degrees of disbelief. They must needs be located within it. If in any sense there is a scale of disbelief or of potential surprise, its range must be the epistemic interval. If such a construction is permissible, how can we translate our core-argument into its terms?

I think it natural to suppose that the power of any imagined sequel of some course of action to arrest the chooser's attention will rest, in the first place, on its own desiredness or counter-desiredness and on the degree of disbelief in which the chooser holds it. Its power to arrest attention, what I have been accustomed to call its *ascendancy*, will I think be an increasing function of its desiredness or counter-desiredness and a decreasing function of its potential surprise. When desiredness–counter-desiredness is represented by some variable such as money profit or loss, it may well be the case that, in contemplating some enterprise–investment, a businessman will assign zero potential surprise, or zero disbelief, to a considerable range of quantities on either side of zero for the total discounted operating profits-to-come of the investment. Beyond the upper and lower bounds of this 'inner range' any larger supposed profit, or larger loss, will have assigned to it some greater than zero degree of disbelief, and this degree, it seems natural to suppose, will be an increasing function of the excess. At some point, then, there will be a constrained maximum of the ascendancy on the 'profit' side and another on the 'loss' side, each being a point where increasing suppositions of profit, or of loss, are just offset by increasing disbelief. There is, of course, no reason at all why the configurations on the two sides should be symmetrical. Many questions present themselves in regard to this illustration of my suggested reform or refinement of the core-argument, the suggestion of degrees of possibility in the interior of the epistemic interval. The supposition of a continuous inner range of hypotheses assigned zero disbelief is only appropriate to such a context as profit–loss. Another question concerns the 'neutral' hypothesis which, being neither desired nor counter-desired, serves as a bench-mark from which to state the distances of other hypotheses as expressions of their degrees of desiredness. At first sight it might seem that the individual should be able to name or locate the neutral outcome by a direct consultation of his desires. But except where the effect of rival hypotheses on him is aesthetic or where they possess some other absolute value or dis-value, he must ground his selection of a neutral outcome on some less immediately intuitive or instinctive principle. We might suggest that the neutral outcome is one whose realisation would make him neither better nor worse off. But on what basis does he judge how well off he is? This will depend on the entire range of outcomes that seem possible, not merely as the sequel of one particular course but as sequels of any available course. The neutral outcome ought on some principle to divide all possible sequels into two groups of equal ascendancy. I cannot doubt that the individual, envisaging some specific sequel of a contemplated action of his own, can decide, perhaps by an arcane thought-process such as constitutes the bulk of our psychic being, whether the sequel is desired or counter-desired.

The two constrained maxima of ascendancy, whose existence it seems to me reasonable to postulate very generally, may themselves be accepted as the focus-points of the extended construction. One objection which may be raised is that each of these is a point in a two-space and that they are thus not directly comparable on a single scale: they are not 'scalars'. They can, however, be reduced to scalar quantities by means of the notion of ascendancy. In a three-dimensional Cartesian frame let the west–east axis stand for desiredness–counter-desiredness, or gain and loss, with a point dividing it into two rays, the eastern for gain and the western for loss. From this same point or origin, let the south–north axis stand for degrees of disbelief, with a range extending from zero disbelief or perfect possibility at the origin to an absolute maximum for impossibility. Within the region defined by the two axes and by a line of absolute maximum disbelief parallel to the west–east axis, any point will stand for an association of some gain, or some loss, and its assigned disbelief. Let a third axis orthogonal to the plane of gain–loss–disbelief represent degrees of ascendancy. In our illustrative case, the points representing ascendancy will lie in a surface of two sheets, one for gain and one for loss. On each of these sheets, equal-ascendancy curves will enable any point with greater-than-zero disbelief to have found for it a point having equal ascendancy and zero disbelief. Thus the two constrained maxima can be substituted by points respectively of lesser gain or loss, and zero disbelief. These points will lie on the gain–loss axis and their distances from the origin will be scalar quantities. In the deepened or refined version of my argument they are the focus-points.

It will perhaps be asked whether, in putting forward a wholly unconventional and even eccentric view of the nature of choice, and grounding it in ideas unusual and even unheard of in economics, such as the notion of uncause in thought, the imaginative and originative source and nature of the choosables, and the endless proliferant creation of hypothetical sequels of choosable action, I wish to emphasise what I am calling the core-argument in its rather spare and harsh simplifications, or by contrast the deepened form which recognises levels of disbelief other than zero or absolute, and which lends itself to a number of possibly fertile manipulations. My answer is that the respective purposes are distinct. In order to gain some critical attention for ideas which at first, to 'mainstream' economic theoreticians, are naturally rebarbative, the argument is best presented in its basic and most essential lineaments, by which it must stand or fall. But we are all indoctrinated with ideals of mathematical incisive sculpture of thought, even of achieving, in however modest a degree, mathematical beauty, the surprising revelation of necessity. I am not sure that these ideals and ambitions are true for us, whose subject-matter is the ineffably mysterious, mutable and subtle nature and capacities of man. Least of all am I supposing that my theme can touch these ideals or even glimpse them. These two contrasting purposes, however, are the reason for the presentation of my theme in two editions. What, then, is that cord on which such beads as I have tried to carve are strung? It is an attempted answer to the question: What can the action-chooser, the decision-maker, *know*, and with what content can the word 'know' be used when describing his business of choice?

I have suggested, in effect, that he can tell himself where possibility reaches its limits, he can trace upon his thought map of imagined things a boundary-fence beyond which, given his resources, given his time-horizon for reaping the fruits of action, no action of his can reach. In a sense which has some degree of paradox, his knowledge is of the non-possible. It is beyond the fence that everything can be tagged with effective certainty as not belonging to the attainable. Unknowledge, for him, consists in *the plurality of rival possibles*. The bounds of the possible are bounds of unknowledge.

6 Harrod as Economist

Between the middle nineteen-twenties and the fresh outbreak of war, economic theory was transformed from its foundations. The half-century from 1870 had left in being an edifice whose symmetry, simplicity and seeming inclusiveness had gained it an unquestioned ascendancy over the liberal world. The prices, in terms of a numéraire, of all products and all means of production, the weekly quantity brought to market, and the equal quantity carried off from the market, of each product and each means, the consequent total of incomes of the suppliers of means of production, the total value, in terms of the numéraire, of everything produced in a week, and the crowning and clinching of the whole structure by a proof that those two totals, of incomes and the value of products, each total separately arrived at, were equal: all these things are shown to flow from the nature of human desires and the interaction of their resources. The conception as a whole was the Theory of General Competitive Equilibrium. It seemed by its sheer completeness and its singleness of method to be unassailable. Yet by 1926 there had begun the first of three assaults, in two of which Harrod had a central part to play.

An idea indispensable to the unified simplicity of General Competitive Equilibrium is that of perfect competition. Each commodity, defined by its physical properties, is assumed to be made by an infinity of firms each so small that the difference made by its output (weekly or yearly quantity produced) to the output of the industry (all the makers of this product taken together) is imperceptible. A firm in perfect competition can thus expand its output without affecting the unit price of the product, and it can do so without affecting the cost of the means of producing a unit of the product. If the price of a unit is not less than the cost, what is then to prevent the firm's indefinite expansion? But if it expands indefinitely what becomes of perfect competition? Piero Sraffa in 1926[1] thus showed that, in the long period, perfect competition is self-contradictory. But this rather rarified *reductio ad absurdum* was reinforced by accepted fact. Expansion of output gives a firm economies of scale and actually reduces unit cost. If perfect competition allows it to sell the expanding output at an unchanging price, what will stop it from swallowing the whole industry? Perfect competition was untenable, yet to abandon it as Sraffa proposed would involve, in Hicks's words, 'the wreckage of the greater part of economic theory'.[2]

The problem that perfect competition failed to solve was what it is that settles at an explainable size the output of an individual firm. The principle involved was plain: the firm would seek to make as large as it could the excess of weekly or yearly sale proceeds of product (gross revenue) over the weekly or yearly costs of its production. The firm subject to perfect competition was too small to influence the price, it could choose only its output, and it ought to set this at a size where one additional unit would add more to total cost than to sale proceeds. Under perfect competition each extra unit of output added the unchanging *price* of a unit to sale proceeds (total gross revenue). But if what this extra unit would add to total cost was less than the price and was *decreasing* as output expanded, how could an equality of the extra gross revenue and the extra total cost ever be reached? In providing a verbal solution to the problem of the firm's choice of output (as distinct from a formal mathematical one) by dissecting *marginal revenue* Harrod in 1930[3] inaugurated afresh, ninety-two years after Cournot, the study of *imperfect competition*.

The story of marginal revenue is a strange one. The notion of a marginal quantity is simply a *difference* between two values of some variable. When we climb a hill each step forward makes a difference to our altitude until at the top it ceases to make a difference. To find what value of a variable whose value we can choose will give the largest or the least value of a variable depending on this one, we take pairs of mutually corresponding differences of the two variables until we find a pair where the dependent difference is zero. The firm's net revenue is reckoned by subtracting the cost of producing the output from the sale proceeds of output, and since each of these depends on output, the procedure just described must be applied to the net revenue. It is the sale proceeds which give rise to the notion of marginal revenue. The sale proceeds are equal to the price of a unit of product times the number of units weekly or yearly produced (the output). An extra unit added to output will require the price of all units to be reduced, for we are considering a firm subject to imperfect competition. But at this slightly lower price, it will add its own value to the sale proceeds. Marginal revenue thus has two terms, one negative and one positive. When marginal revenue and marginal cost have been reckoned for a range of practicable outputs, that output will be chosen for which the two marginal quantities, each expressed in the numéraire, are equal.

When net revenue is expressed algebraically, a formal manipulation yields the results of the steps described above. This mathematical procedure was employed by Cournot in a famous book of 1838[4] and again by Marshall in Mathematical Note XIV of the *Principles of Economics*, and thus the equilibrium of a firm subject to imperfect competition appeared as the automatic, immediate step of a mathematician as soon as he had stated the problem in algebra. Are we then to be puzzled at the great labour devoted to the subject by those, like Harrod, who worked more intuitively, and used verbal and diagrammatic arguments, and by the entrenched opposition and perverse ingenuity of those, like Dennis Robertson and Gerald Shove, who believed that perfect competition could be saved, and those, in particular Sir John Hicks, who thought that without it all was lost? It was needful that both the discarders and the defenders of perfect competition should perceive clearly all that the loss of it would entail. The supply curve as an expression merely of conditions of production was utterly undone. The quantity offered on the market now depended partly on elasticities of *demand*, the demand curve and the supply curve were no longer independent of each other. The notion of the industry as a group of firms all producing technologically identical goods between which no purchaser has any preference disappears. A theory centred on the physical commodity was displaced by one centred on the concerns of the individual firm. This position was only reached by critical study of each element of the old theory to see if it could survive. Harrod performed the hardest, earliest part of this task with many shifts of expedient and policy.

Until the 1930s, economic theory held the entire economic scene to consist of the simultaneous choices made by individuals each in the light (effectively) of a perfect knowledge of the choices which would be made by others. All the choices were made simultaneously. How else, except in this Parmenidean world of un-time and un-event could each chooser know the effect of *all* other choices? How, even in timeless simultaneity, could choosers know each other's intended acts? This was the miracle attributed to the market. We may say, if we like, that individuals' conditional intentions were collated and a solution found prescribing that act for each individual, which he would choose given the acts prescribed for all the others. When the acts involved are all of them exchanges of one good for another, the prescriptions required are those of the quantities to be given and received, and the solution can take the form of market prices agreed by all participants for appropriate quantities. Into a world thus conceiving itself, where assured rationality was supposed to exclude unemployment, there burst the Great Depression of the 1930s.

The questions now confronting economics were ones which the whole spirit and aspiration of its central doctrine entirely and essentially disavowed. That doctrine exhibited the order and coherence of a system which virtually negated *time and unknowledge*. What has such a doctrine to do with the essence of the human predicament, the necessity to decide upon action whose sequel cannot be known? Alongside its central doctrine, economics had some radically different theories which recognised an alternation of boom and slump with, very roughly indeed, a nine-year-period. The Great Depression, despite an unprecedented violence and depth, was looked on as belonging to this *business cycle*. Harrod's blueprint for imperfect competition was complete. He turned with zest and fertile brilliance to try to understand the business cycle, and thus arrived at an account of it which illustrates at its topmost bent the encapsulating technique of a discipline faced with limitless heterogeneity and intricacy of subject-matter, and resolving these difficulties by means of portmanteau concepts the content in detail of each of which is relevant only for what its constituents have in common.

Harrod had been allowed in the years of its writing to follow the evolution of the *General Theory of Employment, Interest and Money*. Six months after its publication there appeared his own book *The Trade Cycle*. In that book the sense of elation and excitement is evident and justified. Harrod had confronted with each other the new Kahn-Keynes Multiplier and the long-standing Accelerator of Bickerdike, Aftalion and J. M. Clark, and asked himself what would arise from their conjunction. The Multiplier principle says that an incremental flow of yearly spending by businessmen or government on the enlargement or improvement of their productive equipment will lead by stages to a larger incremental flow of the society's general output and income.

The Multiplier itself is the ratio of the latter increment, that of general output or income, to the former, that of net investment. The Multiplier process comes about because the extra flow of spending on equipment will at first be partly offset by a depletion of stocks of consumers' goods, as newly-employed men increase their consumption. But this will lead to an increase of the output of consumers' goods by means of a further increase in employment. Each extra party of re-employed men, and their now more-prosperous employers, will spend part, and save part, of their extra income. As the total of the 'saved' portions of income approaches equality with the extra flow of spending on equipment, which we are supposing to be constant, this extra flow of equipment spending will be gradually freed from offset by extra consumption, and will count entirely as net investment. The Multiplier will thus attain its full effect in a higher constant level of general output. Whence can come the extra stock of equipment, which businessmen will need, or desire, in order to produce a larger general output? The stock will evidently be built up, more or less rapidly, by the augmented flow of net investment, which itself will be strongly justified, as to its existing level, and perhaps further stimulated in respect of orders for equipment which will now be given. The stimulus will have a large effect on the quarterly or yearly volume of these orders, because of the arithmetical fact known as the Accelerator.

Much equipment is durable, consisting of buildings, plant and tools whose initial construction cost is many times the annual amount needed to be spent on them, once they are built, to keep them in working order. It follows that when a given stock of equipment is to be augmented, the volume of orders given for new plant will be much greater than what has sufficed for the mere maintenance of the stock at a constant size. Net investment is the main source of orders for the equipment-making industries, and the main need for net investment may come from businessmen's desire for extra equipment to produce a larger output. The effects of the Multiplier call for extra equipment, the need for extra equipment calls for net investment, net investment is what brings into action the Multiplier. In these considerations Harrod saw the elements of a self-sustaining process, the ***regularly progressive economy***. This idea he encapsulated in a 'Fundamental Equation,' where the left-hand member is a percentage of itself by which general output might grow in unit time, and the right-hand member is the percentage of income saved (by the society as a whole) divided by the quantity of equipment needed to produce a unit of general output. Many possibilities and questions spring immediately from this conception.

The meaning of the Fundamental Equation can perhaps be better seen if we move the symbol which represents the quantity of equipment per unit of output (the capital-to-output ratio) from being a divisor on the right-hand side to being a factor for multiplying on the left-hand side. Then the equation will say: the percentage rate of annual growth of output, multiplied by the ratio of required (or desired) equipment per unit of output (the product of multiplication giving us the percentage by which the stock of equipment, supposedly in full use, must grow in order to sustain the growing general output at a constant annual percentage), is equal to the percentage saved out of general output (or income). Let us otherwise express it thus: The annual percentage growth of general output must evidently *be linked with* the percentage saved out of a year's output, for saving provides the needed means of extra production. What is the link? It is the capital-to-output ratio.

Now let us examine, first the purpose, then the assumptions, and lastly some of the implications of this proposition.

The equation contains three variables, any one of which can be determined from it, given the numerical values of the other two. Harrod elects as the unknown the percentage annual growth of output. There will, he says, be some numerical value of this which, by satisfying the equation, will generate self-sustaining growth, the 'regularly progressive economy.' The assumptions which are needed in order to validate this result include some in which the very nature of economics as a style of thought appears. Economics is inescapably concerned with expressing as a scalar quantity the 'size' of a heap of things extremely diverse in technological character. This can be done by valuing the things and adding together their values, if we can justify any principle of valuation on grounds of the purpose served by our exercise as a whole. The capital-to-output ratio exemplifies this character of economics in a very thorough-going way. It is an encapsulation *à outrance*. Yet the inferences that Harrod is able to draw, by some further steps of simplification, seem, to me at least, to justify not only his own argument but the method of encapsulation as a virtually indispensable and inherent tool of our discipline.

In his conception of a process of growth of general output depending on the balanced mutual sustention of the working of the Multiplier and the Accelerator, Harrod had constructed a bomb capable of blowing the economy into violent boom or collapse despite the various stabilisers which he had examined and described in such detail in the earlier part of *The Trade Cycle*. The regularly progressive economy, supposing it to get started, rides on a razor-edge. So far from any failure of balance engendering corrective forces, a departure from the path of regular growth must inevitably lead to an increasing divergence. Harrod here achieves a startling paradox. It is when the businessmen are producing *less* than the society's propensity to save and the technological ratio of capital to output require for a balance between growth of demand and growth of the stock of equipment, that the insufficient pressure of the low production on existing equipment will weaken or destroy the incentive for net investment, halt or reverse the Multiplier and produce the symptoms of *overproduction*. If the businessmen are producing *more* than regular growth requires, excessive pressure on the stock of equipment will make net investment seem insufficient and give the appearance of *underproduction*. These seeming paradoxes are due at bottom to the nature of the Accelerator (Harrod's 'Relation'). They are startling, they add to the sharp flavour of Harrod's argument, but they seem also in some sense to over-reach themselves and be thus confusing. Have we not here an effect of something that *has* happened upon what men now *expect will happen* and thus upon their choices of action and the sequel of these choices? Is there not here a need for careful distinction of sequential phases, of *ex ante* and *ex post*? And it is here that Harrod may, in eyes not yet adjusted to the deep elusive subtlety of economic time relations, seem inconsistent.

The Fundamental Equation from which in principle we can find the quarterly or annual percentage of its size at the threshold of such an interval, by which general output needs to grow in order that net investment may generate through the Multiplier just such demand as it can provide for by extra equipment, is looked upon by Harrod as referring to a point of time. There is no contradiction between our statement of its meaning, using such terms as 'annual' and 'interval,' and Harrod's view of it as describing the events of a moment. We need appeal only to the classic Newtonian limiting process, by which, in measuring velocity, associated intervals of time and space are conceived to make an ever-nearer approach to zero length without attaining it. It is not this formal matter which calls for discussion. The telescoping process as a formal device is acceptable, but we ought to remember *what* is being telescoped, and this 'what' is the individual's range of thoughts, backwards and forwards from his present. He looks at the volume of demand in his today and ascribes it to the Multiplier effect of the net investment which is proceeding today as a consequence of the orders for equipment which he and others gave 'yesterday,' last month, last quarter or last year. He sees those orders justified by the matching of the extra demand and the extra equipment in which they have resulted, and he gives fresh orders in just such larger volume, compared with yesterday, as the justified growth suggests will itself be justified in turn. The thoughts of each businessman take place in his present moment, but they consist of his scrutiny of the past and the present, and his decision for the morrow. Harrod has many passages in which such a structure of thought is recognised and suggested, but he eschews the formal frame which makes it explicit, the distinction of the conjectural, figmental, essentially imaginative filling of a time interval on whose threshold we have arrived and whose supposed content we see *ex ante facto*, from the study of recorded events from an interval which has elapsed and can be seen *ex post facto*.

Harrod was a man who revelled in thought, who followed the scent of reason through endless turns and thickets, and who trod the field of scholarship with a sort of dancing zest. Once an idea had seized his interest and exhibited an incisive explanatory power, he advanced it with unswerving assurance. He led the investigation of imperfect competition, and was one of the two, mutually independent, inventors of the regularly progressive economy, on which he built an explosion-collapse theory of the business cycle, deserving to be called dramatic. For his books, *The Trade Cycle*, and *Towards a Dynamic Economics*, and the articles in the *Economic Journal* which developed or led up to them, he should have been acclaimed as an innovator of the topmost rank. He was, of course, a very famous economist, yet I doubt whether his original powers got their true meed of undivided praise.

7 Levels of Simplicity in Keynes's Theory of Money and Employment

The elemental core of Keynes's theory of money and employment can be stated in two sentences. To buy the means (natural resources, produced facilities and human work) of producing goods is to gamble on the eventual sale value of those goods. From time to time businessmen can lose their nerve and refuse this gamble, preferring to keep their wealth in money rather than embark it in the products of employment. To carry conviction and full understanding this statement needs to be elaborated with the answers to many questions. We may say that in *The General Theory of Employment, Interest and Money* Keynes answered many of the questions without, at any point, incisively presenting the statement itself. The level of simplicity that the statement attains had to wait for the article in the *Quarterly Journal of Economics* of 1937.

Two questions present themselves at the outset. Does not our epitomizing statement confine itself to the 'supply side', whereas Keynes's theory is thought to emphasise the demand side? And does our statement allow sufficiently for the available resort to forward contracts? A single theme is the answer to both these questions. Plans to produce goods rest upon hopes that the goods when the time comes will be demanded. It is these hopes which can give way to panic. But cannot the demand be assured by a forward contract? Only if the gamble on the circumstances of time-to-come is shared by the potential demanders, who may be wholesalers, retailers or the ultimate consumers or users of the goods, but who will only sign a forward contract if their own views of time-to-come do not embrace too great a possible misfortune. We can substitute for our epitomizing statement another more general one. To buy things with a view to using or to selling them is to take an action in unknowledge of its sequel. The kind and degree of this unknowledge can be extremely different from one set of circumstances to another, and the study of these differences is a vital step to understanding how the demand for human work, the giving of employment, can fail. A first renouncement of simplicity must be made.

What are the circumstances which make the question: What will the sequel be if I buy such-and-such a thing? especially open to a wide variety of answers? One such circumstance is the distance in time-to-come at which important aspects of the sequel will declare themselves. The greater this distance is, the more unlike each other some of the supposable sequels of the purchase will be, and the more hazardous that purchase will seem. The pace at which various aspects of the individual's circumstances can be plausibly supposed to change from those of his present will be limited by principles of nature and of the human psyche, and by the character of social organisation. The more distant the time-horizon, the more different the state of things in that day can be from the present. The distance of the time-horizon thus divides goods into two classes: those which are to serve the immediate, familiar and known needs of everyday life, and those which are to embody the plans of imaginative enterprise. The former are consumption goods, the latter are investment goods. The hazards of investment are greater also through another circumstance. Investment goods are often large indivisible systems which must be acquired as a whole, whose purchase is a non-repeatable experiment, either through its expensiveness or its crucially innovative character. And because of the difference in their respective purposes, the buying of investment goods can be more easily postponed or forgone than that of consumption goods.

If these are the differences between the two classes of goods, two more questions present themselves. Is the output (time rate of production) of investment goods more exposed to large rapid changes than that of consumption goods? And, do the respective levels of output of the two classes affect each other?

Richard Kahn had formalised the effect of a change in investment output on consumption output and thus on output as a whole in his conception of the Multiplier process. This became a vital component of the *General Theory*. It showed that changes in investment output might cause changes in the absolute level of output as a whole several times as great as that of investment. Also there had long been in existence a theorem which said that changes in the level of general output (embracing both consumption and investment output) could exert a powerful leverage on planned output of investment goods. This was the Accelerator theorem of Bickerdike, Aftalion and John Maurice Clark. It depended on the arithmetical fact that if, for example, a fleet of twenty ships can be maintained at constant size by building one ship a year to replace one which is worn out, the output of ships will have to be doubled in any year in which the size of the fleet is to be increased by one-twentieth.

It was Harrod who seized upon the question how these two influences of one class of output on the other could be fitted together. By a brilliant stroke he showed how their combination fixed the conditions for growth of general output at a constant percentage per unit of time, and how the extreme fragility of this 'regular growth' provided a dramatic explanation of the succession of boom and slump known as the business cycle. Why were not these results attained in the *General Theory*? We could say that Keynes had enough problems on hand without the Accelerator, of which he makes no mention. He may also have distrusted its mechanical air, which might superficially be seen as dispensing with references to human choice. But I think there is more. Keynes wishes to prescribe a test by which the businessman can know that the building-up of his stock of some kind of productive facility is proceeding at the right, the most profitable, pace. This test requires that when the excess of product value over operating cost of the new facility in each of the years of its assumed life is discounted at such a percentage per annum that the total of these discounted gains is equal to the construction cost of the facility, this percentage (the marginal efficiency of capital) shall be equal to the prevailing market rate of interest. If a general increase of the pace of investment raises the hoped-for gains from new facilities, investment may prove self-stimulating and no 'optimal' pace may present itself. By contrast with Keynes's test, Harrod provided a growth equilibrium, but insisted on its precarious and inherently unstable nature. Keynes's omission from the *General Theory*, except in chapter 22, of any study of how an increase of output as a whole might affect businessmen's judgement of their need for investment goods seems to me a deliberate policy. To acknowledge this influence would invalidate Keynes's test, which requires the marginal efficiency of capital to be a decreasing function of the pace of production of investment goods in general and not merely of that of particular kinds of facility. However, we cannot suppose each businessman to be informed of the investment plans of all the others. His awareness of those plans must come from observing their effects, and this implies a process of sequential mutual reactions, not the immediate and perpetual fulfilment of a test.

I think we may venture further. To allow that businessmen's

desired pace (size of flow) of production of investment goods is judged by them partly by reference to their saleable output of goods in general would have seemed to imprison Keynes in a *closed* system, a system with 'a will of its own', a theory, like Harrod's, of regular growth or of the business cycle. This would have robbed his theory, in some sense, of its generalness, its claim to omni-competence, its free-ranging applicability to all situations. We may even say perhaps that the *General Theory* explains what *could* happen in this or that set of circumstances, not what *must* happen in the only possible set of circumstances.

Keynes's treatment of the inducement to invest is thus somewhat paradoxical. He uses an equilibrium formulation in describing the violent weather and climatics of history itself, yet it is the general principles of this weather and not its seasonality that he allows himself to study. In such a perspective, chapter 22 is a curiously anomalous digression. In defiance of the main policy, it claims to explain the business cycle by appeal to the principles set out in the body of the work, but the phases of the cycle are individually characterised without any indication of why each phase is the inevitable, or at least the natural, sequel of its predecessor. To supply such linkages, however, would be contrary to Keynes's seeming purpose of describing the building blocks rather than the building.

The attempt I am here making to show Keynes's argument as the elaboration of a single and simple theme has now taken several steps. The theme itself is our need to act in unknowledge of what each of the rival courses that present themselves would lead to. This is the unchangeable face of our human condition. Its effect is more daunting when the relevant sequel stretches far into time-to-come and thus it divides the services and goods we buy into consumption goods and investment goods. The levels and the changes of level of the output of each of these classes affect that of the other.

How are these influences transmitted? The businessman will take the gamble of production only if there is evidence to suggest that his products when they are ready will sell. The evidence he wants is the sight of like products which have already been produced selling as fast as he can replace them. Demand must be seen at work to suggest the need for supply. In the closed economy that Keynes considers, the only buyers are the earners of income, those who in some capacity collaborate in production. If all the goods they produce are to be sold for as much as the expense of producing them, the whole of this expense, namely the incomes of the collaborating producers, must be spent on goods of one sort or another. But at this point another step must be taken away from the pristine encompassing simplicity.

People on the whole do not wish to spend the whole of their income on consumption goods. But not all of those who spend less on consumption than they earn are ready to spend the remainder on investment goods. Investment goods must be bought in the first place by businessmen, either as facilities for their own business of producing, or as 'consumer durables' such as houses, which other members of the society will buy from them gradually. To buy investment goods is hazardous, and circumstances may from time to time specially discourage it. There is, then, a gap between the society's income and its spending on consumption, and the question how big a gap can be filled depends for its answer on how big a flow of investment spending the imagination and bold spirit of businessmen can induce. If, when general output, employment and income are high, the saving gap can be filled by the buying of investment goods, then those high levels can find enough demand to allow them to persist.

In thus expressing the matter, I have remained on a level of simplicity which Keynes leaves behind from the outset. He regards it as unquestionable that at the higher of two levels of income, in otherwise like circumstances, the society will both spend more on consumption, and save more, than at the lower level of income. The proposition so stated is sufficient for Keynes's purpose. He does *not* require that the *proportion* of income saved should be higher at a higher income. If the absolute saving gap is larger at a larger income of society, and so long as this larger income corresponds to a larger general output and thus a higher level of employment, it can be said that employment can be maintained at a higher level if the quantity of investment goods demanded per time unit can be maintained at a higher level.

When we have got thus far the questions which the argument prompts begin to proliferate. I have been setting out the relations between income (or general output measured in money) on one hand, and consumption spending and saving, on the other, in terms of comparative levels, not in terms of a process leading from one set of levels to another. This, broadly speaking, is Keynes's policy. He thus stays on a level of greater simplicity than if he had sought to describe a movement in which successive phases follow each other by nature or even by necessity. However, a stylised account of such a movement had been provided by Lord Kahn. He assumed that a once-for-all raising of the level of output of investment goods would generate extra income which would be partly spent on a continuing extra take-off of consumption goods, and that this would soon lead to an extra output of consumption goods, the earnings from making which would call for a further increase of consumption output, and so on in convergent steps until income and general output had risen to a size of flow at which the saving gap was equal to the extra flow of spending on investment goods. The famous article in the *Economic Journal* of 1931, in which this Multiplier conception was described, did not depend for its meaning or validity on supposing that the successive phases were attained at weekly or any other particular time intervals, or even on claiming that they would be individually distinguishable. It did, however, indicate a time-taking process whose reality Keynes admitted. On the same page of the *General Theory* (page 122) however, he refers mysteriously to 'the logical theory of the multiplier which holds good continuously, without time lag, at all moments of time'. This must, I think, refer to the inverse of the propensity to save, which may indeed 'hold good' at each moment but still operates only in a time-taking process. This inverse is numerically equal to the sum of the convergent Multiplier series.

The Multiplier process described by Lord Kahn vitally illuminates reality, but entirely leaves out the feedback of growing general output on the inducement to invest. The output of investment goods is the element which, for Keynes, proximately dominates the scene, and it is therefore essential for us, if we subscribe to his broad vision, to consider what influences govern the size of this output.

Investment goods are required both to make good the wear-and-tear of productive facilities and to augment and improve them. The making-good is part of the business of producing a steady stream of consumption goods at a constant time rate. It is needful in order to maintain income at a constant level. Only that part of investment goods output which augments or improves facilities can serve to fill the saving gap. It is the strength and nature of the incentive for this *net investment* part of the total, or gross, output of investment goods that we have particularly to study. Keynes's treatment of this question is a massive puzzle. Repeatedly throughout the *General Theory* the importance of uncertainty is referred to. It looms always on the skyline of the argument. Yet it is not until the article in the *QJE* that we are close enough to it to see the whole of business and economic affairs lying in the shadow of this mountain. I have myself been charged with nihilism, yet in the *General Theory* by default, and in the *QJE* by uncompromising and decisive avowal, Keynes himself rejects the relevance of probability techniques and ideas for the reckoning of the prospects for enterprise investment and puts nothing in its place. Of such prospects for productive facilities whose initial cost, at best, will take many years to be recouped, he says: 'We simply do not know.'

It is the theme of the inducement to invest and of how the size of flow of net investment is determined that raises most acutely the question how best to conceive and express matters. In the *Treatise on Money* the Fundamental Equations represented a disequilibrium method and tacitly employ the distinction between the expectation and the eventual record of a given proper-named time interval. By this means the proximate causes of movements of prices and quantities can be exhibited. In the *General Theory* Keynes retreats to equilibrium and comparative statics, and so, in chapter eleven, we find that the size of the net investment flow will be pushed to that level where the marginal efficiency of capital is equal to the rate of interest.

The marginal efficiency of capital is that percentage per annum at which the sale proceeds, less operating expenses, of the produce of a proposed new facility in each year of its assumed life would have to be discounted to bring them in total to equality with the first cost (construction cost) of the facility. The argument of chapter eleven implies that each businessman proposing to invest in a new facility can reckon its marginal efficiency without knowledge of what other investments are being proposed or what the aggregate Multiplier effect of them all will be or what will be its feedback on the earnings of his own facility. But this is only a particular source of a general condition, the precariousness and mutability of the conjectures on which, if on anything, decisions to invest must be based, a condition on which, in chapter 12 immediately following, Keynes insists with the famous passage about 'animal spirits'.

Did Keynes's return to an equilibrium method conduce to simplicity? This question is a version or an aspect of a deeper one. Are business affairs in their broadest sweep, and the economic affairs of society, best illuminated by treating them as emergent history or as calculable science? Two views seem possible of the nature of *history in the making*. We can regard it as *organic*, in the sense that what takes place is the natural or necessary outgrowth of what *has* taken place. Or we can regard it as *original*, the product in part, at all times, of thoughts and endeavours whose character could not have been inferred by means of any knowledge, however perfect, of their antecedents. If in this sense history is in some respects *original*, if it is in part *originated* by human thoughts, then it cannot be appropriate to treat any department of it as completely explainable. If so, equilibrium can be no more than a frame of reference. In the *General Theory* Keynes was seeking to explain aspects of the anarchy of history. Why did he choose a method which supposes human affairs to express an informed and co-ordinated rationality?

The theme of the *General Theory* could be expressed more briefly still. Unemployment arises from the preference of liquidity over enterprise. *Liquidity preference* is the idea by which Keynes broke out from the closed self-optimising system of General Equilibrium in which the rate of interest is one of the prices of goods-in-terms-of-goods, being the price of goods now in terms of goods deferred. If a high rate of interest, which the marginal efficiency of capital can only match when the flow of investment is held down to some low level, is due to a strong desire for goods now rather than goods deferred, this strong desire for immediate consumption will imply a correspondingly small saving gap, and employment will be at the level responding to the balanced wishes of the society. Keynes repudiated the notion that the interest rate is determined by time preference. It is determined, he said, in the bond market by the *speculative motive* for holding wealth in the form of money rather than in the form of a borrower's promise to pay stated sums at stated deferred dates. Keynes showed that the size of flow of net investment was influenced on one side, not by the price of *savings*, whose scarcity would imply high consumption and thus give an aid to employment, but by the price of *liquidity*, the desire for which had no counterpart in increased consumption, and was purely a drag on the incentive to invest. The *General Theory* has been said to lack a clear design. Yet Keynes sought by an intense intellectual effort to unify its argument and bring all to an ultimate inclusive formula. This, I think, is the purpose of the allegedly 'mysterious' Chapter 17. But this is approached by an extensive discussion of the nature of liquidity and of the sources of the desire for it, a discussion which overshadows by its length the references to other factors in the inducement to invest.

The fascination of the concept of the interest rate is extremely powerful. Its nature as a reflection of time, its influence on human purposes, which of necessity look to time-to-come, its power almost to draw knowledge of the world of experience from purely logical considerations (as when we find the maximum absolute effect of an interest-rate change on the discounted value of equal variously deferred sums to be located at that deferment whose number of years is the reciprocal of the interest rate),[1] its engenderment by uncertainty and the speculative exploitation of uncertainty, and its invocation by Erik Lindahl as the essence of the concept of income: such are its compelling claims upon thought.

Between the *Treatise on Money* and the *General Theory* there is a change of feeling. In the *Treatise* Keynes was a modern Cantillon describing the business world from an insider's viewpoint; describing with zest the flowing tide of events and the climatic changes. In the *General Theory* he had withdrawn into the classroom and adopted the language of formal analysis. This change appears vividly in his treatment of the interest rate. In the *Treatise* he pictures the Bulls and Bears of the gilt-edged market going into and out of bonds as they individually come to think that the next price movement will be up or down. In this speculative market the price of bonds and thus their yield, the interest rate, can only settle if opinion is divided, so that those who wish to sell for fear of a fall find their offers matched by the bids of those who wish to buy in hope of a rise. It is thus, as Keynes says, a *variety* of opinion in the gilt-edged market which gives stability to the interest rate and some control over it to the monetary authorities.

The necessity for a positive interest rate, in distinction from the manner of its determination, can be shown by an argument which Keynes did not offer. In brief, to lend money in exchange for a promise of stated payments at stated dates, is to part with a known sum of money in exchange for an unknown sum. For if, at some date earlier than that by which the borrower has promised to complete his payments, the lender should come to wish that he had his money back, his only resort will be to sell the borrower's bond for whatever price, now unknown, it may at that unknown time be marketable for. To give the lender some presumption that he will in one way or another get back the whole amount he now lends, and to hold out to him the possibility of getting something more than bare repayment as a reward for his willingness to bear uncertainty, he and all other lenders will require a borrower's promised payments to exceed in total the sum initially lent. That excess is the source of interest.

The *Treatise on Money* shows us the interest rate as the ripples and surges of a market in process, the *General Theory* shows it as a function, representable for the most part by a smooth curve, of the size of that part of the money stock which is not needed to mediate the exchange of real goods and services. In both books, however, the interest rate is a phenomenon of *money*.

It is on page 173, in the first sentence of section three of a chapter called 'The General Theory of the Rate of Interest', that Keynes says 'We have now introduced money into our causal nexus for the first time, and we are able to catch a first glimpse of the way in which changes in the quantity of money work their way into the economic system.' What, then, is money, that its particular discussion occupies eighty pages of the *General Theory*, as compared with thirty for the marginal efficiency of capital? Money as the reflection of uncertainty is one of the elemental forces of history. Money is liquidity. Its nature is intimately fused in that of choices of business action and policy. Its introduction is another, and a necessary, step away from simplicity.

It is artificial and unreal to seek to compare a money-using economy with one where money is absent. The *market* economy, where the business of choice and decision involves everyone, the *free* economy, is inconceivable without money or some equivalent means of 'reserving judgement'. But if, *per impossibile*, we could conceive an exchange economy without such means, an economy where goods must be exchanged for goods and not for money, it would be needful for each exchanger to specify in technical detail, in some degree, what he would accept in exchange for what he offered. By contrast, money allows a producer to defer the decision what he shall get in exchange for what he gives. Why wait? Because he does not yet know what at deferred dates he is going to need. Money is called a medium of exchange, but it might equally be called a medium of search. If so, Keynes's transactions motive for holding a stock of money can be assimilated to the other two motives, which can themselves be resolved into the speculative motive. The three motives are one. Liquidity preference is the negation of enterprise when the sequels of enterprise are especially hard to confine within bounds. Liquidity is the means for the individual to 'keep his options open'.

In his consummate and masterly appraisal of Keynes's work, called *Keynes's Impact on Monetary Economics*, Professor J. C. Gilbert has one judgement which a little surprises me. He says that the *General Theory* 'lacks a clear design'. I would say rather that the design is obscured by the need that Keynes felt to deal with semantic difficulties as they arose, and to insert long chapters contrasting his views with those of others. In this present article I have proposed a reversal, in some sense, of Keynes's plan, which proceeds as it were from the outside inwards, while I would first seize upon the heart of the matter and then consider what is its integument of physiological mechanism. Keynes begins with great aggregate quantities and posits relations amongst them; presents a formal frame of ideas about investment, but proceeds at once to show that this frame is unreal; comes at last to his decisive innovation, the sundering of investment incentive from the urge to save, by discarding the notion that the interest rate is determined by the interaction of these two, and therefore co-ordinates them. Instead he makes the interest rate to spring from and to manifest liquidity preference, and so investment can be insufficient to match the potential saving gap out of a full employment income. Employment declines and fails when enterprise is abandoned in favour of liquidity, in face of the unyielding human unknowledge of the sequels of its rival available courses of action.

The *General Theory*'s most momentous, radical and decisive service was to release the interest rate from its imprisonment in the mutually self-determining equilibrium system of prices of goods in terms of goods, and to make it a response to uncertainty. Liquidity preference was Keynes's great discovery, suggested by the accustomed language of the business, and in particular the banking, world. This work of liberation was accomplishment enough for one man and one book. Keynes was content to leave some vital ideas as mere names or terms, their nature and working not gone into. Above all, he does not at all suggest how the notion of the marginal efficiency of capital incorporates the effects of uncertainty. The gulf which divides chapter eleven from chapter twelve is left unbridged. In the end, probability as a bridge is dismissed. Keynes destroyed the calculable system and he did not replace it with another.

The account I have here given of Keynes's theme urges its essential simplicity, but seeks that goal by a route not always the same as his own. The distinction between investment and consumption is based here upon a difference in the degree of unknowledge, and thus of hazard, which the two motives for production and acquisition respectively involve. To me this difference appears as one of degree, though a very marked and even dramatic degree. Keynes does not treat consumption as involving any uncertainty. Some effect of unification is obtained by my view, which receives support from the modern habit of referring to 'consumer confidence'. A more radical departure, which is encouraged by the brevity of an article as compared with a book, is the omission, from my account, of any discussion of units. In the *General Theory* the stride of the argument is retarded by Keynes's explanations of his units and his terms. This was needful in order that his treatment might put on the armour of quantitative logic that economics has traditionally worn. Traditionally, however, in Keynes's day economics had for generations concerned itself with the price-quantity affairs of market participants rather than with the broad movements which are now called macroeconomics. I find it hard to accept that the notion of involuntary unemployment depends on the failure of prices to rise a little in relation to money wages. Something more elemental surely must be at work? On page 21, lines 10 to 18, Keynes suddenly abandons the fine shades of relative price and in one incisive statement brings in the theme that designed investment can fail to fill the saving gap until employment and income have fallen far enough. Perhaps the economics of general output as a whole should lead us away from the pursuit of an illusory precision.

8 On Hicks's Causality in Economics: a Review Article[1]

The Hicksian vineyard over very many years has yielded a wine of a special and exquisite flavour all its own. Clear and dry, it is a choice companion of the studious hour. No ingredient has been allowed that could grate on a reasoner's taste for exact lucidity and sharp and definite conclusions. Sir John Hicks hitherto has wished economics to be a precise and rigorous discipline, a science, and has sought to exhibit it as such. But now there has been a change which is not, I think, a mere exploration of further territory not until now surveyed by him, but some transformation of basic sentiments. He seems himself to wish to regard his new book as an addition, not a modification, to his existing body of writings:

> 'I came upon [the subject of this book] quite recently and rather suddenly.'

One of the shifts of view to be found here is a seeming acceptance of the idea that we need a variety of theories respectively apt to various problems, and, as I have maintained,[2] not *capable* in general of being made consistent with each other. Different tasks need different tools. Economics, it seems that Sir John would now agree, is an outfit of tools and not an omni-competent computer answering every question by means of the same programme of assumptions. He says:

> The more characteristic economic problems are problems of change, of growth and retrogression. The extent to which these can be reduced to scientific terms is rather limited; for at every stage in an economic process new things are happening, things which have not happened before. We need a theory that will help us with these problems; but it is impossible to believe that it can ever be a complete theory. It is bound, by its nature, to be fragmentary.

In the first of these sentences, Sir John is reflecting the opinion of

Marshall himself.[3] The rest of this quoted passage agrees entirely with the thoughts which I have for many years expressed.

The economic landslide of the early nineteen-thirties caused Keynes's book on the influences governing the general level of prices to be turned into a book on the nature and engendering process of general unemployment. The latter, *The General Theory of Employment, Interest and Money*, has two natures and two levels, though these are united by one exceedingly powerful idea essential to both. On one level the *General Theory* is a working model resolvable into three distinct component members, each of them a loosely-indicated mathematical function connecting two or more variables. On this level the book was already a repudiation of received economic theory (but not of Wicksell's; from him it drew inspiration). Established theory regarded the rate of interest as the price which equalised the demand for saving (a flow) and the supply of it. The demand for the proceeds of saving arose from businessmen who wished to order additional or improved equipment, it was a demand for the means of *investment*. Thus the rate of interest was viewed as the equaliser of saving and investment. But if all the income which the society, when as fully employed as it desired to be, did not want to spend on consumption, was spent instead by businessmen on equipment, did it not follow that all that could be produced could be sold, and thus all who wanted work could be employed? This theory, which thus concluded that involuntary unemployment was impossible, was confronted in the early nineteen-thirties with such events as the halving, in money terms, of the United States' national income, and its reduction even in real terms by a third. The *General Theory* provided a new conception of the interest rate whereby it did not ensure an investment demand for all the income which, at full employment, people would have liked to save. The interest rate, Keynes said, was the reflection of liquidity preference, and liquidity preference was the response of businessmen and others to uncertainty. This explanation of interest was already present in the *Treatise on Money*, where the Bears on the Stock Exchange are those who hold money because they fear that the prices of securities are about to fall. By attributing the existence and the level of the interest rate to *uncertainty*, Keynes made it possible for economic theory to accommodate the notion of massive and widespread general unemployment.

The *General Theory* on this first level was a working model showing, as Sir John's new book would put it, the stages of causation by which changes in one variable brought about changes in another and another. The description of this process is the central and main concern of Sir John's book. But this is the mere stage machinery of Keynes's play. Its meaning and its moving spirit are something simpler and more elemental. Men decide their policies, their enterprises and their steps of action in essential, irremediable unknowledge of what their consequence will be. Cantillon's merchant must buy goods now at a price which he knows, in order to sell them in time-to-come at a price which now he cannot know. This is what every employer does when he engages labour. The enterpriser is a gambler, most of all when he is an investor in durable equipment. Yet in a society which insists on saving, someone must invest if there is to be employment. It is enterprise, the gambler's act, which gives employment. At times the enterpriser's nerve will fail and employment will evaporate. The businessman, at such a time, has retreated into liquidity. This vision is the *General Theory*'s second level.

In the *General Theory* itself this vision is glimpsed in a flickering light. Brief passages express it vividly, and then give place to expositions of mechanism and to baffling searches for some kind of pervasively unifying truth, as in the allegedly 'mysterious' Chapter 17. Those searches are important, they account also for the Keynesian mystique, but they muffle the trumpet-note itself. In a 'third edition', the article called 'The general theory of employment' in the *Quarterly Journal of Economics* for February 1937, the pretensions of the boardroom to far-seeing wisdom were dismissed in a few impatient sentences.

This 'second level' of the *General Theory* failed utterly to seize the minds of the profession. One article there was, accepted by Keynes as editor of the *Economic Journal* and published there in the month following his own, which understood this second level at its full strength and expounded it in terms that surpassed the force and completeness of Keynes's own. Hugh Townshend's 'Liquidity premium and the theory of value' appeared under the classification of a Note, but it was a full-length article. For many years, so far as I know, it remained unnoticed in the literature except by myself.[4] In the decades after the Second World War the economists spent their time and effort in argument about the first level, the describable mechanism whose working could be accommodated in some sense in the model of business as a rational and assured optimising process. Thus the matter of uncertainty was shelved until, in 1973, history again took a sledge hammer to economic affairs and the accepted doctrines by the sudden trebling and quadrupling of the price of petroleum. The depth of the crisis was disguised in Britain by the decisive action of the government and the Bank of England, whose 'lifeboat' of some one and a quarter billion pounds protected the depositors of the 'fringe' lenders, which collapsed along with the property developers they had financed, whose half-built developments could neither be sold nor completed. Had it not been for this rescue, the experience of 1929–33 might have been eclipsed. As it was, the *Financial Times* index of 30 blue-chip share prices fell within a year to less than a third of its level at the start. Even the 'mainstream' economic theoreticians have been shaken. The word uncertainty has burst into their vocabulary with a new force and meaning.

It is this challenge of events to basic policies of thought which has impelled Sir John to write his book. The phenomenon which political economy is concerned to understand is history in the making. That phrase, however, already begs a question. Is the history that we experience truly 'in the making' or is it merely being shown to us, hour by hour and moment by moment, like the turning of pages in a picture-book long since printed? This is the age-old enigma of determinism or its contrary. Sir John feels obliged to confront it for his purposes, and this at least is a recognition which most economists have never felt the need of. Sir John, however, seems to me to wish to practise an illusion. He holds that we are obliged to treat the past as determinate, so that everything which happened in human affairs is fully explainable by reference to circumstances. Despite this, he claims to regard the decisions we take in our present as in some sense free. In what sense, if his claim were granted that past events can be completely explained? I must quote his relevant passage in full:

> It is through this double vision, once he can attain it, that [the economist] is enabled to transcend the old controversy between Voluntarism and Determinism. People (you or I or our masters) do make decisions now, with an eye to the future. There is no reason, when looking forward, to doubt that we are free, as we feel ourselves to be, to choose one course of action rather than another. But no decision made now can affect what *has happened* in the past. Decisions were made in the past, but *now* they are past events. They cannot be affected by what is decided now, so there can be no free will about them – now. So with respect to the past, one can be fully determinist. That is to say, as we have seen, there are no events in the past that one may not attempt to explain.

There are here two questions. We must ask first, whether the nature of decision or choice can be deemed to be different when the historian looks at an example of it which took place in the past, from what it is when a decision-maker is in the act of making a decision in his present moment. Then secondly, we must ask: What do we mean by applying to a decision the expression *non-determinate*?

Decision is non-determinate when it is in some respect *uncaused*. The elements of a decision are the thoughts which involve the individual's desires and his knowledge. If his desires and knowledge, when completely known to an observer, were such as to explain the decision entirely, we should have to say that the decision was determinate. His desires are inborn or else the product of experience. In either case they have been formed by history, by the past. His knowledge, whether or not correct, has come to him in similar ways. If a decision is wholly explainable by desires and knowledge, it is the product of history, and in the individual's business of decision we see history regenerating history, all-pervasive cause ever engendering fresh causation. In what sense is such decision non-determinate? Let us ask what the incentive is for the individual to engage in the business of decision. It is some conception of the sequel. Can the evolution of his affairs which will follow his decision be envisaged by him as a solitary and unique story? It will be partly shaped by the consequences of decisions to be made by others and by himself in time-to-come. Of these, in his present moment of decision, he can know nothing. His knowledge when he makes a decision cannot enable him to exclude all but one sequel. It must instead leave open endless variant possibilities. These he must, in some sense, *originate*. They are works of imagination. If uncause can enter the business of decision and liberate it from determinacy, its natural locus, we may think, is the origination of the sequels, in a sense more absolute than the mere putting together of ingredients. Our language lacks a name for the idea of the absolute non-existence, and then the existence, of something (thought, atom or event) in respective moments one succeeding the other, the idea of creation *ex nihilo*. The best we can do is to speak of the absolute origination of some part of the decision-maker's thought, its *uncause*. This, rather than a notional, inoperative 'freedom' of the individual to act in conflict with what he thinks his own interest, is the non-determinism by which we can suppose men to be the true authors of their own history.

The nature I have here suggested for non-determinate decision is entirely incompatible with the passage that I quoted from Sir John. If decision can contain an element of uncause, a decision made in the past cannot in general be completely explained by an historian who now examines it. Yet how can we assign two different natures to decision-in-process and decision-in-the-past?

In a passage preceding that on determinism Sir John dismisses what he calls the Old Causality. The Old Causality ascribed momentous episodes in the affairs of a person or a society to the deliberate act of some individual or the Deity himself. It has in late years been argued (if I rightly understood a theme with which I was pre-disposed to sympathise) that if the tracing of causes is to have any limits in a finite time and space, and not become simply an appeal to the universal interlocking of things, the spreading ripples must be deemed to start somewhere, and the somewhere which suggests itself most conformably to our necessarily anthropocentric view is men's voluntary acts. Sir John makes no such speculations. He is interested only in cause as mechanism, in how perceptible circumstances bring about each other. The bulk of his book is a dissection of causal mechanism with the purpose of examining the mechanism of Keynes's *General Theory*.

Sir John's first chapter contrasts economics with the natural sciences, and even with meteorology or medicine, in the 'uncertainty' of the knowledge that it can claim. In reference to some of the chief concepts (or rather, terms or expressions) of the theory of output-as-a-whole, ('macro-economics'), he uses the words 'errors', 'ambiguities', 'imprecisions'. He does not define 'uncertain knowledge' or explain whether its uncertainty consists in the plurality or the wide diversity of its answers to particular questions, or in the quantitative imprecision of these answers, or in the scepticism and distrust with which they must be treated. But the main difference between economics and the natural sciences, he says, is in their relation to historic time. The reason why Alfred Marshall's work survives all the batterings which events have inflicted on economic theory is because Marshall realised this and proclaimed it. Marshall's endeavour, in pursuit of which he, a man trained in mathematics, was willing to combine in one argument ideas not strictly consistent or compatible with each other, was to discover the *permanent* laws of a constantly *changing* society. Marshall knew and insisted that the economic story must be told in a language of history, of evolution, of the various speeds of adaptation. It is this understanding of the nature of the economic field of study which sets Marshall apart from those other writers of the second half of the Victorian age, who pursued the pure rational ideal, the conception of a deductive science whose conclusions, resting on a few hardly-questionable axioms, would have the standing of impregnable scientific laws.

The shift towards the Marshallian view, which seems to have given Sir John part of the impulse to write his new book, has raised for him the question how the validity of theories of the *economic process seen as part of the historical process* can best be examined. Such theories are sometimes (but inappropriately) called dynamic. This name suggests a degree of regularity and precision which the *General Theory*, on the whole, implicitly, eschews. Sir John has found an approach in the notion of causality, which he treats as concerned with patterns (temporal and, in some sense, atemporal) rather than with quantities. His discussion has a freshness, boldness and ingenuity which, by a familiar paradox, will satisfy his admirers in the very act of surprising them. He disclaims a professional knowledge of this field, and since for my part I must more strongly disclaim it, I shall venture on very few comments.

A view of the cosmos which does not seem obviously untenable, is that it is essentially continuous; that its seeming division into ultimately distinct and separable elemental items is illusory; that all such items are strands spun into a common thread, or particles composing and subject to a common field of force. If so, must not any discernible or supposable causal nexus be something of profound and fathomless subtlety, too fine by far for any dissection to give more than the crudest sketch of it, too elusively complex for any simple labelling of 'this' as cause and 'that' as effect to be grounded in any reality or genuine meaning? Sir John's proposed treatment of causality seems to me to assimilate it to the game of chess, where in principle, perhaps, the potential sequels of any move could be written down. The player does not know, of course, what sequel out of the vast plurality of those which the laws of chess allow will follow in fact, but this is not the aspect that I wish to attend to here. It is the *discreteness* of a chess move, considered as a step which limits somewhat the array of courses which in a formal sense are open to the game from the point it has reached, which seems to me to reflect one character of Sir John's mode of envisaging cause. Even if there are quanta of cause and effect, still the number of these impulsions must surely be too immense to give meaning to any attempt at dissection we can make, other than that of distinguishing tides and mass movements of causes, banded as it were in great regiments and armies. The battle is won by the acts of the individual soldier, but the observer can say only 'The infantry cleared the mines, the armour advanced.' I am very far indeed from wishing to trivialise a subject as fundamental and engrossing as that of causality, and I am filled with admiration at the virtuosity, the rich resource of thought, which in this book Sir John has brought to bear on it, but I am a little reminded by his treatment of it, of the card games called 'patience'. The moves which are permitted, and their effects, are discrete and can be recorded, if he wishes, by the player. How can we conceive of our ever attaining to a detailed insight into the unthinkably complex fabric of thoughts, feelings, impressions, suggestions, utterances, gestures, that take place in any market process? It is in his discussion of 'Contemporaneous Causality' that Sir John's account of things raises the most insistent doubts. At the start of his direct discussion of Keynes, Sir John says:

> I shall mean by the Keynes theory just the formal theory which has gone into the textbooks. We have been forcibly reminded (by Leijonhufvud and others) that there is much more in Keynes than there is in the formal theory. When we lose sight of him, he is further up the mountain; but this [i.e. the formal theory] is a place where for a while he had pitched his tent.

He adds in a footnote:

> For the textbook formalisation I must myself take some responsibility; for ISLM first saw the light in a paper of my own ('Mr. Keynes and the Classics', *Econometrica*, 1937).

In August 1936 there took place at Oxford a meeting of the Econometric Society, which I think will always stand in the minds of those who attended it as the Econometric Society's most brilliant occasion. A glittering company assembled. In one room there were Ragnar Frisch, introducing his Confluence Analysis (bunch maps) to deal with the problem of multicollinearity, and listening to him Jerzy Neyman. They differed, gently, on which of the several sets of equations should be included in the final count. We gathered in another room for the historic symposium on Keynes. Sir Roy Harrod had just brought out his new book *The Trade Cycle*, a jewel box of ideas and inspiration for whose riches he has not always been given due acknowledgement. Harrod's brilliant originality never received a full recognition, though Samuelson acclaimed it with generous praise.[5] Harrod was one of three who each read a paper on Keynes, the other two being Sir John Hicks and James Meade. Others present at the Oxford meeting were Kalecki, Jacob Marschak, Sir Henry

Phelps Brown and David Champernowne. Sir John's paper proposed the ISLM apparatus. I am not sure that Keynes ever staked his principal claim at a spot represented by the 'formal theory', the *mechanism* of change of the level of employment and of output-as-a-whole. The mechanism was essential. It contained important ideas such as the Multiplier and the different reasons for desiring liquidity. But what the *General Theory* was scenting and pursuing, sometimes from afar, was the skein of notions bound up in the terms uncertainty, expectations, and liquidity preference. It is because these are intractable to the kind of formal treatment which economics has borrowed from natural science, and indeed are alien to it, that they are not the centre of Sir John's interest.

In his technical discussion of causality as a general and abstract idea, Sir John gives much attention to the question whether cause must always precede effect, or whether they can be 'contemporaneous'. He expects his reader to be 'startled' by the notion of contemporaneous causality, but he holds that it is 'the characteristic form of the causal relationship in modern economic theory'. This is the case, he says, when the cause is a flow variable, as for example when we say that if in some past year the number of million pounds' worth of net investment in equipment had been larger than it was, the income of the society would also have been larger than it was, and by a greater difference than that of investment. This 'Multiplier theorem' has been variously presented. The *locus classicus* is the famous article by Professor Lord Kahn, called 'The relation of home investment to unemployment.'[6] In Lord Kahn's Multiplier, a group of men hitherto unemployed are taken on to build roads. When they start to spend their first week's pay on consumption additional to what they would otherwise have afforded, a further group of unemployed will be recruited to make the extra consumption goods. After another week, the second group will start to spend their pay and in consequence a third group will be engaged, and so on. Eventually the whole body of newly-employed people, and their employers, will together be earning a flow of *extra* income of such a size (attained by a convergent series of weekly increments) that the part of it which is saved will have approached equality with the weekly cost of the road building, which is assumed to be still going on. In this Multiplier process, there is in an evident sense sequential causation. In the *General Theory* on page 122 Keynes refers to the Kahn Multiplier as involving 'an increase in the output of the capital goods industries which was not fully foreseen' and says:

> It is obvious that an initiative of this description only produces its full effect on employment over a period of time. I have found, however, (Keynes continues) in discussion that this obvious fact often gives rise to some confusion between the logical theory of the Multiplier, which holds good continuously, without time lag, at all moments of time, and the consequences of an expansion in the capital-goods industries which takes gradual effect, subject to time lag and only after an interval.

It is, I think, this passage that Sir John is referring to when he says (on his page 74):

> There are two versions of the Multiplier theory: the Kahn version, which is clearly sequential, and Keynes's version, which is not sequential. The Keynes version is not at all easy to take. Modern students, indeed, have got used to swallowing it.

A Multiplier which *works* without time lag requires, as Keynes suggests, that the whole effect should be exactly foreseen, and the whole business put into synchronous execution, by everyone concerned. Any other 'timeless' Multiplier is simply a trivial manipulation of the marginal propensity to consume. If we are simply comparing two different *suppositions* about the size of the society's income, and asking what will be the ratio of the difference of income to the difference of saving, given a marginal propensity to consume of k, the answer is $1/1 - k$. Here there is no question of *process*, or of *change*, or of *causation*, or of course of *time lag*. We are simply comparing two different suppositions.

Sir John was doubtless right to raise the question of 'contemporaneous causality' but this motion seems to me to be a Pandora's box. In physics we have the phenomena of gravitation and magnetism. The massive object accelerates towards the centre of the earth as soon as it is released (its motion having usually also a horizontal component). The compass needle begins to swing at the instant the ship begins to turn. These seem to be examples of cause being reflected instantaneously in the effect. But they refer to inanimate Nature. In economics we are concerned with the actions of individuals. These, if caused, are surely caused by impressions, perceptions, suggestions, which have to be 'processed' in thought before they can lead to action. A perception is itself a thought, but if action is to follow, there must surely be more than the 'mere' perception. Sir

John refers to a time series of sales of some commodity, and to, let us say, the income out of which these purchases are made. Such time series extend over a period. If one series were different, the other also would be different. But can we regard a causal relation as subsisting between one series *as a whole* and the other series *as a whole*? If we were to cut the two series up into, say, months instead of years (or even to segments of irregular length, such a thing is not unheard-of) and regard the monthly figures as cause and effect, we should get a quite different picture. Eminent statisticians have sometimes made peculiar use of this fact. Is not Sir John thinking of accounting relationships as though they were genuine instances of the influencing of one phenomenon by another? Cause may indeed be present, and be sought by correlations, but is not its reality buried deep?

Sir John treats the word *probability* as the name of a unified field of discourse. I think this can be a source of confusion, since the purposes which can be served by procedures and schemes of thought all labelled probability are often entirely and essentially different in nature. He heads his chapter Probability and Judgement, but the vital distinction to which this might lead is not finally pinned down. He says:

> There are two theories of probability – or it may be better to say there are two concepts of probability, for the mathematical structures that have been raised on the one concept and on the other seem largely to correspond. They are the frequency theory and the axiomatic theory.

I think there is a need for further steps of dissection and of classificatory boxes than Sir John here suggests, but the first and vital matter is to ask what 'probability' in any sense is *for*. Probability as relative frequency is surely a form of *knowledge*, and such an activity as the building-up of life tables by insurance companies is the pursuit of knowledge. When mathematical methods with a frequency content are used by geneticists or other natural scientists, they also of course are tools for gaining and expressing knowledge. By contrast there can be a need to delineate and delimit *unknowledge*. The decision maker, the chooser of a course of action or of a comprehensive and far-reaching policy, is conscious that even the foreground of his field of action in time-to-come is a shifting mist and that all beyond it melts into a void. He needs to assess, to *express* in some way his hopes and fears, what he can envisage at best and what he must be ready for at worst.[7] Choice of a course of action, of an enterprise, an ambition, is not an experiment which can be repeated indefinitely under broadly unchanging conditions. The very making of this experiment will alter the conditions irreversibly, such an 'experiment' is by its essential nature inherently self-destructive, it is once-for-all. Relative frequency cannot apply to it. Can the *language* of relative frequency nonetheless be used to describe the chooser's prospect when he commits himself to such a venture?

Relative frequency receives its meaning from a carefully defined context. We suppose that a system, whose material components remain unchanged and whose mode of use varies only in certain respects and in limited degrees, is the means of making a 'long' series of trials, the possible outcomes of which are exhaustively classified so that any outcome belongs unequivocally to one or other member of a finite list of classes. Then the relative frequency belonging to such a class is the number of times it scored (by containing the outcome of a trial) divided by the total number of trials which have been made. If each such class is assigned a numerical (e.g. money) value, and the value of each class is multiplied by the fraction representing its relative frequency, the sum of all the products of multiplication is the *mathematical expectation* which would have been justified, *ex ante facto*, at the outset of the series of trials. If, then, a chooser's proposed course of action can be treated as a long series of repetitive trials, in the foregoing sense, if it can be treated as a 'divisible experiment', and if he can find in some record a frequency table validly applicable to his own situation and intention, then he has knowledge of what will be the relevant consequence of his course. The 'ifs' in this sentence show how hard it is in this matter to avoid begging the essential question. The claim to knowledge is valid only on a number of conditions. The consequence, of which he has knowledge, is that of the series of trials *taken as a whole*, and in calling it the *relevant* consequence we are supposing that nothing outside the outcomes included in the mathematical expectation matter at all to the action-chooser. What, then, can be said about the outcome of any one particular trial?

Relative frequencies are knowledge because the classes of outcomes they refer to are not *rivals*. The truth of one by no means denies the truth of another. Every face of a die can appear if I throw the die a few score times. But if I only throw it once, only one face can appear. If I intend to throw it once, the faces are *rivals*. What can relative frequency tell me about the outcome of one identified, 'proper named' throw? When a chooser of action contemplates a course which cannot, by its essential nature, be treated as a divisible experiment, and cannot be pooled with a number of similar experiments, then to speak of the 'chances' of its having some specified result seems to invoke a 'population' with only a tenuously meaningful existence.

I find Sir John's page 105 rather confusing. Having distinguished the frequency concept from an 'alternative approach [whose] chief proponents have been Keynes, in his *Treatise on Probability* (1921) and Harold Jeffreys, in his *Theory of Probability* (1939)', he goes on to prefer Jeffreys's version of the alternative without making clear the difference between them. That difference is important. Keynes insisted that 'In the sense important to logic, probability is not subjective. A proposition is not probable because we think it so. When once the facts are given which determine our knowledge, what is probable or improbable in those circumstances has been fixed objectively, and is independent of our opinion'.[8] In contrast to this we have Sir Harold Jeffreys's view, which according to Sir John is first introduced as 'a valid primitive idea expressing the degree of confidence that we may reasonably have in a proposition'. Sir John proceeds:

> One can welcome Jeffreys's insistence that probability, in the widest sense, is a matter of judgement. If we call it subjective, that does not mean that it is, or can be, irrational; it is a matter of rational judgement.

Then, if there is a probability which does not depend for its meaning and validity on the making of long series of quasi-repetitive experiments within an unchanging envelope of constraints, is this alternative concept the Keynesian one, which Keynes insists is objective and logical, or is it the Jeffreysian one, which rests essentially on judgement; that is to say, *not* on a rigid, objective structure of logic? The two concepts are quite different. Sir John does not make explicit the existence or the nature of the difference, nor tell us which to prefer.

To review Sir John Hicks's book is like viewing exciting scenery from a car travelling at speed on a newly-constructed corniche with many abrupt turns on precipitous edges, a rather rugged surface and an occasional desire for signposts or a milestone. Sir John has here renounced or repudiated much of the outlook, many of the arguments, tenets and claims of textbook or 'mainstream' economics. He has shortened sail somewhat before the High Wind of History. Yet the resource and flexibility, the virtuosity and zest which he abundantly displays serve in the main, I think, to disguise the very limited extent of the retreat which he has found it acceptable to make.

9 On the Nature of Profit

Let us consider a class, or range, of conceptions formed by a decision-maker, of which *policy* indicates one extreme and *act of investment* the other. The conceptions we have in mind compose a class by virtue of more than one character they have in common. They are all of them schemes of action. All of them are things imagined or conceived, not yet, or not wholly, applied to practice and turned into past history. For each of them, therefore, success or failure does not yet exist and valuation is a matter of judgement and conjecture. Each is in some greater or less degree adapted to live in this environment of uncertainty by containing, and consisting in, a branching tree of alternative developments, and further than this, by having the power to put forth fresh branches of shapes yet unthought of and in numbers which are in principle unlistable. This power of adaptation is the character which enables these conceptions to be ordered from greatest to least variety, at each stage or named future date, of branching paths: policy offering the greatest variety, act of investment in some plant or system whose purpose, technology and design are fixed, the least such variety. Yet there must attach to any conception which is to fall in our class a self-identity, a recognisable permanence. For we are going to speak of events which can cause the abandonment, or radical change, of such a scheme of action, and that which has no identity and recognisability cannot be abandoned.

A scheme of action, in the sense we have in mind, will be tested continuously, or repeatedly, by the passage of time. Such a scheme will be adopted in the first place on account of some supposition that it will yield results falling within some specifiable region of variation. Such expected results will be assigned, as it were in instalments, to specific future dates. As each such date arrives at the present and passes into history, the question will be answered whether, and to what degree, the event of that date, now something no longer expected or hoped for but recorded, has fulfilled what was expected. A sufficiently conspicuous departure of the realised from the expected, on any occasion, will induce the abandonment of the policy, plan, investment or whatever the scheme of action in question is. Such a divergence between the running result and the expected result of a scheme of action, sufficient to cause its abandonment or radical transformation, is the first and most general meaning we suggest for *profit*. It will be evident that profit of this sort can be negative as well as positive, can be a disastrous failure as well as a dazzling success.

We are to think, then, if you please, of a system of thoughts, and the assignment to this system, as a unity and as a single whole, of a valuation which is a function of the most recent history. That valuation arises from the comparison of that part of this system of thoughts which refers to the most immediate past, with the recorded events of that immediate past. If the suppositions about what would emerge were much inferior, according to the desires of the conceiver of this system, than what has happened in reality, he may decide to discard this system in favour of another which would take fuller advantage of circumstances, and of an environment, which evidently, by the test of his misjudgement, he did not properly or fully understand. To discard this system, which is a scheme of action combined with hypotheses as to its results, in favour of another, is to take, in the immediate future, some move not provided for under any of the alternatives of the system to be discarded. The adoption of this move is in a special sense a *decision*, a cutting loose in some degree from past policy. *Profit leads to decision*.

The newly adopted system or expectational action-scheme will have to be constructed. This is work of the imagination drawing upon knowledge of the nature of things, of the nature of human beings, their conduct and institutions, and of the circumstances of the present.

Plainly we have here two notions of change. A scheme of action may prescribe different moves for different future dates. And one scheme of action may be exchanged for another. Decision, as we use this word, is involved only in the second of these meanings. At each step or stage of its execution, a scheme of action can be felt to be succeeding within the original hopes, or to be far exceeding those hopes, or to be conspicuously falling short of them. Only in the first of these cases will it be reasonable to retain the original scheme unchanged. To speak of what flows from such a scheme as capable of exceeding or falling short of what was hoped for is to treat this yield as one-dimensional, as capable of being expressed by a scalar quantity. In the most general formulation, we might wish to regard it as many-dimensional, requiring a vector for its expression. But one of the claims of economics is to be able to reduce complex and elusive skeins of human thought, desire and conduct to relative simplicity by the ready-made tool of market price or even by that of subjective, individual valuation. Profit is something expressible in money value. This does not guarantee us against the need for many dimensions, each one a different money value. But it may enable us by a suitable scheme of thought to reduce things eventually to simple comparisons of the numerical values of a single variable.

A scheme of action, a policy or plan, may embrace a long stretch of future years. Yet it is only in each succeeding present moment that the efficiency of this scheme can be tested. A policy, plan or blueprint for enterprise or business is a figment of imagination cantilevered out over the void of future time. The piers which will support it can be built only one by one. The strength of their foundations cannot be known until they are built and tried. A conception in the mind of a decision-maker, such as we referred to in our first sentence, is like a great wheel rolling over an unknown track on a single point of contact, the ever-moving present moment. At each such moment it may be derailed or jarred to destruction. Or we may say that in trying to conceive a scheme which will best take advantage of the evolving environment and the stream of circumstance, a man is like a paleontologist seeking to re-construct a vast skeleton from a few bones successively discovered. Each bone, for the businessman, the enterpriser, is his daily or monthly trading result. If it lies within a range which he has specified to himself, the creature is still, for him, what he thought it was. But if the emerging results lie far outside that range, his picture must be transformed. Let us reserve the name of *profit*, in our first sense, for the *difference* between the recorded result of business in the just-elapsed month or quarter, and the upper, or the lower, bound of what was thought to be a reasonable hope. This formula, however, leaves us with a whole system of difficult questions.

In what I have been saying, I have sought to suggest broadly some lines along which we might think. But now we must be more systematic. Let us first systematise some definitions. By *decision* I mean choice amongst rival available courses of conduct. But not courses to each of which the individual assigns with perfect assurance one and only one relevant outcome or total result. For if he could do that, choice amongst courses would be no more than a consultation of his preference for one particular outcome over all others. If decision is to be more than the mere exercise of taste, if it is to be interesting, and if it is to be realistic, decision must be choice amongst courses of conduct each of which seems to the decision-maker to be capable of leading to one out of many different sequels. It must, that is to say, be choice in face of uncertainty. But again, not of such uncertainty as amounts to pure chaos and anarchy of ideas. If the decision-maker felt that *any sequel whatever*, without bound or limitation, could follow each of the conduct-courses open to him, there would be no purpose or advantage in making a choice. No course would have anything to offer that was not offered by every other course. Decision therefore must be choice in face of bounded uncertainty. And lastly, we shall reserve the name decision for a psychic act that implies a cut between what has been hitherto accepted and what is now to be adopted. Decision, after all, means precisely a cut. Decision, for us, will mean the election of, and commitment to, a new course of conduct, whether or not its desired end or criterion of success is the same as before. Let us then define decision as choice, amongst alterations of policy, made in face of bounded uncertainty. Policies or conduct-courses or schemes of action are chosen in view of their results for the sake of their results. What is the nature of those results? Are they something that can be observed, found out, in advance of the decision, by means of experiment or calculation or consultation of a book of tables? Of course not. Decision, and all *choice*, aims at results in the future. But the future cannot be observed. There are no eye-witnesses of the future. Such a phrase is a contradiction in terms. And there is no strict calculation of the future. It may be that the life of the cosmos, the cosmical process, the history of the world and everything in it including men and their affairs, is the process of solution of a differential equation of unthinkable complexity. But even if so, we do not know that equation. There may be, for all we can tell, no such equation. Then the future is the void.

At least we can say this. In practical human terms, the respective outcomes of the courses of conduct amongst which a man is free to choose, is *still* free to choose, are things imagined, conceived in thought, hypothesised. Not, indeed, imagined *unconstrainedly*. Mere fictions and fantasies are no concern of the decision-maker, for they can contribute nothing to that *good state of mind* whose achievement is the proximate purpose and the final or teleological 'cause' of decision. The imagined outcomes must pass a test imposed by *practical conscience*, the test of *seeming possible*. In short, in the language we will adopt, they must be *expectations*. By an expectation we mean, then, a conception formed by the decision-maker of the course that events which concern him can follow, if he adopts some one of many schemes of action open to him. An expectation is a thought which, on condition that he takes some one specific action, seems to him, in the moment of decision, able to come true. When he is meditating his decision, the outcome of any course, which he must compare with the outcomes of other courses open to him in order to choose amongst them, is a skein of such expectations, a skein to which, in general, he will be adding fresh strands up to the very moment of commitment.

Schemes of action can be as detailed and precise as the script of a stage play, or as general and capacious as the injunction to love one another. By a policy I mean a prescription of classes or ranges within which action should fall, so that when, at future dates not now foreseeable, circumstances of now unforeseeable character arise, the question for the then administrator of the policy is in which of the classes, that the policy allows him, his action should fall. The precise nature, quality and degree of that action will be suggested to him by circumstances of which the policy-framer can take no cognizance, since their possible diversity and complexity is too great. By a business enterprise I mean a detailed blueprint for the type of products, the technology, the plant, the markets and methods of sale. It is plain that a business enterprise, in this sense, is a policy, but with a restricted and specialised field of application. Thus I suggested at the beginning that for the investigation of useful meanings for the word profit it would be appropriate to consider a class of action-schemes of which policy in the more usual and broad sense would form one extreme type and business enterprise with its closely specified technical purpose and methods would represent the other.

The inducement or incentive power which moves a man to choose this course of action rather than that is some consequence imagined as possible, some expectation. It cannot, of course, be something which has already happened, something recorded and observed. I do not need to choose one action rather than another in order to bring about something which has already been brought about. Yet on the other hand the suggestions which lead me to form this expectation or that of the possible consequences of available acts must, in the ordinary course, be things which I observe, things which have happened. Is profit, then, something which has happened or something which is expected, that is, imagined? Perhaps we ought to have made this question explicit at an earlier stage, since we have all along been assuming the answer. Profit is, for our purpose, a conception involving *both* recorded events or comparisons and the expectations suggested by them. Forty years ago, such a conception was schematised and provided with an appropriate vocabulary by the Swedish economists who were seeking to clarify Knut Wicksell's ideas about the origin of continuing, self-regenerating increase of the general price level. Gunnar Myrdal gave us the essential concept. He said, in effect, that a time interval must be defined of such length that its events could reasonably be regarded as the mere execution of decisions taken at its beginning, and not in any way modified in the light of their own effects by fresh decisions taken within the interval. At the threshold of such an interval, when all relevant decisions were assumed to be taken, the events and the outcomes of the interval were free to be pictured by each individual according to what notions he happened to have of the immediate past and the actual present, and of the way things worked and the structure of economic affairs. Such an individual, conjectural picture was an *ex ante* view of the content of the interval. When this interval had gone by and become history, the true events which had occurred in it could be seen from its end-date. Then a comparison could be made, by, for example, each businessman of the expectations concerning this interval which he had held at its threshold and the recorded history which had now emerged. This comparison would then be the basis of his fresh decision-making concerning the *next* interval. And so on. Quantities or measurements conjectured for this interval from its threshold were called *ex ante* quantities, those which could be read off from a careful and self-consistent record at its end were called *ex post* quantities.

Swedish sequence-analysis, as it is called, is evidently artificial. Like all theory, it squeezes reality into an unnatural mould, rejecting masses of detail and forcing the rest into a shape chosen for its convenience in logical or mathematical manipulation. How damaging to Nature's own image is the Swedish method? It requires that all decisions, by businessmen concerning production and by income disposers concerning the disposal of the income earned in that production, and by businessmen concerning improvements and enlargements of their equipment, shall be supposed to be taken at one and the same moment, namely the threshold of a time interval all of whose events will be the resultant solely of these decisions. Within the interval nothing further is decided, but things work themselves out to throw up results visible at the end of the interval for comparison with the expectations which guided decision at its threshold. We may claim, perhaps, that this scheme is no worse than a disentangling of the elements or phases which, in the real process, conceal themselves by the rapid shuttling of their interactions and have the appearance of a continuous flow of activity rather than a sequence of distinct stages. Some such dissection seems at any rate indispensable if there is to be any analysis or understanding of the process. *Decision in flow*, a concept proposed by Professor B. S. Keirstead by analogy with what happens in a fast moving, continuous physical game, seems to suggest very excellently the reality of business or political life, but it also seems to defy representation by any model more fluid and vital than the sequence analysis. And in the last analysis it is surely true that however bewilderingly swift and complex the total flux of events and however complex their influence on each other via the perceptions and reasonings of men, there must of necessity be for each man on each occasion a *sequence* of phases: gathering of impressions and their interpretation; decision and action; waiting for the sequel of action to emerge and be observed. It is this inescapable pattern that is formalised by the Swedish scheme of thought.

One more sub-system of our complete engine needs to be constructed. This is the hardest of all to design, for it has to cope in some fashion with what are essentially insoluble difficulties. We have defined uncertainty as the entertaining of plural rival hypotheses concerning the outcome of each of a number of rival available courses of action. Two questions present themselves. First, how is choice to be made amongst courses of action when it is admitted by the decision-maker that each holds out the hope of some very good outcomes and at the same time presents the threat of some very bad ones? For we shall show that the price of the enjoyment of hope, of freedom to construct and regard as possible some pleasing figments of imagination, is anxiety or apprehension, the compulsion exerted by practical conscience or the instinct of survival, to imagine and regard as possible some very displeasing outcomes. If the outcomes hypothesised for action A run in ascending order of desiredness from Q to T, while those for action B run from U to Z, and if Q and U are each regarded as a worsening of the decision-maker's situation while T and Z are each regarded as an improvement of it, which is the valid comparison, T with U or Q with Z? Plainly it is not sufficient merely to list the hypotheses associated with action A and those associated with action B, nor even to list them in order of their desiredness in themselves. Each must be qualified in a respect entirely distinct from its desiredness or face value, it must be qualified in respect of its seriousness, its seeming power to realise itself. We need at first a word for this second qualification which shall be as neutral and non-suggestive as possible, and we will call it *standing*. Thus we shall say that each hypothesis must be assigned by the decision-maker a degree of desiredness and a degree of standing, and he needs some scheme by which these degrees can be stated. The nature of this scheme, however, will depend on that of the two qualifications themselves. The second difficulty that the scheme must deal with is merely another version of the first. Besides providing for comparisons between rival skeins of hypothetical outcomes, one such skein for each of the rival available actions, it must provide for comparison of the actual, uniquely true *ex post* outcome of a course of action that was in fact adopted, with the skein of rival expectations concerning the outcome of this course, which the decision-maker entertained when he adopted it. If the expectations were Q to T, and the actual outcome has proved to be R, more desired than Q but less desired than T, has the adopted course produced a better or worse result than was expected?

We said that all these questions ask for the solution of the insoluble. They ask that choice of action be made in the same way in the face of uncertainty as it could be in the presence of relevantly complete knowledge. They ask that the difference be ignored between knowledge and the negation of knowledge. Decision, choice of action in face of a fragmentary and conjectural state of thought concerning its consequences, requires an extra stage in the psychic process of choice. It requires something logically and chronologically prior to the exercise of reason, namely, the substitution of absent and essentially unattainable knowledge by the product of controlled imagination. If a man cannot choose amongst rival available courses by knowing what *will* be the sequel of this choice or that, he must choose by imagining what *can* be the sequel. *Standing* must be an expression of adjudged possibility. Imagination must be controlled by reference to such conceptions as we have of the nature of things and such knowledge as we have of existing circumstances. A theory of the kinds of transform to which an existing situation can be subjected, and of how much time any process of transformation, any chain of sequential comprehensive events, would take, will tell a man whether a given hoped-for state of affairs can be supposed attainable from the state of affairs existing at his moment of decision.

Let us represent desiredness of hypothetical outcomes of an action-course by distances measured on the horizontal axis of a Cartesian diagram from a point standing for what we will call the neutral outcome. The neutral outcome is such as the decision-maker deems neither an improvement nor a worsening of his existing situation. That existing situation draws its quality in large part from what it seems capable of leading to. Thus when the decision-maker can discern many rival available action courses each with a wide diversity of possible outcomes he will be inclined to locate his existing situation somewhere between the best and worst of these outcomes. Any *relevant* action-course will be one whose possible outcomes, conceived by the decision-maker and judged as possible by him, lie on either side of his existing situation interpreted as his neutral outcome. For any course, all of whose outcomes seem worse than the worst of another course, will be of no interest to him. Distances of points on the desiredness axis, representing outcomes better than the neutral one, will be measured towards the right of the neutral point, and those which seem worse, to its left. Now on the vertical axis of the same diagram, let us represent degrees of possibility.

Desiredness and possibility are not qualities inherent in the entities to which they are ascribed. Those entities themselves are thoughts, namely hypotheses or suppositions about what might be the time-filling sequel to some choice of conduct on the part of the decision-maker. The ascription of desiredness or of possibility is itself a thought, an act of the psyche. Thus these ascriptions are thoughts about thoughts. Let us not be disturbed by this depth of subjectiveness. What is the aim of the psychic act of decision, what does it serve to do? Proximately its purpose, and the test of its success, is to engender in the decision-maker a *good state of mind*. The instinct to try and survive, what I have ventured to call practical conscience, presses a man not to base his actions on unexamined fantasy concerning their supposed effects. He feels the necessity to try to exclude suppositions which are incongruous with what he knows of the way things work, in human nature and human ambitions and affairs; and with the speed at which situations can be transformed one into another and the amount of time that is available for those trains of transformation which he is inclined to consider or to hope for. But having applied these tests, he is left with a skein of hypothetical sequels, for each available course of action, amongst which there is no worthwhile basis of discrimination in regard to their *degree* of congruity. They are all possible. There may be other hypotheses, more desirable or more disastrous than this 'inner' subset, which appear to him somewhat less than perfectly easy to reconcile with his general knowledge of affairs and his particular knowledge of the existing circumstances. He may define for himself in some way several steps or degrees of less than perfect possibility. But some such classification of hypotheses according to an *ex ante*, personal judgement is as far as he can go in subserving the demands of practical conscience and qualifying hypothetical outcomes according to their 'seriousness', it is as far as he can go in assigning them *standing*.

Why should not this judgement of the standing of hypothetical outcomes of an available action-course be expressed by a subjective, judgemental counterpart of statistical probability? I shall here suggest only one of several semantic or logical objections. This one arises from the essential nature of the decision-making process in a context, like that of real life business, where knowledge is in the nature of things always incomplete because necessarily always being increased at one edge and eroded at the other and always being transformed and re-interpreted. At all times, some of our information is losing its relevance to decision because it refers to what is now an increasingly remote past. Its place is always being taken by fresh information relating to the more immediate past. And all the time fresh scientific discovery and fresh invention are rendering some knowledge obsolete or showing it to be false. Within this flowing stream of ever-changing information and insight, the decision-maker attempts his endless task of inventing, imagining the possible outcomes of each of a list, very likely itself increasing as he works, of rival available courses of action. His task, even in respect of any one action-course, is *endless*, and this is the point. There is no list of possible outcomes, complete and known to be complete. The situation is utterly different from that of a game with known rules, even such a game as chess, where the number of possible sequences of moves leading to a result, the so-called chess maze, is believed to be of the order of ten to the power one hundred and twenty. Now probability, in its statistical or empirical derivation, is a ratio of a class of contingencies to all possible contingencies, as judged by a long record of trials all conducted under the same constraints or limited variability of circumstances. But can the businessman really fill in a list of every kind of sequel that could arise from his experiment of setting up such-and-such an enterprise, constructing such-and-such a plant, or adopting such-and-such a new business policy? Business is not chess with its finite list of possible moves within an unchanging frame of known rules. The task of defining the list of contingencies, in an ever-unfolding environment of technology, politics and markets, would take an infinity of time and still run a losing race. As for the assigning of probabilities to the items of the list, even if its perpetual incompleteness could be ignored, what basis or meaning could there be for the attempt? Let us suppose the businessmen to consider, not probability but possibility.

I shall not here suggest how possibility can be shaped into a variable quantity in some precise sense. Our purpose can be served by the supposition that 'perfectly possible' means roughly the same thing for everybody; that perfectly impossible means the same thing for everybody; and that many people can give meaning to a series of fairly fixed steps leading from perfect possibility to perfect impossibility. It is this scale which we shall represent on the vertical axis of our Cartesian diagram. Now if the decision-maker considers only those of his imagined sequels to some action, which lie on some one level of possibility, it will, we suggest, be only the extreme members of that set of sequels which will interest him. For if a disaster seems equally possible with a minor misfortune, who will trouble his mind with thoughts of the minor possible damage? Or if a vast prize seems to be brought, by the action-course in question, as much within reach as a minor gain, what is the latter's relevance to the decision whether to adopt this course of action or another? The decision-maker might perhaps, on a working approximation, be supposed to disregard all but his 'perfectly possible' hypotheses. He may venture further, and deem some extra gain or desiredness, or some extra degree of disaster or undesiredness, to outweigh the associated loss of possibility, so that what we shall call his *focus hypotheses* are outcomes to which he does not assign perfect possibility. In such a case, the primary focus outcomes, the hypotheses which have the greatest ascendancy in his comparison of rival available action-courses, can be replaced by equivalent standardised focus outcomes which would exert the same ascendancy by a combination of somewhat less desiredness or undesiredness and correspondingly higher possibility.

It is the focus outcomes, understood broadly in the way we have indicated, that represent those *bounds of uncertainty* to which we referred in our definition of decision. With the apparatus we have now set up we can attack the central difficulty of an expectational analysis of economic events. This is the problem of how to compare an actual, recorded, *ex post* outcome with what had been expected. In the first place we can make the obvious distinction between those instances where the recorded outcome has fallen *within the bounds* of what had been expected, thus leaving intact the structure of inference on which those bounds were set up; and those instances where that structure has been proved faulty by a recorded outcome falling outside the bounds. The idea of some distinct bounds to what the decision-maker regards as congruent with his conception of the world and his knowledge of his existing situation is thus essential to the scheme of thought we are proposing.

Let us bring together the strands that we have laid out. These strands are *policy*, a mode of conduct; the *sequel* of a policy, ascribed to some named future time or recorded for some past time; an *expectation*, a hypothetical future sequel not disabled by some visible incompatibility with the nature of things, with human nature and affairs, or with the existing particular circumstances and the time available for transforming them into the circumstances constituting the sequel; *uncertainty*, the compulsion of practical conscience, the instinct for survival, to entertain many rival expectations concerning any one future time; *desiredness* and *possibility*, the two elements of an expectation which determine its ascendancy in the thoughts of the decision-maker; *focus outcomes*, the 'best' and the 'worst' of the expectations concerning the sequel of any one policy, the expectations having the greatest ascendancy, and serving to mark the bounds of uncertainty; *profit*, negative or positive, the degree to which a recorded sequel is more desirable, or more undesirable, than the focus outcomes that were assigned to its date; *decision*, the psychic act of abandoning one policy in favour of another, an act induced by the experience of recorded profit.

This scheme of ideas enables us to show the conduct of any businessman or board of directors as falling into two kinds: the pursuit of a given policy; the recognition of the need for a new policy. There will be no unmistakeable precise dividing line between the adoption of the more 'far out' and untried measures envisaged, more or less explicitly, by the existing policy, or tacitly allowed by it, and the breaking out from the bounds of that policy or its reversal. The abandonment of policy is likely to be marked by anxious, prolonged and intense thought and debate, perhaps with changes of board or Cabinet membership. We are defining profit as that degree of success beyond expectation, or of disaster beyond what was reckoned possible, which can bring about such an upheaval. In this construction we think of the conception or entity, the policy or business enterprise, as something which takes a view of a long future stretch of time. Comparison of what had been reckoned possible with what has occurred and become recorded fact can be supposed to be made at short intervals or even continuously. Such comparison can be formalised or schematised by supposing that, for all such coming occasions in common or for each occasion individually, a pair of focus outcomes is determined and the *ex post* results located in relation to it. Such a proposal requires outcomes to be in some way reducible to a single dimension. The business context (perhaps in contrast to the political or diplomatic) naturally reduces them to the money measure. In business, change of policy will also be often represented by the embarking on some fairly self-contained and easily defined adventure, a large-scale *investment* in the economist's sense of the construction of new facilities. When change of policy consists in a massive enlargement or improvement of facilities (new plant, new organisation, new marketing policy) the effect of profit in our meaning of the word can be expressed by a special use of the economist's familiar tool of elasticity. I propose to define two *elasticities of profit*.

The present value or discounted value of a series of deferred receipts of money is reckoned by multiplying each such deferred sum by a factor of the form $(1 + r)^{-i}$ where r is some percentage by which a quantity of money now in hand will have grown, after one time unit, when lent at interest, and i is the number of time units' deferment of the particular instalment Q_i in question. Thus a present value can be expressed as

$$V = \sum_{i=1}^{L} \frac{Q_i}{(1 + r)^i}$$

where L is the longest of the deferments involved.

This formal conception depends for its meaning on the status of the deferred receipts of money in question. They may be promises made by a borrower whose honesty and solvency cannot be questioned without calling in question the stability of the entire frame of business life. In such a case they are not only held as certain in the mind of the lender, but he can show public reason for this certainty. But they may instead consist of the trading revenue of a business in future years. By trading revenue of any year I mean the sale proceeds of product less the expense of *running* the business. This expense does not include any allowance for the depreciation of the plant and equipment. The earning of trading revenue is the process of getting back, with something over to make good the deferment of the instalments of trading revenue, the first cost of the plant and equipment. In deliberating the question of whether to invest in such equipment at the time of establishing or enlarging a business, the decision-making investor businessman is only concerned with depreciation in so far as it affects the length of future time during which he can expect the equipment to continue earning trading revenue. When a man puts petrol in the tank of a car, he is interested at any time in how much there is left. How much has already gone is merely a piece of information useful in reckoning how much is left. The future trading revenue of a business in any named year of the future is, needless to say, highly conjectural and uncertain, and we shall suppose the businessman to entertain plural rival hypotheses in its regard. In terms of our formula, he will assign many rival hypothetical numerical values to each Q_i. In this case he will need correspondingly to entertain plural rival valuations of the business, each such valuation resulting from the use of an expression of the form $V = \Sigma Q_i(1 + r)^{-i}$ by assigning to each Q_i some one or other of his rival conjectures concerning the trading revenue of the ith year into the future. Amongst these rival valuations he will further be able, we suggest, to determine or discern an upper focus valuation, the highest valuation which his judgement of the possible trading revenues in the years up to the horizon L commends as acceptably possible. Such an upper focus valuation may be derived by simply taking for each year the highest of his rival conjectures as to its trading revenue; or he may assume some auto-regression or meaningful fluctuation implying that it is illegitimate to suppose that trading revenue could be at its best in every year together. We can suppose him similarly able to determine a lower focus valuation.

Let us return for a moment to the nature of the concept of focus outcome and focus valuation. It depends on the two notions of boundedness of imaginative uncertainty (uncertainty looked upon as a release of the imagination) and of neutral outcome. The boundedness of uncertainty is achieved by an appeal to a general conception of how the natural and human world is constructed, and of its immediate state or situation in comparison with the one conceived for a future date. The abandonment of a focus value of the outcome of any proposed course of action therefore implies that a structure of assumed data, and reasoning based on them, has been found untrustworthy. This failure of the bounds of expectation to hold fast in the case of some named interval or date which the moving present has reached and has turned into history, is thus bound to call in question, in the decision-maker's thought, his expectational structure concerning dates still in the future, those on which his valuation of the business or its system of equipment wholly depend. (The value of a business is what it *promises*.) It follows that the decision-maker's recognition that his focus value for some Q_i was below what has proved the actual outturn of trading revenue for that year, must impel him to revise his focus values for those Qs which lie still in the future, and thus his valuation of the (discounted) series of these Qs as a whole. Let us write G for the excess of his upper focus valuation of the business over the neutral valuation, and H for the excess of the neutral valuation over his lower focus valuation, and let ΔG stand for the extent of upward revision of G due to some excess ΔR of realised trading revenue over the focus value R of the trading revenue for that interval or date. We may now call $(\Delta G/G)/(\Delta R/R)$ an ***elasticity of profit*** for this particular decision-maker and his business.

However, even the new values which he assigns to the Qs will represent only a revised view of the trading revenue which can be got from the same plant and organisation as before. Our contention is that a trading revenue which exceeds the upper focus value that was assigned to it will in general induce investment in improving or enlarging the plant, in order to take advantage of newly appraised circumstances which now appear more favourable than they had been thought, and capable of more effective exploitation. An improved plant and organisation will have its own valuation, differing from, and exceeding, the revised valuation of the business in its old form. Let us write ΔJ for the excess of the upper focus valuation of the new business over the new upper focus valuation of the old business. Then a second meaning for the elasticity of profit will be $(\Delta J/G)/(\Delta R/R)$.

The elasticities of profit which we have just defined serve the purpose of insight and discussion rather than of econometrics. They exhibit the powerful leverage with which a small observed event, namely an unexpectedly large trading revenue, can bear upon valuations on a much larger scale, namely, valuations of the entire enterprise, and thus lead to decisions concerning expenditures far greater than the trading revenue in question. This mechanism is a psychic or expectational counterpart to the much discussed Accelerator. It can be even more dramatic in its effect. For whereas the Accelerator, coefficient of induced investment, or capital-output ratio, whichever name for it we prefer, may have a numerical value of the order of 3, the elasticity of profit could be several times as large, the last straw which breaks the back of hesitation to launch a big enterprise or investment. I commend these concepts to any seekers after a theory which explains both stability within some range, and violent explosive movement once the bounds of that range are crossed. Trading revenue can vary within the bounds of the focus values assigned to it without triggering any action. Once they are exceeded, once, that is to say, the decision-maker's expectational system has shown itself inadequate, large changes of policy and great investments can be initiated. Mechanisms like that invoked by Sir Roy Harrod and Sir John Hicks in their trade cycle theories seem to provide too sensitive and too ever present an instability. Our conception offers an alternative.

The reader has doubtless recognised, in the meaning we have adopted for the word profit, an analogy with the use made by Keynes and others of the expression *windfall profit*. The character of windfall profit is to be something unexpected. An unexpected event is one which reveals the mistakenness, or the incompleteness, or the insufficient open-mindedness of the individual's structure of expectation. Something has happened which was not bargained for, and so the bargaining has to some extent failed and must be re-done. Things must be thought out again. An even more radical fresh start is no doubt called for by a recorded trading revenue which is less than the lower focus level which was entertained for it, and which is perhaps even negative. Having defined *windfall profits* and shown how they arise, Keynes makes them the source of the suggestion, which he supposes that enterprisers will in general respond to, that they should increase their output in the hope of reaping still larger absolute amounts of profit. Profit thus plays in his scheme of analysis a complex role, not all of which, in the *Treatise*, is made quite explicit. Windfall profit is an *unexpected* thing. It accordingly carries a suggestion that the expectation system which left it out of account was faulty or incomplete, and should be modified. The nature of the modification, and that of the action required in consequence, are also roughly implicit in the character of what has happened.

The Fundamental Equations of Keynes's *Treatise on Money* were a highly efficient shorthand for stating a comparison between expected and realised results. They expressed an embryonic, non-explicit sequence analysis, and their nature can be best seen if we interpret them in Swedish terms. Keynes is here taking as given the quantity, in some quasi-physical sense, of consumers' goods of all sorts which are offered for sale in some time interval defined as to length, or even, in principle, named as a portion of the historical calendar. It is evident from a reading of the *Treatise* that this quantity is not, within the time interval concerned, subject to change in the light of the prices which are being realised. In other words, we are free to regard this quantity as having been decided on by the enterprisers (each deciding on *his own* output) at the threshold of the interval, and therefore to have been, as it were, thrust upon the market for whatever it would fetch. What would it fetch? Whatever quantity of money the income disposers in their capacity as such had decided, at the threshold of the interval, to spend on consumption goods. The income disposers do not wait to see what their money will buy before deciding how much to spend, any more than the enterprisers wait to see what their goods will fetch before deciding how much to sell. We are not here in an equilibrium in the Walrasian or Edgeworthian sense of a *pre-reconciliation* of intended sales and purchases by means of *tâtonnements* or re-contract. We are in a *dynamic* process, that is, a process whose later events are influenced or determined by its earlier events. Keynes's businessmen determine at the threshold of an interval of specific length what quantities of their various products they will offer to consumers, and their expectation of the money which this quantity will fetch is expressed by the first term of the first Fundamental Equation. These *expected* sale proceeds are simply the total of the pay of all sorts which will be earned in the interval by all those collaborating in the production of a quantity of consumers' goods equivalent to what is intended to be sold in the interval to consumers. This pay includes the businessmen's own *expected* reward for their productive efforts. Thus if the businessmen's expectations are realised, the consumers' goods which they sell in the interval will fetch just their own cost of production. Keynes is evidently here relying on the working of an implicitly perfectly competitive market, where new firms press into any industry where more than the cost of production is being earned, and increase its scale until no additional firm can expect to find any remaining excess of sale proceeds over cost. All firms in the industry will then, if expectations are realised, be just covering their costs.

But these expectations need not be realised. There are two other possible sources of money for spending on consumption goods. There is the money which will be earned in the interval in producing goods intended to become net additions to the society's equipment, its stock of buildings, plant and tools. If part of this money is spent on consumers' goods, the prices of the latter will be higher than their unit cost of production. And thirdly there is money which can be withdrawn from preexisting stocks in the hands of income disposers, or by the exercise of hitherto unused permission to overdraw at the bank. Such dissaving, however, can be negative, it can be positive saving; that is to say, less money than was earned in producing consumers' goods may be spent in buying them, so that the sale of consumers' goods brings in less than their cost of production. All this is summed up in Keynes's first Fundamental Equation, where E' stands for income earned in producing consumers' goods, that is, their cost of production; I' for the income earned in or cost of production of, net investment goods; and S for saving. Then if we write U for the total money spent in the interval on consumers' goods, $U = E' + I' - S$. Dividing this by the physical output R, however measured, of consumers' goods, we have for P, their price level, the two-term expression $P = (E'/R) + (I' - S/R)$. Keynes goes on to explain that if between one period and another the price level of consumers' goods changes, this change must necessarily consist either in a change in the cost of production of consumers' goods, that is, the term E'/R or in the presence of an inflationary term $I' - S/R$, the excess of the cost of production of those goods which constitute net investment, over the saving of income disposers in the same period. These two terms correspond respectively to the modern notions of cost-push and demand-pull inflation.

While Keynes was writing the *Treatise*, Gunnar Myrdal was publishing in Swedish the essay called *The Equilibrium Concept as a Tool of Monetary Analysis*, which appeared in German under the editorship of Professor Hayek in 1933, and at last, fatally delayed so far as attention and influence went, in English in 1939. This brilliant and path-breaking work, modestly called by its author an immanent criticism of Wicksell, provides both a parallel and a contrast to Keynes's work in the *Treatise* and the *General Theory*. Wicksell, perhaps inspired by Ricardo, invented the notion of monetary equilibrium, the state of affairs where price stability is not excluded by a divergence of society's intentions to save and its intentions to enlarge and improve its equipment. Myrdal took Wicksell's formulation of this concept and showed the necessity to express it (as we have just done, glossing Wicksell) in terms of *intentions*, in a language involving the distinction between *ex ante* and *ex post*, the expectational, conjectural picture from the threshold of an interval contrasted with the recorded, self-consistent picture available, in principle, when the interval has passed into history. We ourselves in this paper have taken one further step. Keynes and Myrdal both worked at the formal level in terms of single-valued expectations. The businessman, even if aware of the conjectural nature of his *ex ante* quantities, was assumed to assign nonetheless to each only a single numerical value. Keynes tempered the violence of this simplification in a footnote:

> An entrepreneur, who has to reach a practical decision as to his scale of production, does not, of course, entertain a single undoubting expectation of what the sale proceeds of a given output will be,

> but several hypothetical expectations held with varying degrees of probability and definiteness. By his expectation of proceeds I mean, therefore, that expectation of proceeds which, if it were held with certainty, would lead to the same behaviour as does the bundle of vague and more various possibilities which actually make up his state of expectation when he reaches his decision. (*The General Theory of Employment, Interest and Money* p. 24.)

The interesting question is, how this 'certainty equivalent' is derived from the underlying rival hypotheses. This plurality and rivalry are the form in which a conscious lack of sufficient knowledge, or a conscious freedom of imagination, express themselves. It seems better that our notion of profit, the capacity of our wrestling with life to produce unexpected results, should belong to a scheme of thought directed to uncertainty.

Let me summarise the view I have proposed. Decision is the act of making a fresh start. A start is the start of *something*, and that something lies in an imagined future. What is imagined is a scheme of transformations of the present, existing, situation into a series of other situations, a scheme which can be formalised by stating either the situations or the transforms, the events. The scheme requires the decision-maker to act according to a policy or, more restrictedly, a plan, and it holds out the hope of a flow of desired attainments. In the course of execution of the plan or of adherence to the policy, a series of milestones will be passed. These may prove to be on the route foreseen; or they may be off it, to one side or the other. A tract of country of unsuspected richness may have opened up, and the old route may be diverted to take advantage of it; or the way may have led into a Slough of Despond, and may have to be drastically altered to escape disaster. These changes of direction, these fresh starts, are decisions, and the recognition of unexpected outcomes, good or bad, that call for them are the recording of profit. To rank as profit in the decision-eliciting sense which I have adopted, the outcomes must fall *outside* a range of envisaged possibilities. Not necessarily wholly rejected in expectation, profit must be something *surprising*. It would be unreal in the extreme to suppose that in a world which can yield surprises, and continually does so, men blinker themselves to a single line of view, to single-valued expectations. Dispassionately regarded, their knowledge of the state of affairs at any present moment, their understanding of how things work in the natural world and especially in its human department, and their knowledge of each other's evolving thoughts and presently crystallising intentions, is fragmentary, shifting and elusive. Were it not so, where would be choice, freedom and origination? But since it is so, expectation must consist in a range of diverse possibilities for every envisaged outcome. Profit is the registering of the failure of that range to be capacious enough. Profit is history's irony.

10 The Romantic Mountain and the Classic Lake: Alan Coddington's *Keynesian Economics*

Alan Coddington brought to economic theory an extreme sensitivity to ideas and a rare subtlety of thought; a willingness to examine widely differing and mutually opposing views, but also a capacity for incisive choice among them; a lightness of touch and even a high-spirited enjoyment in the delicate handling of precise but elusive argument. He was exceedingly careful and even fastidious in expression. His cast of mind was 'classical' in the general cultural sense, in contrast with the 'romantic' urge of some writers on economics. His reasoning was qualitative and a little given to overlook the question of relative force and importance. He would have been an outstanding ornament to the judicial bench.

In this book he has gathered six papers, severally written over a span of years and, I think, considerably revised and reoriented. They are a selection from a stream of papers which he must have worked on, it seemed to me, as a grateful recipient of them, steadily and continuously. They were philosophical in a very practical manner, spare in expression, richly subtle in content, and beautifully organised. The principle of selection for this book has been that of relevance to Keynes's *General Theory of Employment, Interest and Money*. Inevitably, much space is given to examining and dismissing one or two of Keynes's more tiresome and unconvincing ideas, such as the definition of involuntary unemployment. But even in discussing these, Coddington is invariably suggestive, intriguing and illuminating; often he is surprising. If we wish for an epitome of the book's main, fundamental purpose, I should say it is to exhibit and explain a contrast in styles of thought, which we might loosely call the classic and the romantic. Keynes in this classification was a romantic, as the zestful, electric personality displayed in face-to-face encounters instantly told one. Writers in these latest years have become uninhibited in their animadversions on the *General Theory*, describing it as 'lacking a clear design' (Professor J. C. Gilbert) or an 'obscure and discursive work' (Coddington), or 'an exceedingly bewildering and vexatious book' (Coddington).

The *General Theory* is, as Keynes himself described it, a record of struggle. A book that arises from a vision, like a mountain appearing fitfully amongst its clouds, must inevitably present an uncertain outline, a series of glimpses lit by transient gleams of understanding, offering mysterious gaps in the total view which must be intensely considered, not always with conclusive success. Keynes had to construct what seemed to him (and largely was) a new landscape of ideas, a coherent assemblage of many different elements. It is small wonder that the *General Theory* presents a wild and craggy scene, compared with the clear placid surface of the 'classical' lake. This comparison is not perhaps inapt. Coddington in debating how the term 'correct foresight' should be understood refers to my interpretation of general equilibrium as general pre-reconciliation of intended actions. This was not meant as a description of a market *process* but as a pure abstraction where like the lake-water everything was in immobile harmony. A book which, like the *General Theory*, describes a long wrestle with elusive concepts owes much of its value to this very character of showing traces of the tentative exploratory starts and ventures which the author had to go through. Being in some degree with him on his expedition, rather than merely seeing his camp at the end of it, we have a more comprehensive grasp of just where and what that camp is. The *General Theory* has provided Coddington with an incomparable field for the exercise of his rare gifts, and he has revelled in their use. A reader, young or old, who is genuinely hooked on the fascination of economic theory will learn more from Coddington's book, about how to think, how to argue, and how to express ideas, and above all, how to exercise self-critical care and detached, impartial judgement, than from the great majority of books on economics.

* * *

Economics has a singularly intense, and indeed a double involvement with epistemology, for besides the concern of every scholarly discipline with the question how to gain knowledge about its subject matter, that subject matter itself in economics has a first-rate, essential and elemental concern with the question how individuals gain such knowledge as can exist about the circumstances on which the success of their practical endeavours depends. The concern of economics with practical matters has led it to neglect or repudiate a need to envisage the ultimate enigmas, the question of determinism or creative freedom, and that of the existence, or not, of a world outside the individual mind. But belief in an objective world outside our minds does not entail a belief that objective knowledge of that world is attainable. An objective world, if we assume it, makes suggestions to us about itself through the five senses. But what we make of those signals is another matter.

In earlier years Coddington gave the impression of being a subjectivist, of accepting the idea that the world of each individual is an architecture of his own, even if the bricks he uses are mostly much like those of other people. But a man naturally tends to picture a kind of world where his own gifts have the greatest scope and play, and Coddington's exact judicial mind, reaching for impartial truth, sought the coherence, stability and intelligibility of an objective universe where permanent principles could be discerned. With delicate forceps he wished to tease out the fibres of reality. Such a mind and such an ambition we may call classical in the cultural sense, and we are surely bound to admire it exceedingly, even if we are ourselves romantics.

Coddington was sometimes present at the seminars of untrammelled thought organised by Professor Littlechild at Birmingham, where the ultimate questions could be broached and long thoughts entertained. Littlechild himself, Jack Wiseman, Brian Loasby, Israel Kirzner, Murray Rothbard, Terence Hutchison, Professor Mahony and others set going a discussion oriented to subjectivism, and Coddington of course was fully in the swim of such high-powered explorations. Yet in his book he has by implication somewhat reproved us. Joan Robinson once pointed out that the brightly-coloured fish that look so various while swimming in the water are not nearly so different when reduced to bare skeletons after they are caught. The reader of Coddington's book may feel that he has reduced the 'classical' (in the economist's sense) and the Keynesian theories to skeletons which are much alike. But the legitimacy and relevance of this reduction is the questionable point. The fish of human affairs are live flashing darting forms, not dissected carcasses. In order to do justice to Coddington's intensely intellectual, salutary but too ascetic book, it must be considered at close range.

* * *

Coddington's first mode of skeletising the 'classical' theory and Keynes's *General Theory*, performed in his Chapter 2, is to reduce the difference between them to a matter of what they respectively hold in focus. The classical theory at first assumes that economic phenomena can be separated into the 'real' (those which would prevail if money had no existence except as a numéraire for expressing *relative* prices) and the monetary, those which engender and explain changes in the *general level* of prices. It thus at first divides the economy into two systems and, at first, studies the phenomena peculiar and endogenous to each system by itself. In a second and subsequent stage, it considers what modification of the first-stage conclusions will be called for when we admit that the two systems will in fact interact. The analysis of the first stage will be formal and rigorous, but that of the second will be informal and impressionistic. The *General Theory*, Coddington says, reverses the sequence of stages. It considers first the interaction of monetary and real phenomena, and makes this its prime concern, turning afterwards, and informally, to consider the phenomena peculiar to each system separately.

In regard to this comparison, I would say that we are not justified in treating the 'under-employed' economy as exempt from scarcity. General output in conditions of heavy general unemployment is *less* than in the 'fully' employed economy, and scarcity of goods for consumption must therefore be more, not less, acute. What is scarce, and what causes the extra scarcity (the extra poverty) in the under-employed economy is *enterprise*. The willingness to embark resources in the production of specialised, techno-vulnerable goods is what we used, forty years ago, to call a *limitational factor*. It is a *sine qua non*. Coddington believes that the *General Theory* 'lacks a theory of the allocation of resources' (p. 18). I do not quite follow this. Keynes can still appeal, even in the under-employed economy, to the marginal productivity theory of allocation. But we should have to disallow that appeal if we regard heavy general unemployment as due to entrepreneurial uncertainty. For that can make marginal productivity unascertainable, the object of guesswork, and perhaps zero or negative.

Coddington's argument leads to the view that both schemes of analysis must converge towards the same result, since both of them cover the same field of phenomena, only differing in the sequence in which they take things. This difference of procedure does have one consequence. It means that one of them treats rigorously and holds in sharp focus the phenomena endogenous to each separate system, while the other focuses on interaction of the two. Already in his Chapter 2, Coddington thus presents the classical theory and Keynes's theory as ultimately the same.

Coddington's distrust of the claim that the *General Theory* is irreconcilably opposed to the classical construction appears further in his Chapter 3. Here we find more markedly a piecemeal deconstruction of the idea of massive general *involuntary* unemployment. He admits the dramatic force of appearances, the overwhelming impression of a deep-seated malfunction of the system. Yet he questions the meaningfulness of treating even the state of things in the early 1930s as *involuntary* unemployment. This questioning does seem to me, in a large view, perverse. One need not appeal merely to the extraordinary *scale* of the unemployment, surely betokening some sort of economic distemper of an endemic kind. In later chapters Coddington discounts the part played in economic affairs by uncertainty, or presents its effect as something quite different from that of causing unemployment. But this is where the follower of Keynes must plant his flag and keep it flying. We need only look to Cantillon. The merchant buys goods (or the means of making goods) at a price which he knows, with a view to sell the goods, or the product, at a price which when he buys it, he cannot know. How, then, can he know the marginal product of the man he engages today, whose work will not yield a product till next week, or next year? If the marginal productivity of any kind, or all kinds, of people seeking employment is judged by employers to be zero, negative or merely unknowable, there is nothing that those people can do, except to become entrepreneurs and employ themselves, and the difficulties, delays, and discouragements of this are plain enough, when established businesses are holding off.

It must be admitted, I think, that Keynes's definition of 'involuntary unemployment' is a needless pedantry uncharacteristic of the usual spirit of his work, and is a concession of the kind he felt obliged to make in the *General Theory*, to what he took to be academic respectability. He said that unemployment is involuntary if a small rise in the price of wage goods would increase both the demand and the supply of labour. In the 1970s and early 1980s there has been a very large rise in the price of wage goods, but it has not increased employment.

* * *

Coddington heads his chapter four 'Deficient Foresight.' But if, in an absolute sense, we make our history by our decisions (however differently from what we hope, our interacting plans take their effect) surely it is *imagination* rather than *seeing* that we are engaged in? So I have thought and written for more than forty years, and thus no doubt must have earned some disapproval from Coddington by the time he came to write his book. For his views had changed since he reviewed my *Epistemics and Economics* in the *British Journal for the Philosophy of Science*. In his book he is the wholly consistent, resourceful and committed advocate of economics as an account of rational and coordinated conduct. This is the picture reflected in the clear classic lake and not what is seen in Keynes's romantic mountainscape.

In 1921, Keynes published a *Treatise on Probability* which looked back to a remark of Leibniz rather than to the calculus of chances. If it were true, as Keynes in that book supposed, that probability is a *logical* relation giving rise to degrees of rational belief in hypotheses concerning singular episodes or questions, rather than series of trials made under constrained variation of circumstance, then probability might have given form to his discussion of investment decisions. But this conception of probability, though able to captivate both Leibniz and Keynes, seems to have remained a seduction of thought. When he came to write the *General Theory*, Keynes had no use for probability, his own or that of others. He gave a central place to our inability to know what will be the distant outcome of this course of action or that, but he gave no hint of a procedure of thought or judgement by which the place of knowledge could be filled. For me, this unknowledge, naturally subject in its psychic effect and impression to surges and recessions of intensity, provides the core of the explanation how general massive unemployment can occur. Coddington will have none of this:

> What is problematic about Keynes's discussion of uncertainty in the *QJE* article is the question of what its scope is intended to be. On the face of it, the object of attention is economic activity in its entirety; specific categories of decision are mentioned – in particular the decisions underlying private sector investment expenditure and the (stock) demand for liquid assets – but no reason is given why the considerations advanced should either be confined to these cases or should apply with relatively greater consequence in these cases. Such differentiation, however, is precisely what would be required to sustain the argument that is being advanced.

Coddington's argument seems to me wholly fallacious through its neglect of three essential and commanding differences between two broad categories of economic activity. A decision to invest in highly expensive, highly complex, extremely specialised and technologically indivisible systems of productive facilities which will need many years of profitable operation to repay their first cost, is an utterly different thing from a decision to satisfy the immediate pangs of hunger and thirst by spending a few dollars on goods of the most familiar and relevantly simple kinds, the consumption of which has been and may well be repeated many thousands of times. The great differences which converge to make an investment in a productive system vastly and momentously more hazardous than the purchase of a meal, a garment or even a piece of furniture seem plain. They are the long stretch of time-to-come which must provide the circumstances of success or failure for the productive system; the novelty which in these days its design is likely to incorporate and which can be tested only in those coming years; the specialised complexity whose performance is hard to judge in all its various aspects; the exposure to inventions which may render the plant obsolete before it has earned its cost; the huge outlay in relation to the individual's or even the large firm's resources. Time, novelty, complexity, specialism and massive outlay make investment an enterprise whose imaginable consequences embrace both high success and deep disaster. The expenses of keeping oneself alive are extremely familiar, extremely repetitive, highly divisible, made in small instalments, and they are *unavoidable*. Great contemplated investments can be postponed or abandoned in a cold wind of technological or political threat, or an adverse tide of public sentiment.

I think that in his Chapter 4 Coddington is arguing as follows: Economic activity is undertaken in uncertainty concerning its results. But this condition would not of itself explain why that activity in the aggregate is greater at some times than at others. To explain this variation by appeal to beliefs about future circumstances, we have to suppose that these beliefs can change without the occurrence of suggestive changes in currently prevailing circumstances. But to suppose this is, in Coddington's words, to 'drive a wedge between behaviour and circumstances.' Coddington speaks of the circumstances prevailing in any observer's present moment as 'objective,' and of the supposition of independent change of beliefs about the future as subjectivism. Subjectivism in this meaning of the word is the repudiation of belief in a fully rational, calculable economic world, and it is this repudiation against which Coddington in this book has thrown the whole effort of his resourceful and ingenious mind. Coddington is defending his scholarly discipline, and those who practice it, against what he regards as a threatened dissolution. His stance is an honourable and highly understandable one, not to be disdained by those like myself who find in the idea of the freedom of thought from total governance by experience the means of escape from determinism.

Coddington has been intensely interested and exercised by the response of Hicks to Keynes's ideas and the relation of Hicks's interpretation to his own. Coddington's instinct for reasoning which shall be subtly but perspicuously exact and rigorous naturally finds a great deal to admire and sympathise with in Hicks. However, he finds Hicks to be divided in mind in regard to the *General Theory*. Hicks by instinct is in the cultural sense a classic, in the intellectual sense a puritan, but one who gave way to Keynes's irresistible romantic spell. At the source of all the sound and fury over Keynes lies a mistake about the subject of his thought and work. That subject was the human affair in all its ambitious thoughts and passions, the heart of man unsearchable even in its business manifestations. He did not seek to reduce the picture of the tumultuous market place to a cool play of well-instructed reason. In terms of painting, Keynes was a Turner, not a Canaletto.

The central theme in Coddington's Chapter 5 is the rate of interest. It perfectly illustrates the mutual incomprehension of classics (in the cultural sense) and romantics. There exists a great mass of government and other fixed-coupon debt, what we may for short call bonds. These are traded on the Stock Exchange in huge volumes by participants hoping to make speculative gains or avoid losses. The yield of such bonds, because of their fixed coupon, varies inversely with their market price, and this yield, or these yields of the bonds of different lengths of remaining term to repayment, powerfully influence other rates of interest for current borrowing and lending. Money available for use in this and other securities markets is held for the *speculative motive* which Keynes explained in the *Treatise on Money* and again, more explicitly, in the *General Theory*. The purchaser of a bond, whether a newly-issued or a previously-existing one, parts with a known sum of money *in exchange for an unknown sum*. Does not the bond promise him repayments of fixed date and amount? Yes, but for all he knows he may want to repossess his money sooner, and how much he will be able to repossess depends on the state of the bond market at that now-unknown time when repossession will be desired. I have here added my own gloss to show, as I did long ago, that lending money at a fixed coupon is speculative, and this uncertainty accounts for the *existence*, and not merely the level, of an interest rate.

Against this account of the genesis and nature of interest rates, Coddington advances the 'bootstraps' argument, which claims that to ascribe interest to uncertainty is to make it pull itself up by its own bootstraps. (I think Lord Kaldor was the first to use this phrase.) What I have referred to above as my gloss is my answer to this objection. Nonetheless, we must surely admit that even in a society where money had no existence save as a numéraire, it would often happen that one man would see a more profitable use for some tool or beast of burden than its owner was making of it, and would borrow it at a price. The fact that borrowing and lending would occur without stocks of money and without a bond market does not do away with the fact and effects of uncertainty.

Coddington endorses Dennis Robertson's rejection of 'the claim that Keynes's liquidity preference theory of interest is either novel or in substantive conflict with the "classical" loanable funds approach'. Coddington's presentation of the brilliantly insidious and fallacious argument must be quoted in full:

> The point, as it turns out, is a purely logical one: that whatever something *is*, there are many things that it is not; and it hardly makes much sense to say, of the various things that it is not, that one of them, rather than another, is what it *really* isn't. . . .
>
> The individual trader may dispose of his money income by allocating it between the following three exhaustive and mutually exclusive categories:
>
> (1) spending (on commodities);
> (2) net lending, i.e. buying bonds;
> (3) hoarding, i.e. additions to money holding.
>
> The 'classical' idea was that interest is the reward for *not-spending*, i.e. it is the inducement to refrain from spending. In apparent contrast, the Keynesian doctrine is that interest is the reward for *not-hoarding*, i.e. it is the inducement to part with liquidity. The resolution of the apparent conflict between the 'classical' and the Keynesian doctrine now emerges. In terms of our categories for the disposal of income, the resolution is that lending is, at one and the same time, both not-spending *and* not-hoarding.

It is astonishing that Coddington at this point fails to ask and answer the question that thrusts itself upon us: Which of the two distractions from lending, namely the urge to spend or the urge to hoard, is the effective one which has to be overcome by the payment of interest? Which, that is to say, is the *opportunity cost* of lending? Whichever is the stronger of the two urges is the forgone satisfaction, the sacrificed next-best thing. The interest rate must attain a level sufficient to overcome this greatest counter-inducement, whichever it is for a particular individual or firm in its particular circumstances of a particular moment.

Even after reading with close attention and thought the whole of Coddington's book (the greater part of it several times) I am still a little surprised at the vehemence of his reaction against the Keynes-style liquidity-preference theory of interest. He says:

> It had long been known that the market rate of interest (which, of course, is a money rate) can diverge from the 'underlying, real rate' – the rate that would have obtained in the absence of monetary disturbance, if the monetary system worked so as to reveal rather than disguise the real forces. . . . Keynes introduces, and indeed focuses on, such monetary disturbances in the determination of interest rates. What he does not tell us is what it is that is being disturbed: what the monetary disturbance is a disturbance *of*. Keynes's theory of the speculative demand for money must therefore be seen as an essay in the economics of pure chaos.

The eight and a half page section three of this chapter is all devoted to showing that Keynes left unscathed the body of theory which pre-existed his work, provided the proper application of that body is understood. The classicals, Coddington insists, were fully aware that *during the process* of adjustment of prices and wages to an expansion of the money stock, this expansion will encourage an increase of output and employment. It is only in the long period that things will settle down to the *status quo ante*, except for the higher level of prices. However, it is long-period equilibrium that the classicals were interested in.

The final section of Chapter 5 is concerned with the Multiplier and its role in theories of the trade cycle. It was Harrod who first centrally embodied the Multiplier, in combination with the Accelerator or, as he called it, the Relation, in a fully worked-out theory of the cycle. *The Trade Cycle*, appearing in August 1936 at the famous meeting of the Econometric Society where Hicks, Meade and Harrod himself each read a paper on the *General Theory*, was dramatic, startling and convincing, was generously praised later on by Samuelson, and was the first phase of Harrod's invention of a 'dynamic economics,' a theory of regular growth. Harrod's name is briefly mentioned in passing, somewhere in the text, but that is all. It does not appear in the index or the bibliography. But this is only one instance of the massive failure of our profession to give Harrod his due as one of its most brilliant innovators.

Chapter 6 stands in odd contrast with the rest of the book. It is called 'The Search for First Principles' and the seven pages of its Section 2 give an excellent account of the position of those who see businessmen's unknowledge of time-to-come as the central theme of the *General Theory* itself and, in more incisive language, that of the *QJE* article of February 1937. That theme was expressed with even greater uncompromising insistence by Hugh Townshend in the *Economic Journal* itself of March 1937. Eleven lines at the top of Coddington's page 95 admirably epitomise my own views.

This section explains why such views are neither accepted nor understood by the profession at large, and had become repugnant to Coddington himself when he came to put the book together. Coddington says:

> What, then, does fundamentalist Keynesianism amount to? It does not provide any sort of determinate theory or model of how the economy functions at the aggregate level; it does not enable one to make any definite predictions about the likely effects of alternative policies or circumstances. On the contrary, it is a viewpoint from which such constructions would appear as rather desperate makeshifts of transient applicability. Fundamentalist Keynesianism is concerned with the texture rather than the direction, as it were, of the economic process. To stress the basis of all economic activity in more or less uncertain expectations is precisely to emphasise the openness and incompleteness of economic theorising and explanation. It does not itself provide any kind of fixed mechanism according to which the unfolding of events takes place, but it does show how one would set about constructing a narrative of events.

This is as good a brief description of the effect of my own view as I could reasonably wish. From this description, it is perfectly plain why those who wish to build an economic science rivalling celestial mechanics in certainty (notwithstanding the three-body problem) or even to compare with medical science, cannot listen to Keynesian 'fundamentalism.'

Throughout his book, Coddington's discourse proceeds on the highest level of intellectual integrity and an impartial seeking of true insight. Despite the author's skill, ingenuity and wit in exposition, the subtlety of some arguments will appear extremely demanding. The astringent excellence of the author's thought, his zest and dedication, repay any efforts on the reader's part that may be needed. In the end it must be said that Coddington has no use for the *General Theory*. It has given him some impression of the vivid charisma of Keynes's personality, his hard-riding delight in the intellectual chase, his power to excite his reader and gain uncritical allegiance. But to suppose that this glittering presentation is the measure of Keynes is deeply mistaken. Keynes in the early 1930s saw that economic theory as it stood was failing to cope. Something was deeply wrong. I will not here argue yet again what that something was; Keynes made it entirely plain in the *Quarterly Journal of Economics*. He rode the race to a finish and was not pipped on the post by the running-out of his years and strength.

11 Marginalism: The Harvest

THE NATURE OF MARGINALISM

Economic theory is about the sources of individual conduct and the consequences of its interaction. It is the intimate fusing together of the two questions, concerning the mode of choice of conduct and the outcome of the combination of many men's choices, that constitutes economics as a distinct body of ideas and a discipline on its own. Its identity and separateness are especially confirmed by its possession of an incisive and, once its presuppositions are accepted, all-conquering principle. The method of the economic analyst is to assume that men pursue their interests by applying reason to their circumstances. A man will do what reason dictates: that is the key to all conduct in the business sphere, in the view of the economic theoretician. Therefore the theoretician has only to apply his own reasoning powers to a general, universally applicable description of men's basic predicament in order to know not only the essential character of a correct policy for the individual in each of his various business capacities but also what, in fact, the individual will do. The law of gravitation is hardly simpler in essence, and economics can aspire, so it might seem, to rival celestial mechanics in its sweep and certainty. It is small wonder that marginalism, the necessary reflection of reason confronted with diversity of need and scarcity of means, should have seized and held the imagination of the economists of the competitive world for half a century.

There were further considerations. Social experiment is possible, if at all, only to governments, and then only to governments willing to interfere with people's lives. But in a climate of austere liberal individualism, such a government attitude is a contradiction of its essential beliefs. A method of study which can eschew experiment was a solution of an otherwise insuperable difficulty. Economic theory, it seemed, could become a deductive science with ready-made, and exceedingly few, necessary and sufficient axioms. The temptation to follow this inviting road, once the nature of that road had been grasped, was irresistible. As has so often happened in the history of science, inspirations came to individuals here and there in time and space, without any notice being taken until some peculiar illumination of the intellectual and the social scene caused these scattered veins of gold to show up all at once and unify themselves in a striking pattern. This is the event we are here to discuss.

Even Robinson Crusoe, despite his unnatural situation, would have economic problems to solve. How often is his name invoked for this very reason. Yet these problems become more interesting when, with the arrival of Man Friday, they become interactive. Edgeworth invented the indifference curve and the contract curve to give an account of that central economic phenomenon, the bargaining process, but Crusoe could not bargain while he remained in solitary state. The chief difference between the Crusoe situation and the Crusoe–Friday situation is that it might, just conceivably, be possible for Crusoe, while alone, to have sufficient knowledge of his relevant circumstances to be able to act rationally, that is to say, to discern and adopt that course of conduct which was demonstrably the most advantageous for him. But with the advent of a second mind, *another* chooser, that knowledge could be attained, if at all, only by means of the most special arrangements and the most unlikely accidents. It requires only the presence of *other minds* than that of the particular chooser whom we are studying, and his awareness or acknowledgment of *other moments* than his present moment, to destroy the basis of *demonstrably optimal choice*. Rationality, as the method and basic procedure not only of the economic chooser under the microscope but also of the economic analyst with his eye to the instrument, thus makes two imperious demands in any non-Crusoe situation: first, for a *market*, and secondly, for a *timeless system*. It was the eventual recognition, in the post-Victorian era, that timelessness is an illusion of a peculiarly, extraordinarily stable and tranquil age, the kind of age which has scarcely occurred in history save under the Antonines or Queen Victoria's navy, and that as a general and universal assumption of economic analysis it totally removes us from reality, which led in the interwar period to the decline in the importance of marginalism. It would of course be grossly misleading to suggest that the harvest of marginalism is over. Logic, like Nature, can be expelled with a pitchfork, but it ever returns. But logic, the pure logic of choice, is seen since 1936 as only a constraint and not a complete and all-sufficient guide. It provides some prohibitions, but it does not tell us positively what to do. Marginalism, however, solved a crucial difficulty which technics had failed to solve.

By technics I mean that view of the field of economic phenomena which assumed their essence to belong to the visible, tangible scene of *things*. The difference, expressed with some oversimplification, between the earlier economics and that of the Jevonsian or Mengerian era, or to be more just, that of the Gossenian era, was the difference between an economics of *things* and an economics of *thoughts*. The effects of the division of labour is a theorem in the subject of industrial arts, a very general theorem, but one concerned with industrial efficiency, with *techne*, with the organisation of manipulative processes, with manufacture not with ingenio-facture (you will perhaps forgive a little verbal ebullience on this exciting occasion); it is a theorem which could have served as the ideal foundation of a new discipline of industrial process organisation, the heart and soul of the management education of what was then the future; it could have opened this path had the observer of the pinmakers been, let us say, James Watt the engineer instead of Adam Smith the moral philosopher. The notion of a *commodity*, as that word is used in the theory of the perfectly competitive determination of price and output, is a concept whose operational basis is an operation of the chemist or the physicist or the housewife in her kitchen, making *physical* tests to discover whether two specimens belong to one and the same commodity. The basic theory of value is an account of the exchange ratios of things whose identity and nature is established *prior to* the discussion of their value. These commodities are *objects*, valued by economic *subjects*. But since the recognition of imperfect competition, that is to say, since the early 1930s or, again to be more just, since 1838, the notion of object and subject have become inseparably interfused.

Whether two specimens do or do not belong under the same heading, are or are not representative of the same commodity, is a question which can only be answered by the *buyers*. Two specimens are one commodity if I and all other potential buyers are indifferent between them and unwilling to distinguish them; otherwise they are two commodities. Technics, in this respect, has survived as part of the mainstream of economics. It is scarcely recognised even nowadays that the competitive determination of price and output, in the old *simpliste* formulation of stable intersecting curves of supply and demand, mutually independent, refers to a technically and physically defined commodity, not to a *thought-commodity*. When economics was technics, value rested on technical considerations. The cost-of-production theory of value was a direct appeal to technics, for it regarded the physical character of the valued objects as dominating and almost exclusively relevant. If they were buried deep in the rocks, necessarily they were valuable, since so much labour was required to get them out. It was not thought necessary to add that they were valuable if *in fact* they were got out, since then someone would have actually given much labour to acquire them and must have thought the effort worthwhile. In the cost-of-production theory of value, value is *ex post* (as indeed it is in the revealed preference theory of value: economics has a remarkable cyclicality). We have to ask, therefore: Is an *ex post* account of value all that we require? May it not be argued that since the conduct chooser whom we are studying needs to be able to discern value in a thing *before* he makes efforts to possess himself of it, value ought to be such as the analyst also can discern in advance? There is an answer to this question, which might make us content with an *ex post* conception of value if we were living in a period of stable tranquility and technological stagnation. For then a man's *ex ante* picture of a proper-named calendar interval would be much like his *ex post* view of that interval. The unchanging society with an unchanging economy does not require the *ex ante/ex post* bifocal view. But this answer involves a sacrifice of generalness. Even Marshall would have been dissatisfied with it, for though he left many ideas unformulated, unseparated, and unnamed, he did refer habitually to what men expect.

But there is a more incisive and readily appreciated argument against our being satisfied with a physical, *ex post*, and cost-of-production basis of value. For if the relative values of two things, or the respective quantities of them which are deemed to have equal value, are made to depend on cost of production, *which* such cost are we to take? The cost per unit may vary greatly with the number of units produced per unit of time. What will be the *relevant* output? Will it depend upon price? But we are making price depend upon output. We have two unknowns but only one equation – the technological equation which makes the cost, and thus the price, of one thing in terms of another to depend on the relation of their respective daily quantities produced. It is this *indeterminacy* that is removed by marginalism. Marginalism provides the needed second equation, so that price and quantity depend upon a schedule of cost and a schedule of desire; or the needed third equation, so that quantity supplied, quantity demanded, and price, depend on the function which binds quantity supplied to price, the function which binds quantity demanded to price, and the stipulated equality of these two quantities. The length of the elastic string of output depends upon the tension, value; but there will be no tension unless there is a pull, or an anchorage at *both* ends of the string. Cost of production is only one anchorage.

We have suggested that economic theory itself consists of the unified answer to two questions, concerning the mode of choice of conduct and the consequences of the interaction of the courses of conduct that men choose, when the mode of choice itself is an endeavour to take account and advantage of those consequences. Marginalism also has a similarly dual character and is a fusing of two conceptions. For marginalism is (if I may be allowed to invent yet another word) simply maximalism or minimalism, when those are conceived in the formal mathematical sense. It is an application of the familiar technique offered us by the differential calculus, whereby those numerical values of an argument-variable are sought to which there correspond extreme values of a function depending on that argument. It is the technique which consists in setting the derivative equal to zero and solving the resulting equation. Now setting the derivative equal to zero will not give us an equation in which the argument appears, unless the function in question is nonlinear. What happy circumstance is it that ensures the nonlinearity of the function connecting the total satisfaction derived from the daily quantity consumed of a good with that daily quantity itself? It is the circumstance of diminishing marginal rate of substitution, or (let us pay some tribute to historical modes of expression) diminishing marginal utility, a fact of human nature. Marginalism makes an extraordinarily felicitous use of a characteristic of the human psyche, or should we say, of the human predicament or the Scheme of Things Entire, to justify the appeal to a formal mathematical technique of the utmost generalness of application and total freedom from any essential connection with any particular subject matter.

THE PRESUPPOSITIONS OF MARGINALISM

We have ascribed to the economic analyst a particular view of human affairs and a method of procedure which follows from that view. Men pursue their interests by applying reason to their circumstances. Thus if the analyst can specify their circumstances, he can predict their action. Between these two propositions there is an unstated premiss of vital effect upon the resulting body of theory. We have to assume that reason dictates at each moment to each individual interest (each person or firm) only one course of action. This implies, on one hand, a certain character of the circumstances and a certain character of human interests, and to this we shall return. But it requires also that 'applying reason' shall be interpreted in all strictness. For if our proposition meant merely a loose reflection by each man on the impressions casually gathered from his environment, and an impulsive response guided by some rough notions of logical implication, there would be no telling at all what action would result. In especial, there would be no telling what aspects and details of his real circumstances he might take into account or might, through indolence or ignorance, neglect. On the contrary, if the ascription to him of reasoned conduct is to mean determinate conduct, that reason must be applied in a strict manner to a *sufficiently known set of relevant circumstances*. It is the necessary *knowledge* of circumstances which economic theory may be thought to have overlooked and failed to provide for in its assumptions. Let us therefore reformulate the first of our two propositions. Men act *rationally*. And let us define rational conduct as that conduct which the individual can *demonstrate* (at least to himself) to be the most advantageous for him. If conduct is to be rational in this sense, the individual's knowledge of his circumstances must be relevantly complete, and known by him to be complete. What are those circumstances, and what is required in order that we may fairly suppose him to know them?

He will evidently need some technological understanding of the world, but we shall not consider the question of the advance of knowledge of technique. We shall suppose him to have some self-consistent picture of the physical structure of things and of how things work. If this picture is primitive by some standards, no matter, for we are going to show that the question of its improvement does not arise. He must also have a full knowledge of the effect upon his feelings of every attainable set of supplies of the various goods which he is aware of. The exact dependence of his comfort and efficiency upon a variety of specific sets of daily or weekly quantities of the various existing goods must be a matter of certainty and not of conjecture. For the freedom and the need to make conjectures would destroy determinacy. Who is to know what guess I may evolve from a stream of assorted impressions and suggestions?

Beyond all this, however, there is a requirement of a different order. If an individual's choice of his own conduct is to be demonstrably the best for him, he needs to know what choices are being made by others. For the character of their actions must inevitably affect the outcome of his own. This requirement is the foundation of much that economics has to say. For of course when we speak of 'the individual' we mean the *general* individual, any and every individual. What is true of one, what is conceded to one, must be true and conceded in respect of every other. *All individuals simultaneously* must, if they are each to act rationally, have a knowledge, at the moment when each makes his choice, of what each other individual is choosing. Each must be free to choose, but each must know what the others' choices will be. In this paradox, in its mode of escape from it, we see economic analysis at its best. General equilibrium, which solves the problem by supposing the *pre-reconciliation of choices*, is a remarkable idea both in its powers and in its limitations. Its power to solve the paradox of rational choice is intellectually beautiful and must give it a grip upon our thoughts. But this power is conditional upon the choices we are studying being *simultaneous*. If we are to claim that the world of men's actions is rational, that world or system of actions must embrace *every* action: there must be nothing left outside. If all such actions are simultaneous, it follows that the world we study must be deemed a timeless or momentary world. Rationality and time are alien to each other. This is the severe limitation imposed upon the analyst by his chosen method, that method to which marginalism must be taken to belong if it is to have its full meaning and effect.

Marginalism belongs essentially, and finds its role only, in the conception of general equilibrium. Marginalism is an aspect of a world of rationality, and a world of rationality must of its nature be all of a piece. A rational world cannot be a curate's egg, rational in parts. One cannot be an efficient railway traveller on a railway system which works chaotically. If there is no knowing what trains will run, there is no knowing how best to plan one's journey. Marginalism is logic, and logic to be applicable must be in possession of its sufficient data, and those data, to be sufficient, must cover the entire system which is being examined.

The notion of partial equilibrium plays a great role in Anglo-Saxon economics, but its special character and purpose ought to be kept constantly in view. It is essentially a means of insight, we might almost say a didactic method, depending upon assumptions which clearly exclude it from realism even of the most restricted kind. For it depends upon *ceteris paribus*, and that dependence forbids the conclusions of partial equilibrium to be built up, or as the statisticans say, blown up, into a description of the system as a whole. When the attempt is made to put all the partial equilibria together to compose a picture of the system as a whole, it is plain that each is thereby compelled to give up its *ceteris paribus* assumption: when all the partial systems, the small bits of the economy, are adjusting themselves to each other, *cetera* are no longer *paria*. If the general adjustment is successfully completed, the result is a general equilibrium. And a general equilibrium requires pervasive perfect relevant knowledge.

The choice which confronted the economic theoretician, at the beginning of the seventies of last century, was between adherence to rationality, strictly defined, as the essential principle of his model of the world and of his procedure in analysing it, on the one hand; and on the other, the abandonment of any aspiration to see the economic aspect of human affairs as a self-contained, unified, and simple whole, every feature of which would reflect one and the same natural law. The marginal principle, uniting logical generalness (the classic method of the differential calculus in locating an extreme value of a function) with an insight into a universal feature of the response of human nature to its desires and scarcities in mutual confrontation, swung him decisively in favour of unity, simplicity, and perfect intelligibility. We do not suggest that this crux was recognised. Alfred Marshall none the less devoted his life to finding an evasion of it, by recourse to partial equilibrium and to deliberate imprecision of argument. He did this in full awareness of an ultimately self-contradictory task. An economist cast in Marshall's mould would have to be protean, changing his assumptions, posture and approach as each fresh kind of problem arrived, yet prepared to draw some distillation of insight from all of the mutually exclusive sets of assumptions; taking them together, by some extralogical or nonlogical process, despite their contradictions.

MARGINALISM AND MEASURE

The task begun by Quesnay, of exhibiting economic society as a system, an organism, and a unity, was essentially completed by the marginalists. Quesnay's invention (perhaps suggested by the physiology which he knew as a physician) was that of the *system of inter-necessary*, or *intertributary*, *activities*, a skein of activities each supporting, and supported by, the system as a whole. The living animal exemplifies and doubtless originated the idea. The organs and their functions compose something which can operate only in virtue of the combined presence and operation of these components, and each component could have no continuing life except as part of the living creature as a whole. Quesnay's analogy showed the Farmers, the Proprietors, and the Artisans as necessary, each to all and all to each. Moreover, their activities had to be conducted each on a scale appropriate to that of the others. There was a *technological constraint* on the sizes of the flows of goods going from one sector to another. The artisans, for example, had to receive enough raw materials, directly or indirectly, from the Farmers to be able to manufacture the wares which they supplied in exchange for materials and sustenance combined. However, the technological constraint did not amount to determination of the flows. Had the Proprietors had a stronger taste for manufactures, relatively to their taste for food, it might (when we consider the matter in the light of our own insights) have been possible for the Artisans to exact from them a larger food supply. The total *value* of the flows supplied by any sector could still have been shown as equal to the total value of the flows received by it, even if the physical quantities involved had been changed. Something more was needed, beyond the bare principle of technological internecessity, to account completely for the precise character of a *tableau économique*. That something was the tastes of the participants. The notion of subjective marginalism made it possible to transform the *tableau* into a *general equilibrium*.

The self-containedness and self-sufficiency of the *tableau* are, of course, necessary to the idea of the general equilibrium. The general equilibrium is an equilibrium of exchanges, and the exchanges form a closed system without loose ends or quantities not brought into a final balance. That self-containedness is equally necessary to the macro-economic conception of society. The heart of the Keynesian theory, in its arithmetical aspects, is the necessity for output as a whole to be absorbed either in consumption or in investment. Both of these conceptions thus involve an accountancy, a procedure involving addition. Things which can be added together are, by the necessities of that procedure, either themselves scalar quantities, one-dimensional entities each representable by *one number*, or else are explicit arrays of such. Now the intersectoral flows of the *tableau* or of the Leontief system or of the Keynesian macroeconomic system are composed of an ineffable diversity of real goods. How can they be so represented as to be *additive*? The answer may be said to be what makes economics possible, the notion of value. Value, however, is not something which resides in objects themselves, in the sense that mass or volume does. Value springs from a relation between the character of an object and the desires or needs of a human individual. Value is *subjective*. How then can value serve as a *public* measure, something recognised by all members of society as a universal standard? How can the value of a given object, or of a given quantity of some commodity, be one and the same for individuals of widely different temperaments, natures, and backgrounds? The public validity of value is achieved by the market. Those who exchange goods on a market adjust the daily or weekly (*et cetera*) quantities they offer or demand to such levels that, *at the margin*, their preferences, their rates of substitution, coincide with market prices, and these latter are, of course, the reflection of the mass of individual preferences taken as a whole. It is the notion of balance at the margin which makes possible the *scalar* measurement of collections of goods of wide-ranging diversity. Marginalism provides measure.

This measure is of course a very different thing from the length or mass which are attributes of an object in itself. Valuation is an act of some one mind. Many circumstances and considerations, unrelated to the object in question except via that mind, can influence and affect the evaluation. In particular, the daily or weekly quantity in which some good is already due to be received by the valuing individual will affect the price he is willing to pay for one extra daily or weekly unit. By altering his intake of this good, he can vary the number of weekly units of some other good, or of purchasing power in general, which he would regard as exact compensation for the loss of one marginal unit of the good in question. Thus he has under his control his own marginal rate of substitution of one good for another. But he will get the most possible anticipated satisfaction out of a given expenditure devoted to these particular goods taken together if he so adjusts his purchased quantities that his marginal rate of substitution is equal to the ratio in which the goods exchange for each other on the market. When *every* member of the society has thus adjusted his shopping list, there will be effective *unanimity* concerning the relative values of the two goods, and this unanimity will attach itself to the market prices, which are themselves a consequence of the mass of individual marginal valuations all taken together. The values of the two goods in terms of each other are thus public and generally accepted facts. For the moment, they represent for each private person as much an objective fact as the barometer reading. They will be seized upon by accountants and by statisticians and used as building blocks of a vast edifice of company accounts or of national accounts; they will enter into the reckoning of GNP and of growth rates and of the balance of payments. The marginal principle will have conjured scalar objectivity and publicly accepted measure out of subjective diversity.

The central enigma, the most elusive and the most important theoretical problem for Adam Smith and his successors in the classical tradition, was that of the distribution of the total product. The length at which they discussed it was in inverse ratio to their success in solving it. It was not solved, in any incisive and complete fashion, until the marginalists in the second wave of their assault brought the new weapon to bear on the factor market as they had on the product market twenty years earlier. If it were asked who was the originator of mathematical economics, the masterly professional style and sweep of Cournot would give him the award. But another name deserves mention as the inventor of ideas peculiarly vital to economists. A conscript to the ranks of economic theoreticians, all unconscious of his plight, was Euler of the theorem. (Of course he has other claims: Euler's differential equation is the general basis of the turnpike theorem.) With Euler's somewhat posthumous assistance, the marginalists solved the income-distribution problem, within their own terms of reference, by means of the notions of diminishing marginal product, constant returns to scale, and perfect competition. The first two of these give us a production-surface generated by a straight ray pivoted at the origin of three mutually orthogonal axes, which at first coincides with one of the two 'horizontal' axes and then swings up and over to coincide with the other. This is the linear homogeneous production function. The third notion, perfect competition, renders this linearity expressible in value terms as well as in physical terms. The demonstration of the exact exhaustion of the product under these conditions was the work of Wicksteed, Wicksell, and John Bates Clark. But let us instead consider the elegant simplicity of Irving Fisher's visual three-dimensional geometry.

Its essential element is a rigid rectangular plate, of which one corner is placed at the origin of the coordinate system while the diagonally opposite corner touches some point on the surface determined by making adjacent edges of the plate lie vertically above the two horizontal axes. We thus have the plate making contact with the surface along a straight line through the origin and the point which represents the actual combination of factor quantities and output quantity that we are going to study. It also makes contact with the two vertical walls of the coordinate system, which, if we call the vertical axis z, will be the xz-plane at the yz-plane. Now let a spider start walking from the production point, say (x_i, y_i, z_i) along one edge of the plate till it reaches the yz-plane. We may suppose without appreciable loss of generalness that this first leg of its walk is downhill. On reaching the yz-plane it turns through a right angle and marches down the next edge of the plate, along its contact line with the yz-plane, until it comes to the origin. It has now 'exhausted the total product,' z_i. But in doing so, it has paid the factor bill for factor x at the rate of that factor's marginal product, for that marginal product is represented by the slope of the first edge which the spider traced, namely, the edge parallel, in the horizontal plane, to the x-axis, while the quantity employed of factor x is represented by the horizontal component of the spider's walk along this first edge. Now the spider has also paid the factor bill for factor y, in walking down the second edge, by an argument precisely similar to that concerning factor x. It has precisely paid each of the two factor bills, and in doing so it has precisely exhausted the total product. It has out-Eulered Euler.

In the adding-up problem and its solution, marginalism is exhibited, I think, as indispensable to economic theory. For the abstract, idealised construction which we call the theory of value, the adding-up problem was a crucial test. All hung on it. To be able to show that Quesnay's self-sustaining, closed economy could be rendered determinate by a principle which met the overriding condition of balance and self-containedness was the conclusive triumph. And this truth, if accepted, illustrates another. Economic theory cannot be a logically unified, omnicompetent, and perfectly general system able to answer all questions and reconcile all insights. For the general rational equilibrium has to be timeless. Rational conduct must be fully informed conduct, the necessary data include the choices being made by others, the possession by each individual interest of a knowledge of the choices being made by all other individuals can be achieved only by a systematic pre-reconciliation, and this must encompass *all* choices with which our universe of discourse concerns itself. Thus these choices must be made simultaneously, the making of one involving and presupposing the making of all the others. Yet what has a timeless construction to say to the real scheme of things, the human predicament of consciousness, which consists in *perpetual finding out*?

What has a world where knowledge is already complete, and everything is known, to do with a world where choice is about the future, but knowledge is only about the past? The whole business of choice, decision, policy making, deliberative conduct, is necessitated by our being at all moments headed into a void, a space empty of observed fact. There is an utter contradiction between the presuppositions of the general rational equilibrium and the actual situation of human beings. Yet the general equilibrium indispensably illuminates our concerns. This is what I mean in claiming that the economist's great mosaic of theory must contain pictures somewhat mutually incongruous. We cannot expect to survey the whole without adjusting our mental posture from time to time.

Great themes are to be found in our discipline which make no use at all of the marginal principle. These themes, it therefore appears, are not concerned with economising, with the search of men for the best use of their resources. In his classic article, 'A Suggestion for Simplifying the Theory of Money,' Sir John Hicks noted that the traditional quantity theory has no place for marginal analysis.[1] Indeed, the quantity theory in the form $MV = PT$ makes no mention of choice, preference, or utility, but is purely mechanical. In its Cambridge form, $M = kY$, it does refer to the desire of people to keep a money stock equal to some proportion of their income. But even here the notion of marginal balance seems to be absent. In the *General Theory*, Keynes says that 'we can suppose that the schedule of liquidity-preference relating the quantity of money to the rate of interest is given by a smooth curve which shows the rate of interest falling as the quantity of money is increased.' A smooth curve can, of course, be differentiated, and thus the notion of margin is plainly implicit in Keynes's statement. Even he, however, does not appear to use marginal terms explicitly. That final terminological clamping together of the theory of money and the theory of value was the work of Sir John Hicks in his remarkable article. There is one puzzle in that article. Although the *Treatise on Money* had long since presented the speculative motive for desiring a money stock (it is implicit in the discussion of the 'two views' and the Bull-Bear position in the gilt-edged market), Sir John does not give it the prominence it seems quantitatively to deserve. Nonetheless, what Sir John Hicks did in his article was in effect to unify the two[2] valid Keynesian motives for holding assets in liquid form: the transactions motive and the speculative motive. Hicks shows that when money is held in preference to the income-earning assets it could buy, this is because of the expense and danger of investing it in such assets. By his explicit marginalisation of the theory of money, Sir John Hicks gave the final touch of formal beauty to the work of Wicksell and Keynes (to leave aside Ricardo) in bringing together the theory of relative prices and the theory of absolute (that is, money) prices in a single whole. Even here, there remains a difficulty and a doubt.

What is money doing in a theory of rational conduct which can, in the nature of things, in the scheme of things entire, be set only in a timeless system? For money is that which is valued only because it can be exchanged for something else. And what would be the use, in a timeless world, of exchanging something which is enjoyable in virtue of its own properties for something which has no *inherent* desirability? What would be the use of a mere exchange counter in a world where there was not going to be any time to exchange it? Money is that asset which enables a man to *put off* deciding what to buy. It frees him from the barter necessity of making up his mind, at the moment of selling a real object, what other object to accept in exchange. In a world whence putting off is excluded by assumption, there is no place for money. Pre-reconciliation must be in terms of objects wanted for their own sake. Money opens the Pandora's box of expectation and uncertainty, the limitless field of imagination is brought into view, and determinacy must evaporate.

Let me try to deal with a contention which may at this stage of my argument be justifiably raised. Even if the materials to which marginal analysis is applied, it may be said, are mere figments and conjectures, does this invalidate or stultify the use of logic? Guesswork may be all we have to go on, but if so, will it not be logical to apply logic to our derivation of conduct and policy from our guesses? I think there are here two questions. First, are fine adjustments worth while, when the whole foundations upon which they are calculated are liable to unheralded and extensive shifts and upheavals? Speculation and marginalism are an uneasy team to drive. Secondly, is not marginalism intended to afford certainty and exactness, an unquestionable guide to the precise character of the most advantageous conduct? It is surely out of place in a world of restless conjecture, invention, and deliberately sought transformations of technology and taste. In the fluid unstable world which has so greatly accelerated from the manageable Victorian pace of change, marginalism must have lost some of its commanding influence and relevance.

And yet, we cannot make sense of things, even from the most pragmatic viewpoint and for the most practical purposes, without a frame of coherence, a glimpse of what *would* constitute an orderly, rational, unified economic organisation of affairs. In finding my way from one place to another, I cannot follow the great-circle course, because there are streets, hills, rivers, and geographical 'accidents' of every sort. But a conception of the terrestrial planet as a spheroid is not therefore dispensable.

12 New Tracks for Economic Theory, 1926–1939

RATIONAL INTER-ACTIVE CHOICE

In order to survive, to live enjoyably, to add to their possessions, men must use their circumstances according to reason. Some formal rules must be obeyed in their choices of conduct. To ignore these will be to get less far towards some goal than their circumstances would have allowed. When the conduct in question can be summed up in the word *exchange*, the renouncing or parting with one thing in order to possess another, the formal rules may take a prominent place. They can be seen as the architectural principles of a system where men of extremely diverse desires and endowments can do the best for themselves that is possible when all alike enjoy an equal freedom with each other from force and fraud. Reason, in this light, seems to show how men *should* act. Cannot the analyst of their conduct then assume that they *will* thus act, and so claim, given details of their tastes and endowments, not only to understand but to predict their conduct? This is the claim made by the Theory of Value, which was established by the end of the nineteenth century as the central doctrine of political economy. It can be summarised by saying that self-interest induces men to live by reason, and that by doing his own reasoning from the tastes and circumstances of individuals, could he know them precisely, the analyst could know what they would do. Let us however inquire what we must mean here by circumstances.

The circumstances which concern a man in choosing a course of conduct are those which will affect the sequel of that choice. Anything which, if it were itself different, would make a difference to the sequel, is relevant to his choice. Among such things are the actions which other people will be taking when the sequel of his present choice is working itself out. Those actions of others will be the result of choices made by them, at the time when our chooser is making his choice, or in time to come. How can he know what actions they are choosing, or will choose? What they will choose in time-to-come he cannot know, if choice means what our unselfconscious use of language takes for granted. Can he even know what they are choosing 'now'? Only if we suppose that all the simultaneous choices are *pre-reconciled*. If each man made out a list of actions, *one or other* of which he would perform according to the actions promised by others, it is conceivable that when all the lists were collated, a set of actions could be found, one from each list, such that each man would choose that action out of his own list, given that each other man promised to perform the action prescribed for him out of his list. Such a set of pre-reconciled actions can be called a *general equilibrium*. It consists of actions *all chosen at the same time*. What of actions to be chosen in time-to-come? There must be no such actions. In order to have a general equilibrium, *time-to-come must be abolished*. The general equilibrium, where every person's action springs from fully informed reason, can exist only in a timeless world, a world of a single moment with no future.

The notion of a general pre-reconciliation of choices is easier to entertain when the actions involved are confined to exchanges of goods between the members of the society. For then the business of pre-reconciliation need only find *prices* of goods in terms of each other, such that the total quantity of each good offered, and the total quantity of it asked for, are equal for every good. But the discovery of such prices is the business of a real existing institution, the *market*. It does not, however, pre-reconcile the offers of exchange made simultaneously in a timeless world. It works in the continuing stream of history. Moreover, the participants in the market are conscious that there will be market days in time-to-come, when some of the goods now traded will still be in existence, so that any price agreed upon today will later be compared with prices which may prevail on any such later day. Thus the market in *durable goods*, or in *means of production* intended to yield products on later days, will necessarily be speculative. The market in the real world of supposedly continuing history only pursues remotely the ideal of fully informed rational interactive choices. Insofar as it approximates that ideal, however, it achieves a system which embraces all goods, including those means of production, such as the services rendered by human beings or by their possessions, the sale of which provides the members of society with incomes. These incomes consist of shares of the aggregate of goods and services which the members of society are collaborating to produce. Is it sure that the shares which they are individually able to claim will add up to a total neither more nor less than the aggregate which they have together produced?

All will be well in regard to this, the famous *adding-up problem*, if we make some further stipulations. If production is so organised that a doubling, trebling, *et cetera*, of the numbers of workers, acres of land, and so on right through the list of factors of production, will precisely result respectively in a doubling, trebling, *et cetera*, of the quantity of product made per week or per year (the *output*); and if the pay of each person or other factor employed is equal to the difference which his presence or absence makes to the output of the product; and if the suppliers of productive services are paid their incomes *in product* and not in money, then the adding-up problem will come out right. However, in the real world, pay is in money and not in product. What further stipulation will ensure that this does not matter? It will not matter, if the product is made, and sold for money, by firms in *perfect competition* with each other. For then a change in any firm's own output will leave the price per unit of the product unaffected, and it will not matter whether the annual quantity produced is measured in physical or in value units. What, then, is perfect competition?

PERFECT COMPETITION

It is a dazzling piece of conceptual sleight-of-hand. We have to suppose the number of firms making some technologically defined product to 'increase beyond all bounds' (as a technique of thought, not as a piece of history). The total output of all these firms does not, however, in this purely abstract and formally conceived process, increase at all. Instead, each firm is deemed to get smaller and smaller, so that its output 'tends to zero' (without ever reaching zero). Each firm is thus of negligible size in relation to the industry, namely, to the entire collection of firms all making a technologically identical product. No practicable change in its own output will discernibly affect that of the industry as a whole, and thus it will sell its product at a market price which is uniform for the whole industry: it cannot charge more, it need not charge less. The unit price of the firm's product being thus invariant against changes of its output, that output can be measured either in dollars or in litres, kilograms, cubic feet, *et cetera*, and if, by deeming every factor of production to be as finely divisible as we like, we ensure the sort of relation we have described above (called 'constant returns to scale') between factor-quantities and output, then the adding-up problem comes out right no matter whether pay is in dollars or physical units.

FAILURE OF THE RATIONAL CONCEPTION

What picture of economic society and affairs does all this give us? In order to treat all conduct as guided by fully informed reason, it abolishes time, except for a single momentary flash of existence for the world; or, at the very least, a society which lives wholly in such moments, each entirely cut off from others and neither inheriting anything from the past nor bequeathing anything to time-to-come. In order to show how incomes are determined so as precisely to exhaust the total output, it assumes perfect competition, in which all firms are vanishingly small, and the consumers of goods do not mind from which individual supplier they get the commodities, each defined by physical characteristics, that they need.

It was this picture of the economic world which, in the 1920s and, more dramatically, in the 1930s began to seem inadequate and even fundamentally wrong and misleading. The seeds of new thoughts had already been sown while the conception of perfectly competitive general equilibrium was establishing itself, and they had been sown by one of the authors of that conception, Knut Wicksell, who in his *Interest and Prices*[1] had shown that in a society which uses money in the full meaning of the word, money has a powerful and essential influence of its own on affairs. In 1926 Sir Dennis Robertson (as he became) published *Banking Policy and the Price Level*, and in 1930 John Maynard Keynes, influenced by Wicksell and by his discussions with Robertson, published his *Treatise on Money*. Here Keynes used a most powerful, simple, and fundamental invention of his own, which in an alternative form employed the principle concurrently and independently suggested by Wicksell's follower Gunnar Myrdal, expressed by him as the distinction between *ex ante* and *ex post*. Keynes nowhere explained his Fundamental Equations in these terms, failed apparently to see what their essential nature was, and in his *The General Theory of Employment, Interest and Money*, abandoned them in favour of an inappropriate resort to a quasi-equilibrium formulation. To Myrdal belongs the honour of liberating economic theory by an Alexandrine stroke from its assumption that the future and the past were meaningless words.

WHAT CAN BE KNOWN?

At the root of the false views and policies implicit in the Theory of Value, when this theory was consulted about the problems of the post-1918 world, was its neglect of the question: What can the maker of economic choices *know*? On the epistemic question, the Theory of Value had nothing to say, except for Edgeworth's (purely theoretical) proposal that the prices composing a General Equilibrium would be established by 're-contract' (that is, by trial and error) and Walras' reference to essentially the same notion under the name of '*tatonnements*.' (But the invention which performs at unthinkable speed a systematic procedure of trial-and-error was three quarters of a century away.) But the problem of discovering the measurements of a timeless equilibrium is at any rate not essentially, fundamentally, in the nature of the human condition and the scheme of things, beyond the reach of mortal man. Knowledge of the content of time-to-come *is* beyond it, if by *choice* we mean a human capacity and freedom to *originate history*. Suppose my employer, or some other compulsion, tells me to go from New York to Los Angeles, and suppose at the airport a notice gives me a list of flights and their respective destinations, one to Chicago, one to Montreal, one to Miami, and one to Los Angeles. I successfully reach Los Angeles, because I 'chose' the right plane. If 'choice' is a *mere* response to tastes and circumstances, both kinds being given and known, does 'choice' originate anything? No. But if choice does originate something, if choice *starts something new*, something that was not implicit in the antecedents, then there is no foreknowing choice, and there is no knowing what time-to-come will make of present choices. In this foregoing paragraph I have gone far beyond any argument to be found in Keynes or in Myrdal. But if any such argument as the one I here propose concerning choice is accepted, then a frame of analysis such as Myrdal's *ex ante* and *ex post*, or the Fundamental Equations of the *Treatise on Money*, is indispensable and powerful.

MONETARY EQUILIBRIUM

Myrdal's English version, *Monetary Equilibrium*,[2] appeared long after its Swedish and German versions, and still longer (some twelve years) after Myrdal's work in the later 1920s on his doctoral dissertation. *Monetary Equilibrium* is the record of an intense effort to give clear and sharply distinct form to Wicksell's discussion of the engenderment of inflation. An interest rate is a pace of proportionate growth of a debt. If one hundred dollars is lent today on condition of the borrower's promise to repay the lender one hundred and ten dollars one year from today, the debt is going to grow at ten per cent of its initial amount in a year. This is a *pace*, so much per unit of time; and the 'so much' is a *proportion*, ten per cent. If the borrower thinks that what he can buy with the borrowed hundred dollars, or what he can make with what he buys or hires with it, will sell for one hundred and twenty dollars in a year's time, the borrowing will seem profitable. In order to make the loan, the lender may have refrained from himself buying something. Then, perhaps, the market will experience no increase of pressure. But there is a lender who can lend without foregoing any purchases. This is the banking system. If the banking system lends at a lower percentage per unit of time than the gain that businessmen think they can make with such loans, many businessmen will borrow in order to buy materials, build factories, hire labour. The prices of these will rise, the suppliers of them will be richer, they will themselves spend more than before, the prices of goods will rise again. And so on, and on. If the banks now raise the interest rate they charge so that it equals, on the whole, the rate of gain, whatever it may be, that businessmen now hope to make, it will no longer pay these businessmen, or seem to pay them, to expand continually their borrowing and their spending in attempting to expand their production. Thus, said Wicksell, the general rise of prices, the inflationary rise of prices, will stop. The general rise of prices, induced by a money rate of interest (the banks' lending rate) which is less than the natural rate of interest (the gain obtainable from industry and commerce) is a disequilibrium phenomenon, one which, so far from finding a new resting place, is spurred on by its own effects. If the two rates were kept equal, the inflationary process would never start. This theory, this theorem, was the inspiration of three men of very different experience, outlook, and natural tendency. It induced Myrdal to write the thesis which in English is called *Monetary Equilibrium*. It gave Keynes the clue for his *Treatise on Money*. It suggested to Professor Hayek the possibility of a neutral money, explained as one strand of *Prices and Production*, that prophetic warning given forty years before its time.

INVESTMENT AND SAVING

What has all this to do with the 1930s? The problem then was catastrophic business depression and unemployment. Keynes's *Treatise* did not talk about unemployment, only about price levels. But it did talk about the relation beween saving (leaving unbought some of the goods that were produced) and investment (producing goods intended for use by businessmen as such, not for consumers). Provided goods not bought by consumers were duly bought by businessmen *as such*, for use as tools, as means of further production, no one need be driven to fire his labour force by the fear that he could not sell his output. So long as investment absorbed all the output which was in excess of consumption, there would be no *increase* of unemployment. If this equality could be achieved and maintained for an output big enough to employ everybody who wanted to be employed, there need be no involuntary unemployment at all. Keynes decided to turn the *Treatise* argument in a new direction, to explain the size of output as a whole, and thus to explain the level of employment.

The first Fundamental Equation of the *Treatise on Money* said that prices of consumers' goods in general ('the price level') would prove to have risen if it turned out, at the end of some period (a particular week or year) that the money spent in that period on investment had been more than the difference between the income earned in that period and the amount spent in it on consumption. But could those two amounts, investment and saving, differ from each other? They could, because the income in question was the income which had in total been *expected* at the beginning of the period by all those (including the businessmen themselves, the employers) who had collaborated in the production of goods during the period. The amount spent on investment goods, however, was not reckoned until the *end* of the period, it was a recorded fact, and its amount could be quite different from the excess of the formerly expected income over the recorded consumption spending of the period. Money could be spent on investment which had been held in reserve, or which was borrowed from the banks as an addition to the pre-existing quantity of money; or investment could be less than saving, through money being *put* to reserve, or used to pay off bank loans. In short, the first Fundamental Equation treated income as a quantity reckoned before the event, *ex ante facto*, at the threshold of the period when the events would take place, but it treated consumption spending and investment as quantities actually realised and recorded at the end of the period, *ex post facto*. Thus there could be a difference between (intended) saving and (realised) investment, and if the former fell short of the latter, more would be spent on consumption goods than people had reckoned on. Their prices would be higher than had, at the outset, been expected. And vice versa. Keynes did not use the expressions *ex ante*, *ex post*. These were Myrdal's introduction, and it was Myrdal, and by no means Keynes, who made explicit the vital difference of nature between what people envisage as the contents of a period of time-to-come and what they can record as its content when it is past. Yet this distinction is shown by Keynes' spontaneous implicit invention of it, and use of it, to be indispensable.

When he had finished the *Treatise*, Keynes thought he 'could do it better, and much shorter,' if he were to start over again. The new version, *The General Theory of Employment, Interest and Money*, replaces a fragmentary and scattered account of the *inducement to invest* with a massive treatment occupying some forty pages. Yet it is one particular aspect of this treatment which is the truly essential contribution of the *General Theory*, the heart of Keynes' explanation of how unemployment can be involuntary. Keynes was very far from recognising, in the course of writing the book, just what his ultimate conclusion was turning out to be. He left statements standing in the book which are incompatible with his ultimate theme. That theme is that we do not and cannot have knowledge of what will come about in time-to-come, not even a year or two ahead or (as recent events may have impressed on us in 1973, 1974, and 1975) a month or two ahead. Yet in Chapter 2, where Keynes attempts the obviously essential task of showing that 'involuntary' unemployment is logically possible, he endorses the orthodox principle that the wage offered by an employer will be equal (under stress of competition from rival employers) to 'the marginal product of labour,' the difference which the presence or absence of one man would make to the value of output. In a time of deep business depression, when all the foundations of confident expectation seem to have crumbled, what answer can a businessman give himself when he asks: What difference *does* one extra man make to the value of an output which I have yet to sell, in a seemingly disintegrating market where nobody is buying anything he can do without? He must reckon with the possibility that his output is already on a highly price-inelastic part of the demand curve, so that one extra man's output may actually make a *negative* difference to the total value of output. And there is a further question, to be put not by the businessman but by the analyst: What foundation is there in such a time for notions of definite and stable curves as descriptions of the situation facing a businessman?

Keynes, in the *Treatise*, had shown that investment and saving were not *identically* equal, were not merely two names for the same thing. For they should be looked on as two distinct bodies of intentions, two sets of conjectures about time-to-come. But there is another possibility to be taken into account. May not these two quantities be *brought* into equality by some equilibrating influence? May there not be a *price* which makes *demand* for saving, namely investment, equal to supply of saving? What would this price be? It would be a rate of interest, if, as the orthodoxy of those days declared, the interest rate was itself determined at the level which brought investment and saving to equality. To show that investment could be unequal to saving and remain so, Keynes had to repudiate this theory of the interest rate and replace it with another. Liquidity preference, and the essential notion of liquidity itself, is the most original of Keynes's technical contributions.

LIQUIDITY PREFERENCE

A *bond* is a borrower's promise to pay to the lender stated sums at stated dates. The lender cannot tell, when he hands over money as a loan to the borrower, at what date he may wish to repossess his money. If he should need it before the date when the borrower has promised to complete his repayment, what will the lender be able to do? If there is a bond market, he can sell his bond for whatever sum, at the unknown date in time-to-come when he may need his money, it will fetch. In order to give himself some presumption that such a sale will at least restore, or complete, the restoration to him of the initial sum, the lender will require the borrower's promised payments to exceed, in total, the sum he lends. That percentage per unit of time which, when used to discount the borrower's promised payments, gives them a *present value* (a discounted value) equal in total to the initial loan, is the interest rate on this loan. It guards and compensates the lender for parting with a known sum of money in exchange for an unknown sum, it compensates him for his voluntary exposure to uncertainty. Interest is the price which lenders can exact for giving up a liquid asset, money, in exchange for one which is less liquid, a bond. What, then, in essence, is liquidity?

Liquidity is the quality of that asset in which contracts for payment are made, and which, therefore, will ultimately be needed in order to make those payments. So long as the man who has contracted to make a payment (of wages, of a debt, *et cetera*) holds in his possession a suitable quantity of this payment-medium, he can feel sure of being able to pay. He will not be exposed to risk of loss of value, in terms of the payment-medium, of any asset he might hold instead. In 'normal' times the most liquid asset, and the universal medium of contracts for payment, is money. Keynes said that there were three motives which might induce a man to hold money instead of an income-earning asset (land, houses, plant, company shares, or bonds). These were the speculative motive (fear of capital loss), the transactions motive (desire to be immediately able to make unforeseen payments), and the precautionary motive. The last of these, however, is superfluous. Assets held against the need for unforeseen payments could be income-earning assets, were it not for the danger of capital loss in case of a precipitate sale. But to hold liquid assets against *that* danger is the speculative motive. What, then, is liquidity? It is a defence against uncertainty.

The interest rate, or the system of rates on bonds with various terms to run to their extinction, plays a complex and somewhat deceptive role in the argument of the *General Theory*. It is shown there to owe its existence to uncertainty, and thus it fits well into an argument whose central theme is the blankness of time-to-come. It claims its place in the theory of the inducement to invest, since the value placed in today's market on an investment good (a petroleum-cracking plant, a ship, a housing block) rests on some hypothetical series of trading profits that this instrument is conceived to yield in future years. However, today's valuation would not, even if those future profits were guaranteed, be equal to their sum. For an amount less than that sum could be so lent today, various parts of it for various lengths of time, as to yield amounts equal to those supposed profits at the dates in question. The lower the interest rate used for this discounting, the higher would be the *present value* reckoned with it, the more easily that present value could outtop the cost of construction and make investment seem worthwhile. But if time-to-come is a matter so largely of blank unknowledge within wide bounds, will not the shifts of conjecture or ascribed possibility concerning the profits themselves far outweigh any fluctuations of the interest rate? Keynes ascribed a failure of businessmen to fill with an equal flow of investment the potential saving gap between output and consumption at full employment to a lack or breakdown of 'confidence', a failure for the time being of the gambler's capacity for self-sustaining hope. Failure to fill the gap with investment deliberately planned will mean that it is filled at first, after a drop in such investment, by *unintended* investment in the form of unsold inventories of consumers' goods, and that later the gap itself will be reduced by a reduction of output, of employment, and thus of income. It is, unhappily, the mechanics of Keynes's conception of economic society, such features of it as the consumption function, which have claimed most attention, distracting (or shielding?) men's thoughts from the vital proposition that enterprise is the daring, and desirable, pursuit of imagination, not merely or mainly reason that enterprise is *imagination in action*.

The nature and source of a rate of interest was the problem which had engaged Eugen von Böhm-Bawerk in writing his *Positive Theory of Capital* during the 1880s. His central ideas were given a refined mathematical expression by Wicksell and later intensely explored by Professor F. A. von Hayek. Böhm-Bawerk sought to explain interest as the reward claimed by those who contributed the productive services of themselves or their land long before the consumable product could emerge. The embryonic or instrumental products ('intermediate products') which stored up these services and carried them through the time-consuming productive process to consumable completion were the means of a more effective 'division of labour' than the best available in a process leading more quickly from inputs to result; and the result, in each week or year, could therefore be permanently larger for the same input amounts of the services of men and Nature. The intermediate products made up a mass of 'capital' whose size, and whose efficacy as a whole in economising productive services, increased with the 'average period of production' which elapsed between inputs and output. This 'waiting' between input and output was distasteful, and so its fruits, the tools which made labour and Nature more effective, were scarce, high-priced, and able to afford a compensation to those who performed it. Between increasing marginal distastefulness and decreasing marginal efficacy there would be a balance at some particular size of the capital stock, that is, of the 'average period of production'. However, there is a question here. We have to consider that everything that exists, exists *now*, in 'the present'. All goods which compose the capital stock exist simultaneously, and those individuals who are now supplying productive services can be paid *now* with the now existing results of earlier efforts. In a stable and constant capital stock, there is no inherent 'waiting'. It is only when the capital stock is being increased that the results of present effort must be looked forward to by individuals over a span of time. The notion of 'roundabout production' in which an elaborate apparatus of 'produced means of production', or 'intermediate products', enables given quantities of 'original means of production', labour and natural forces, to yield a larger output of the goods wanted by the ultimate consumers, can nowadays be illuminated by one more conceptual tool invented in the 1930s.

In those years a scheme of thought was proposed whose purpose was to make possible the calculation of the changes of output of *intermediate goods* (the direct products of farming or mining, goods intended for further processing, tools of every kind, all sorts of instrumental systems and equipment) which would be called for in response to any change in any items of the list of demanded quantities of *final* products ready for consumption. Leontief's input-output analysis is in fact a pragmatic picture of *coexisting* capital items, a picture of the techno-temporal structure of the capital stock. Leontief was concerned with the technical structure, but within this technical structure there is latent a *temporal* structure, residing in the fact that what exists today as yarn, and what exists today as cloth, and what exists today as finished garments, do not and never will belong in the same physical object, yet today's finished garment was at an earlier time cloth, and that cloth at an earlier time still was yarn. Leontief was not immediately concerned with the temporal structure, but if changes are made in the 'bill of goods for final use' these changes will require time spans in order to have their full effects, and those time spans will reflect the technical capital structure of production. They are the reality of the time structure of production.

The Theory of Value and Distribution (that is, of relative prices and the sharing of income), the central doctrine of economic theory from late Victorian times until after the First World War, drew its ascendancy from its claim to be the logical consequence of a very few axioms easily recognised to be true. That ascendancy was destroyed during the 1920s and 1930s by its gross and fundamental incongruity with what was seen to be happening in the world. Far the most basic and incurable source of this incongruity, the essential reason for the failure and irrelevance of the doctrine, was its entire disregard of the question of what men could *know*. It assumed, without argument, that they could know everything necessary for demonstrably optimal choices of conduct. (Such demonstration would require a means of proving that the available knowledge was indeed relevantly complete.) This total rejection and denial of the human condition, the fact of the void of future time which we can only fill with surmise and figment, left it helpless to explain the events of the early 1930s when, for example, the income of the United States in money terms was halved. But even on its own terms the structure of the theory of value was defective. The notion of perfect competition, on which it rested, is internally inconsistent and even basically unintelligible. Its inconsistencies were explained by Mr. Piero Sraffa in a classic article in the *Economic Journal* for 1926. If perfect competition lets firms expand output freely without reduction of price, and if economies of large scale make their unit costs lower the larger their output, what can prevent any one such firm 'which gets a good start' from swallowing the whole market and destroying competition? This dilemma, posed in essence by Alfred Marshall whose words I have just borrowed, and long before him by Cournot, became in Mr. Sraffa's hands the signal for a great schism. Perfect competition was quite central and essential to the great encompassing, simplifying, and unifying Theory of Value, solver of the problem of income sharing and foundation of the General Equilibrium. In the late 1920s and early 1930s, the move was made by Harrod and Mrs. Robinson (among others) in Britain, by Chamberlin and Yntema in the United States, by Mehta in India, to abandon perfect competition and create a theory of Imperfect, or else of Monopolistic, Competition. But it proved easier to destroy the old symmetry and simplicity than to replace it.

To invent a new tool of thought, or show how an existing scheme can be adapted from another discipline, can have as far-reaching an effect on our field as the proposal of new substantive propositions. In 1934 Sir John Hicks showed how an individual's division of his expenditure over different consumer's goods could be explained by means of *indifference curves* combined with a *budget line*. Indifference curves, an adaptation to economics of the geographer's lines of equal altitude or *contour lines*, had been introduced by Francis Ysidro Edgeworth in his book *Mathematical Psychics* in 1881. Vilfredo Pareto had used a family of such curves as a 'photograph' of an individual's tastes, and Enrico Barone, in order to exhibit the effects of taxes, had added to Pareto's indifference map a straight line which expressed both the prices of two goods in terms of each other, and the individual's income in terms of each good. Sir John Hicks used such a scheme to improve on Alfred Marshall's method of measuring the intensity of a consumer's desire for a small increment of his weekly (*et cetera*) supply of some commodity. Such a desire, Marshall said, could only be measured by seeing how much money, in given circumstances, the individual would pay for the extra weekly quantity. Chief among these circumstances was the size of his existing weekly supply. The larger it was, the less intensely he would wish for any extra. However, this *diminishing marginal utility* would not be quite accurately measured by the diminution of the money he was willing to pay, since the latter would be diminished also by his increasing shortage of money, as he considered buying a larger and larger weekly quantity of the good. Marshall's proposal was simply to ignore this effect of the increasing shortage of income and treat the marginal utility of income as invariant against changes in the amount of income still disposable. By means of the indifference map and budget line, Sir John Hicks was able to separate from each other the 'substitution-effect' and the 'income-effect'. However, Hicks's real contribution, by his article in *Economica* of 1934, was to spread widely an appreciation of the indifference map as a tool. It has been applied in scores of diverse contexts, with surgical effects on obscure economic enigmas.

What has been called the 'Cambridge method' in economic theory consists in a shuttling by the theoretician between the problem he at first sets out to solve and the conclusions at which, with great labour and many false trials, he eventually arrives. It may become obvious, when that solution is arrived at, that it could have been approached more easily, and can now be viewed more intelligibly, as the solution to a somewhat differently formulated problem from the actual starting point of the investigation. Then the argument is (very profitably and at a great gain in *efficiency of insight*) realigned on this somewhat different target. Closely linked with this practice is what may be called the encapsulating method. Difficulties which seem more tiresome than they are worth, obstructive of advance but not seemingly concerned with the essence of things, can be shut up in a black box which is then treated as a thing-in-itself, not to be inquired into but fitted, as a whole and unopened, into any scheme where its contents are broadly relevant. One such simplification is the *capital-to-output ratio* defined independently by Sir Roy Harrod and Professor Evsey Domar. It is essential to the notion of the regularly progressive economy, by which so dramatic a picture can be given of the workings of the business cycle, intractable unemployment, inflationary pressure of demand, and the inherent instability of economic systems.

In the later 1920s and the 1930s, a great spasm of creative effort in economic theory responded to the visible dissolution of the comparatively orderly Victorian world in which Marshall had been able to discern the gradual perfectibility of industrial and social organisation hinting at the perfectibility of human nature itself. The tranquillity had been shattered, and the theory of economic life which reflected it needed to be transcended and even wholly subverted. Not merely the detailed design of the economist's account of things needed to be changed, but its fundamental assumptions, its purposes and ambitions, what it claimed to do had to be essentially reconsidered. Such a reorientation was hard to accept and is still mainly unaccepted.

13 Hayek as Economist

INTRODUCTION – BIOGRAPHIA

Aristocratic in temper and origins; physically, morally and intellectually fearless; clear and incisive in thought; the embodied principle itself of following the logic where it leads; the soul of scholarly generosity; Friedrich August Hayek is one of the outstanding sculptors of this age's thought. He was born on 8 May 1899 into a family academically distinguished on both sides. At the University of Vienna he gained two doctorates, becoming Dr. jur. in 1921 and Dr. rer. pol. in 1923. From 1927 till 1931 he was Director of the Austrian Institute for Economic Research. In 1931 as visiting lecturer at the London School of Economics he gave the lectures which were published in that year as *Prices and Production*[1] and which gained for him, in those days of baffled debate about the causes of the great depression which had struck the industrialised world like a plague, his first sensational prominence. In that year he was appointed Tooke Professor of Economic Science and Statistics in the University of London. He held this Chair until, in 1950, he moved to Chicago. In 1962 he was appointed Professor of Economic Policy at the University of Freiburg, and in 1974 he was made honorary professor at the University of Salzburg. In 1944 he had been given an honorary Doctorate of Science by the University of London, and in that year also he was elected a Fellow of the British Academy. In 1974 he was awarded the Nobel Prize in Economic Science.

At a meeting in 1976 with a Spanish editor of penetrating and sympathetic insight, Hayek answered a question by quoting a fragment from the poet Archilochus, which is well known through its earlier use by Sir Isaiah Berlin: 'the fox knows many things, but the hedgehog knows one big thing'. Hayek was then referring to his half-century of effort to explain to scholars, politicians and people the nature and detailed working of the disastrous, multifarious and recently almost universal monetary debasement of our times. This message was, he told us, the 'one big thing' to which his scholarly life had been devoted. I think it may be permissible to elaborate that statement in two respects. In the first place, though the theme of monetary profligacy and of the imperative need to eschew it is an essential unity, it is also a many-stranded skein of utmost subtlety and complexity. Secondly, there is unquestionably another 'big thing' which Hayek in later decades has pursued with a burning zeal, the idea of freedom. And I think even a third quarry has led his tireless tracking of ideas, of truth itself. This third trail is the question of the method by which human affairs can be effectively analysed and understood.

Our age lives in the glare of natural science, and the supposed methods of natural science have soaked into the fibre of our thought as economists. Yet if we looked at some of the still-central concerns and professions of mankind, we should see the law, based on classification and precedent; and medicine, with its recognition of the deep mysteries of the human psychosomatic personality, *The Self and Its Brain*.[2] Economists would do well to ponder the diversity of Hayek's intellectual horizons. The participant in economic life is a human being. The study of human nature and institutions is not alien to the work of the economist, but fundamental to it. To attempt, however, in the space of some twelve thousand words, to give insight into all of Hayek's interests is impossible. I have confined this chapter to a study of two books and a few articles which seem to me to present the core of his more strictly economic thought. The mountain of his work on *The Constitution of Liberty*[3] and *Law, Legislation and Liberty*[4] I must leave for others to scale elsewhere. The sections of this chapter are labelled with the titles of those books and articles.

PRICES AND PRODUCTION

Hayek's fame sprang at first from a highly individual account of the nature of the trade cycle. This conception was first presented in English in 1931 in lectures delivered at the London School of Economics and printed as *Prices and Production*.[5] A new version, considerably revised from the former, appeared as a long essay in the volume called *Profits, Interest and Investment*[6] in 1939. *Prices and Production* fascinated many minds, not only at LSE, partly, I believe, because of its arcane and obscure suggestion of a radical telescoping together of ideas into some new incisive simplicity. Two of the ideas that were thus treated as one, however, were those that we should now call the rate of profit and the rate of interest, and this conflation was recognised by Hayek in *Profits, Interest and Investment* to have been a mistaken policy. It sprang very naturally from Böhm-Bawerk's view of the nature of interest as that variable (let us define it in the abstract as the proportion of itself by which a capital sum increases per unit of time) which brings to equality the irksomeness of marginal consumptions foregone and the pleasure of gains hoped for from marginal augmentations of equipment financed by those savings. Wicksell in his *Geldzins und Güterpreise*[7] of 1898, and in his *Lectures on Political Economy*[8] published in English in 1934, had based a theory of the phenomenon of a progressive general rise of prices on the relation of the rate of interest charged by the banking system on loans of money, to the rate of profit which could be earned by the use of this money in industry and commerce. In *Prices and Production* Hayek used the term 'rate of interest' as a substitute for 'rate of profit'. One of his chief concerns in *Profits, Interest and Investment* was to dissolve this confusion. This was very necessary, for Hayek's argument ascribes the trade cycle as a whole, partly on Wicksellian lines, to the natural action of the banking system.

The theme itself to be found in these two books is inherently elusive, involving a complex evolution of outputs, prices and profit rates through subtly merging phases. Hayek's statement of it has the vitality and excitement of a work of art seen almost in process of composition. In another mood we might say that successive attacks from various directions (thoughts of Hayek's own, the fruit of an implacable self-criticism) are despatched or fended off by a lithe play of resource. To make such a work intelligible without doing violence to its intricacy and subtlety is a daunting task. I shall first set out in brief the central strand of Hayek's theme, distinguishing between the version of *Prices and Production* and that of *Profits, Interest and Investment*.

The services of men and nature applied in production yield a consumable result only after a lapse of time. The longer the time that can be allowed, over the variously dated applications of human and natural forces as a whole, before their consumable product emerges at some one date, the greater this product can be for given amounts of such forces. This is because such forces, applied long enough in advance, can be used for making tools to make further tools, and so on, in a sequence which goes far in substituting equipment for men and nature. The building-up of the material means of such a system, as distinct from its continued operation once built, requires a lengthening of the pause between effort and consumption, on the whole, as compared with the continued use of a less complex, subtle or powerful system. If for some reason, in the course of building, this endeavour is interrupted before an output of consumable goods from it begins, the part which has been built will stand to be abandoned while all gatherable efforts of men and nature are concentrated at the near-consumption stages of a shorter system. If those who are working at the 'early' and now-abandoned stages are highly specialised to the work of those stages, they will be disemployed by this retreat. Thus we have the seeds of depression. The question now is, what can be the source of an interruption of the building-up of a new, more time-taking, more labour-and-land economical system of production? If the only source of funds to pay for the services of men and nature engaged in the building process during the time when it is not turning out any consumables which can be sold, is the saving done by people at large out of their incomes, it may be reasonable to suppose that the conditions on which these funds are lent and borrowed will in some degree serve to constrain the time-length of the new system to what the savers are prepared to finance out of their abstention from current consumption. If so, there is nothing which need evidently frustrate the achievement of the more efficient system. But if there is a banking system, extra funds, beyond those savings which correspond to non-consumed income earned in production, may be provided to the entrepreneurs seeking to build the new system. This money will be paid, in wages, rent and profits, to those who are building the new system. They will not save all of it. Some will be added to the monetary demand for consumers' goods, which however are not yet being produced in greater daily or annual quantity than before. Prices of consumers' goods will rise and profits for those businessmen directly concerned in making consumables will increase. These businessmen will seek by all means to increase their output quickly, and the only way in which they can do so is by adopting shorter, rather than longer, systems of production, drawing the services of men and nature for this purpose away from those who are seeking to build longer systems. At the furthest extreme from the direct production of consumables, there will thus be firms making equipment for the new longer systems, who will be starved of orders and unable to pay their employees. Thus business depression will set in.

The foregoing passage broadly presents, I believe, the theme of both the two books we are discussing. The differences between those two accounts arise from Hayek's recognition of vulnerable features in *Prices and Production*. Even in the later essay he did not, perhaps, fully come to terms with all of them. His theme appeals essentially to the intimate dependence of elaborate tool-using methods of production on the willingness of people to allow a considerable time to elapse between effort and result. Tools must be made, *then* used. Tools are needed in order to make tools. But there is, I think, a distinction to be made, important in practice though not evidently basic in principle, between the fact that in building up a more elaborate system of equipment-using production, things must be done one after the other, and the fact that when such a system has been established, there will be a difference of date between the rendering of some productive service by men or nature, and the emergence of the identified quanta of consumables to which this service has contributed. For if the postponement of consumption during the building process becomes intolerable, that process can be stopped, and other methods of production reverted to. But when the new system is fully in business, the elimination of its inherent time-lapses would involve its dismantling, that is, its reduction to scrap, in a suicidal vulturine scramble for its flesh. Even in the later essay, Hayek does not seem to keep this distinction always in focus. The necessity and effects of time-lapse in production is one perspective of the use of equipment, that is, of tools in a very general sense, in production. This perspective is the basis of the 'Austrian theory of capital', due chiefly to Eugen von Böhm-Bawerk, whose principal purpose is to explain why the providing of the services of equipment generates and justifies an income, a share in the total product. But the connection between time-lapse and the use of an elaborate division of labour is complex, subtle and elusive to the last degree, and Hayek became aware that his representation of it, or his neglect of its problems, in *Prices and Production* placed the argument of that book at a serious disadvantage. In *Prices and Production* Hayek speaks as though every productive operation and hence every tool used and every person engaged in that operation could be located, in relation to every other operation contributing to the output of a specific kind of consumable at a named date, as either nearer to or further from the final operation from which that consumable directly emerged. Evidently examples of such a 'linear' sequence can easily be thought of. Ploughing the field and rolling it, drilling in the seed, hoeing, reaping, threshing and milling the grain, baking the bread, compose such a process. Even here, however, there are tributary streams of operations: those concerned with the making of implements, the breeding and feeding of horses or the supply of fuel and chemical fertiliser. Hayek envisages such converging lines, but this idea hardly touches the problem. Production in an advanced industrial society needs for its description a Leontief table of input coefficients, where in principle, and in algebraic practice so far as computation allows, every operation or every industry or sector is deemed actually or potentially to contribute means of some kind to every other, both directly and indirectly. Such sectors as transportation, the telephone system and the electric power industry plainly have a hand to some degree in everything that is done by anybody anywhere, even though it may represent only a small part of the cost of a particular item of consumption. But there is more. The web of inter-contributory operations or sectors, though its individual parts may have technically constant kinds of output, can direct these in variable proportions to other sectors. It can change those proportions. The dedication of any sector to the making of a particular kind of machine or material, the *specificity* of the product of each sector, is as we might say a micro-specificity. It does not render impossible a re-orientation of the web of production as a whole to an altered bill of goods for consumption. These considerations by no means destroy Hayek's theme, but that conception needs to be seen in their light.

In seeking greater force of persuasion for his theme, Hayek characteristically went to the foundations. These rested on the Böhm-Bawerkian theory of capital. With an inexhaustible energy, Hayek undertook its re-working and re-expression. I shall attempt below to explain and assess the conception he achieved. Meanwhile I must try to show what those inherent problems of the Austrian theory of capital are, which make it so intractable for Hayek's purpose.

Lapse of time between the input of productive service and the output of a consumable product can be due to different kinds of circumstance. In *Prices and Production* Hayek's dominant assumption was that time-lapse occurs because a piece of material, having an identity which it retains throughout all operations on it, requires to be extracted, shaped, fabricated and finished by operations which individually take time and have to be performed successively, each having an effect which, from the moment of its performance until the object is sold for consumption, remains as it were embodied in the object and adds something to its accumulating value. In the case of the building of a house, time-lapses from this source may be a matter of weeks or months. But what are such intervals compared with those involved in the use of the house? The greatest source of time-lapse in production must surely be durability. A house whose foundations are begun today may be lived in for a hundred years. Even ships and locomotives may be in use for decades. Tools and machines may be in use, after many years of their life, to make other tools. Durability of tools and of products has two consequences for Hayek's theory. It renders extremely difficult and elusive the task of linking the application of measurable productive service by men and nature on one date with the emergence of a measurable consumable product at another date. And durability is a chief vessel of the governance of the present by the past. An existing piece of equipment may cost more to operate per unit of product than one which could now be designed. But unless the savings of operating cost expected from a new design, as compared with the existing tool, have a total discounted value not less than its construction cost, it will not be ordered. Hayek's argument, viewing 'capital goods' as materials which only retain their physical identity through a process of fabrication into consumable form, overlooks the grip that durability has in constraining the businessman's choice of productive methods. The span of the nine-year business cycle, to which his theory was meant to apply, is not long enough for a wholesale discarding of existing equipment during the latter half of its upward phase, say two or three years.

In referring just now to a test of worthwhileness of replacing obsolescent machines by new designs, we spoke of the savings *expected* to be made. This word reflects the most fundamental of all the difficulties which economic analysis faces. Time-to-come is not open to inspection, there can be no eye-witnesses of its history. That history (unless we are fatalists who abnegate the reality of choice) will be created by the decisions which flow from our conjectures as to what it can be made to yield. Time-to-come is the void, waiting to be filled by enterprise, by action which manifests originative acts of mind. *Expectation* names almost the whole business of pragmatic thought. In *Prices and Production*, however, there is no mention of expectation. Even in *Profits, Interest and Investment* this lack is only formally recognised. Yet in a brilliant article in 1937[9] Hayek had asked what the economic choice-maker can know and how he can know it.

A question which, perhaps, even natural science has not attempted to answer, is why things that take place *take time to do so*. Why do events take time? The question perhaps belongs to that region of the inconceivable, which J. B. S. Haldane conjectured in saying that the universe is queerer than we *can* imagine. In natural science, however, we can at least know how much time definable changes will take under this condition or that. To make the same supposition in matters of human action is surely exceedingly dangerous. In seeking to describe and account for trains of economic events, economists have tended to assume that the economic system or organism of society works like a machine, or perhaps like a hydraulic system. Is there not a fluid which flows around the system, encountering goods at each movement and thus registering prices? It has been assumed, implicitly, by many theorists that money needs to arrive and be present in order to have an effect, just as the tide needs to arrive and be present in order to float a ship off the mud. But what we need to ask is, not what will float the ship off the mud, but what will cause the captain to make preparations for the moment when he can cast off and sail away. And what inspires the captain's activity is his *knowledge* of the tide. Money can exert a force upon events by merely being *thought of*. We must go further. Some philosophers in discussing the mind-body problem have spoken derisively of 'the ghost in the machine'. But this phrase fits the nature of the economic system remarkably well. It is a *system of thoughts* before it is a system of actions. One mind can act upon another, in an economic context, without moving money from one account to another or one holder to another. The picture which his words conjure in another mind can be the source of action. When he wrote *Prices and Production* Hayek treated the economic system as hydraulic, as a body whose muscles needed, as it were, a supply of blood, and were determined in their actions by the flows of blood. But the muscles, in a more interesting sense, are actuated by the neuronal system, by the messages which, as we must express it, come from thoughts. The phases of the trade cycle are depicted in *Prices and Production* as due to the flows or constrictions of money. Undoubtedly the muscles need blood, but they work because of thoughts. Hayek later wrote on questions of psychology, and, we are told, was at one time undecided whether to become an economist or a psychologist. Does not the psychologist need a field of real human action from which to draw suggestions? Economics should surely provide it. Like Adam Smith, Hayek was by instinct a moral scientist in the round.

Profits, Interest and Investment in some essential respects moved far from *Prices and Production*. In the latter Hayek felt obliged to start his train of events from a supposed state of full employment. He did so because in the later 1920s and early 1930s it still seemed to most economists that 'equilibrium' had a powerful practical as well as analytical ascendancy, and that it made full employment the natural state of affairs from which deviations had to be explained. In the later essay he assumed 'an initial situation where considerable unemployment of material resources and labour exists'. Here also he distinguished the 'rate of profit' from the 'rate of interest' and spoke of 'the inadequate distinction [he] had formerly drawn between the movement of money wages and the movement of real wages'. *Profits, Interest and Investment* was meant to re-state the theme of *Prices and Production* in a less vulnerable form. But *Prices and Production* had a drive and vitality, however peculiar, which make it a classic, and which the later essay lacked.

THE PURE THEORY OF CAPITAL

Hayek's theory of the trade cycle took for granted a particular view of the nature and consequences of tool-using production, which it regarded as time-using production. Some of the objections raised against *Prices and Production* were due to the inadequacies of its presentation of the theory of capital which it pre-supposed. In order to satisfy his critics, himself chief amongst them, Hayek decided to re-work from its foundations his theory of 'capitalistic production'. As this work progressed through several drafts during the middle and later 1930s, he responded to its ever-freshly multiplying difficulties with an intense and sustained effort nothing short of heroic. *The Pure Theory of Capital*,[10] published in 1941, is as it were a final report on Böhm-Bawerk's proposal.

In the theory which Hayek develops, the word *capital* names an aspect of the technological organisation of production. It might be said in brief to reflect the fact that in order to obtain consumable goods we first make tools and other preparations, and then make use of them. This fact can be looked on in two ways. We can say either that production via elaborate preparatory stages *takes time*. Or we can say that the tools and materials which embody such preparatory work are the vehicles which convey the effect of such work through time and pile it up with an added yield at the date of the emergence of goods ready for consumption. On either view, time is essentially involved in the notion of capital. On the former view, time-lapse *allows* of a highly instrumented method of production, or, in a broad meaning of the term, a highly-perfected division of labour. On the second view, it is the intermediary materials and tools, the *capital goods*, which allow time-lapse to exert its virtue in making the forces of men and nature more efficacious. On either view, there is an intimate connection between time-lapse and the material stepping-stones to consumable goods. There is a temptation, with some excuse, to identify capital, or capital goods, with the operation of time as in some sense a factor of production. The originators of the theory which Hayek has carried, perhaps, to its ultimate pitch of usefulness, had indeed proposed that the endlessly heterogeneous collection of tools and materials in use at any moment could be reduced to a scalar quantity in terms of an average lapse of time between productive activities and their consumable result. Hayek takes pains to show that this notion is fallacious. Instead, we must divide all the productive services of men and nature which are applied at any one moment, into fractions small enough to let us discriminate every different length of time-lapse which occurs between the use of such a fraction and the emergence of the consumable product which constitutes its fruit. The entire assemblage of such time-lapses is the *output function*, and this is one means of describing the *time structure of production* which validly replaces the inadmissible notion of an average period of production. An alternative is the *input function*, which we obtain by dividing the consumable product emerging at any one moment into such fractions as are due to human and natural services rendered at different earlier dates. The set of fractions into which the input of any one moment is divided according to the lengths of time to its maturity as consumables is not the same set as that into which the consumable output of any one moment must be divided according to the lengths of time which have elapsed since their corresponding inputs. For equal inputs will yield different quantities of output if they remain invested for different lengths of time. This notion is itself one of the essential strands in Hayek's skein, and its meaning must be carefully considered.

What governs the form of the output function? This question comprises several others. Is the form a matter of choice? If so, of whose choice? In making the choice, what end is sought? What principle guides choice in pursuit of this end, or what test shows it to have been attained? Is the chooser perfectly free in choosing, or what constrains his choice? Let us take these in turn.

Economic theory is centrally, essentially concerned with choice. If the form of the output function is not subject to choice, the economist need not spend time on it. For Hayek, the effect and the attainability of this or that form, the governance of this attainability by the society's endowment of materials, tools and consumables at the moment when the form to be attempted is being chosen, and its governance by the desires of the individual members, is the central matter of capital theory. The society has before it a range of rival forms of the output function. Other conceivable forms are excluded by the combined effect of the society's endowment and its tastes. How are those tastes, and the consequent constraint imposed on the choice, to be known? Hayek seeks in the first place to isolate the essential effects of time-lapse in production. In order to pursue this question without distracting issues, he at first assigns authority over the whole business of production to a single individual. This controller is assumed first to decide what quantitative mix of consumable goods is to be produced, and then to organise the use of all the productive resources available to him so as to secure the largest output of this mix which can be maintained indefinitely from the moment when he takes charge of affairs. We ought to notice the ingenuity of this scheme. The constraint imposed upon choice of productive method by the need for immediate consumption from the word 'go' is not excluded from it. This need can be met at first by existing stocks of ready consumables, and during the time thus gained, time-taking preparation of tools and partly-processed materials can proceed. As the stocks come to an end, the new process will begin to yield consumable goods, and it will be doing so at the highest time-rate (output) attainable under the assumed condition of constant consumption per time unit from the outset. By this scheme, whose complexity in detail is rather more formidable than I have suggested, Hayek introduces the ideas of building-up the apparatus of time-taking productive method under the constraint of desired consumption mitigated by the possession of stocks of ready goods. He thus illustrates, in a scheme which at first sight may appear highly contrived, two of the essential elements of the economic role of time.

We have viewed in two ways the part played in production by lapse of time between input and output. On one view such time-lapse allows the forces of men and nature (the *original means of production*) to produce consumables through a series of preparatory stages where tools and materials are produced as the means to make further such means until a last stage is reached in which consumables emerge in much greater quantity per unit of time than if labour and nature had been applied more directly. What, if anything, is given up for the sake of this gain in efficacy? It is here that the distinction is vital, between the situation where a time-taking method of production has merely to be continued and maintained, and the situation where its material embodiment of fresh kinds of tools and materials has to be built up in successive stages. In the former, the only sacrifice entailed in continuing the method of production which has been established is the forgoing of such brief higher rate of consumption as could be got by dismantling the apparatus of that method, that is to say, by starving some existing machines of the energy and materials needed for their operation, and even reducing to scrap the machines themselves. By thus subjecting their own apparatus and stores to a process of pillage, the society could enjoy a brief, suicidal orgy. In the second situation, the sacrifice required of an already fully employed society, in order to make the transition to a more time-taking method of production whereby the given flows of input of services of the original means of production would yield a larger consumable output, is a period of lower consumption than they have been enjoying. For some services both of the original means and the existing produced means (tools, systems and inventories of materials) of production would have to be diverted from producing consumables by the method hitherto in use, to building up by necessarily successive stages the new apparatus whose more efficient use of the services of men and nature, once this new apparatus was complete, would provide a permanently larger flow of consumables.

Which, then, of these two situations is the relevant one? Hayek's purpose in *The Pure Theory of Capital* is to develop the most austere and stringent abstract model of the role of time-lapse within a productive technology. For this purpose, he abstracts from money and, with a curiously arbitrary fragmentation, from uncertainty. (How can time as a field of choice (time-to-come) be discussed in any meaningful abstraction from uncertainty? Hayek thus reduces his problem to one which can be treated demonstratively, that is, by rigorous logic. But logic needs its data, which time-to-come conceals.) These two exclusions, of money and uncertainty, would themselves, I think, ensure full employment, but Hayek makes this also an explicit assumption.

In order to build up by successive stages a productive apparatus not hitherto existing, a society whose productive means are fully employed must forgo during some time-interval some consumption which it could otherwise have enjoyed. What is the inducement to make this sacrifice? Evidently it is the permanently higher rate of consumption which can thus be secured. Out of this extra stream of consumable goods, obtained from an unchanged input of the services of men and nature, a continuing reward can be paid to those who went without some of the consumption they could have had during some time-interval. That permanent stream of reward for the definite total of forgone consumption can be called a rate of interest on the total of their saving, for it can be expressed as an annual quantity related to a quantity of capital, a capital sum. A ratio which is the same in form but conceptually distinct in referend is that of the extra stream of consumable goods yielded by the improved method of production. How much saving, how much forgoing of consumption, a sacrifice of what amount per time unit for how many time units, will the members of the society be willing to do? The most familiar notion in economic theory, that of the equalising, at the margin, of sacrifice and advantage, suggests that their saving will be pushed to the point where a little more would be so irksome as to cancel the attractiveness of the prospect of the little addition it would make to the increase of consumption that their saving will yield. However, the sacrifice of consumption involved in building-up by successive stages the apparatus of a technology not previously used (though known) will not be uniform and equal for the various stages, for these are successive. The use of some services of men and nature to build the first stage will mean the withdrawal of these identified (as we might say, proper-named) services for the whole length of time it will take to complete the new apparatus in all stages. Those who forgo consumption, of some specific amount, for this relatively long time will require a greater reward than those who forgo an equal amount merely in order to make possible the final stage. To take account of this aspect of the transition to a new technology is to consider the matter from the side of the *need* for a reward for sacrificing consumption. What, then, of the possibility of supplying that reward? The process of building the physical embodiment of the hitherto unused technology consists in first making tools and materials which are, as it were, the seed of the whole process. The next stage rests upon the shoulders of the first, and the first takes some credit for the efficacy of the second. And so on through the stages. If we accept this view, a greater share of the total gain of capacity to produce consumables must be ascribed to the early stages than to the later. In fact, the early stages will be so chosen that they can claim this extra share of credit for the gain. They will be the natural first stages. How can the two ideas, that early sacrifices of consumption claim a greater reward and that early inputs of productive services to the building of the new apparatus are the source of greater shares of the gain of capacity, be formalised so as to make possible the conception of an equalisation at the margin?

The formal conception of a rate of interest is that of a *speed of proportionate growth*. Growth of what? In the world of business as it proceeds in reality, what grows is a debt expressed in money terms. If the debt starts at 100, and the contract between lender and borrower stipulates that 110 shall be repaid after one year, the debt is set to grow at 10 per cent a year. If at the end of a year the lender agrees to a postponement of the settling of the debt for a year more on the same terms as prevailed for the first year, the lender is effectively lending, for the further year, the 110 he could have received at the beginning of this second year. If he again receives the initial debt, of 110, plus one-tenth, the repayment due at the end of the second year will be 121. And so on. This is, of course, the principle of compound interest, and it is the meaning of a rate of interest in the fundamental formal sense. A rate of interest is conventionally stated as such-and-such a fraction of the initial or of the accumulated debt per annum, but the calculation of the interest due to be added to the debt, and the actual addition of it, need by no means be done at yearly intervals, but can be stipulated to be done at any intervals, say quarterly or daily or *continuously*. The notion that packets of productive service contribute a greater share to the ultimate increase of capacity to produce consumables, if they are applied early rather than late in the process of building up the new system, can be conveniently formalised by supposing these packets to be notionally carried through the respective time-intervals between their application and the emergence of their first consumable products, in the form of entities growing exponentially, that is, by compound interest.

Let us now suppose that a packet of productive service is applied to the building-up of the new system a specified length of time before the system is to be completed, and that the contribution it will make to the system can be measured. Let us suppose that the relation between the value of this input, and the value of its contribution, be expressed in terms of exponential growth, or compound interest, at a certain rate. And let us suppose that the same can be done for another input, of equal value when applied, but applied a different length of time before the completion of the system. And suppose that the 'rate of interest' expressing the notional growth of value is different for the two inputs. Is this a satisfactory arrangement of the affair? If more input could be applied at the higher rate, and correspondingly less at the lower rate, the value of the completed system, its productive capacity, would be increased. On this principle we may say that the aim of those who design the process of building up the new apparatus, under the constraint of a limited willingness of those who finance the operation to forgo consumption for that purpose, will be to make the scheme of time intervals such that the rates of exponential growth of differently-timed inputs are *equal*. This rate, common to the whole process, will be determined by technological possibilities on one hand, and by the amount of saving that the members of the society will do, on the other. For this rate will express alike the gain of efficacy and the reward for forgoing consumption. The idea of this equality between gain and sacrifice at the margin is the familiar one, in economic theory, of maximising a dependent variable by suitable choice of the arguments on which it depends.

In this second section of my chapter I have sought to give, in some two and a half thousand words, an account of a theory to which Hayek devoted some four hundred and forty pages. *The Pure Theory of Capital* emerged in its published form from several manuscript versions which I had the privilege of reading during its composition. The sustained intensity of thought which it cost its author, the astonishing degree to which he has imposed coherence on a mountainous body of reasoning concerning a theme which is perhaps unmatched in economics in its intricacy, show theory-making as a task not for intellect alone, but for high moral courage and implacable resolve. To write such a work, it is not enough to be able to pile brick on brick for year after year until the heap is high enough. In the end there must emerge a unified conception informed by some single principle. A critic would find it hard to show that, on its own terms, *The Pure Theory of Capital* does not attain success by this test. The questions which it must elicit from any reader would be ill-judged if they sought to deny its element of the heroic. None the less we are bound to consider them in their widely various bearings.

What can a theory do, for its author or his readers? It can, in its most elevated role, give his spirit the ultimate satisfaction of the contemplation of beauty. It is hard to say what we mean by beauty, in this or any other context. But intellectual beauty involves, perhaps, an element of surprising conviction. Beauty is felt in a proof or an explanation, when this conception seizes the mind in a single thought. Beauty is sudden and dramatic in impact, no matter how still and timeless its form. Next we may say, I think, that a theory sets thought at rest. It provides a faith. This surely is the effect we demand of a theory, even if we reserve the thought that other theories may displace it. A theory which commands our assent is a stroke of

Alexander's sword, cutting through a tangle of confusions. It is thus a powerful classifying agent, revealing unity and an essential strand in common amongst ostensibly diverse and unrelated things. A problem, may we say, is an ostensibly incomplete presentation of elements. To solve a problem is to reveal a hidden completeness or completeability. It is for this that a theory can serve.

In reading *The Pure Theory of Capital* one is likely, I think, to conjecture that Hayek very early in his scholar's life gave his allegiance to Böhm-Bawerk and to Wicksell, that his mind was seized by an arresting idea, namely, that in investigating the nature of capital we are investigating an aspect of the nature of time. Such a conviction gives an immense impulse to intellectual effort, for it removes at one stroke any fear that the problem in hand may prove trivial or peripheral. In seeking to grasp some manifestation of time we are driving at the heart of things. Some such influence seems needed to explain the huge effort which Hayek devoted to refounding the Böhm-Bawerk–Wicksell theory of capital. That such an effort was needed, that Hayek encountered numberless and daunting troubles, that so long a book was required to contain the implications of an ostensibly incisive idea – capital is the working of time-lapse in production – suggests inevitably that too much was expected of a tool which had, at first sight, so brilliant a glow of promise. Which of the purposes of theory does Hayek's intricate and elusively subtle construction serve? He has pursued to the uttermost the possibilities of his theme, and the conceptions involved in it are often beautiful in themselves. But the very austerity and unappeasable thoroughness of his detection of difficulties and his determination to cope with them have had the opposite effect of the presumably intended one. In his prodigious effort at final vindication of the Jevons–Böhm-Bawerk–Wicksell idea, Hayek has disdained the principle of benign imprecision without which so much of economic theory cannot breathe. He explains in detail why the skein of different lengths of time elapsing between the input of original means of production at some one date and the emergence of the quanta of consumable goods respectively attributable to various fractions of that input cannot be reduced to an *average period of production*. Yet is seems inconceivable that any statistical or practical use can be made of the Austrian theory of capital unless it can be epitomised into some such form.

The reader of Hayek's *Pure Theory of Capital* will, I think, find some particular difficulties or objections in addition to its general extreme complexity. In specifying those which seem to me important

I am saying nothing which casts any shadow on my recognition of a masterpiece. In this book, Hayek has nailed his colours to the mast and has pursued to the uttermost limits the logic where it led. The result is a remarkable contribution to knowledge which could have been attained in no other way, and, I will venture to say, assuredly by no other man.

At the outset of his account of the output function and the input function, Hayek simply assumes that 'each separate unit of available input is expected to make a definite and determinable contribution to the output stream of the future'. He expressly defers the question 'on what principle particular parts of the future output stream can be attributed to particular units of input'. The discussion of the input and output functions, their meaning, the influences that govern their form and the possibility of determining it (finding it out) is spread over many chapters, one of which deals with the special difficulty posed by durable goods. In order to decide whether the problems of attribution of particular dated quanta of output to particular dated quanta of input can be solved so far as the structure of inference resting on this attribution requires, the reader needs to be alert through these many chapters to note and consider each reference to the matter. Hayek has preferred to deal first with the problem of describing supposedly determinable output functions and input functions, by means of ingenious and beautiful three-dimensional diagrams, rather than confront in one chapter at the outset the essential question of whether and how far the attribution, and thus the determination of forms of the functions, is possible. Yet this question is fundamental to the whole edifice.

The problem of assigning particular dated quanta of output to particular dated quanta of input (or vice versa) is made immeasurably more difficult by a fact which Hayek seems quite to ignore. In *Prices and Production* it is taken for granted that when services of men and nature are applied in some productive operation, the direct product of that operation is unqualifiedly nearer to the ultimate consumable good than is the material on which they work in that operation, this latter being the product of an earlier operation, more remote from the consumable. Productive operations, it is thus assumed, fall naturally and distinctly into what we may call a linear sequence, each being merely a preparation for the next in the series. Hayek recognises that contributory streams of such operations may converge into the making of a consumable good. But this is not the essential matter. Production in a modern economy is a network of operations every one of which, in some large or small degree, helps to provide means of every other. At what stage in the production of the goods that lie on the grocer's shelves are we to locate the work of the Post Office, the railways, or the electricity supply industry? The universal inter-necessity of all types of productive operation is pictured (with unavoidable simplification and aggregation of widely different things) by the Leontief table of input coefficients, a square matrix where every sector is present in the list of suppliers of materials or tools to any randomly-chosen sector. Thus every sector is deemed to be in principle directly supplied by every other sector, and indirectly by every supplier of its direct suppliers, and so on, in a pattern which only algebra can completely and intelligibly describe. The notion of 'stages of production' is not essentially absent from the Leontief scheme, but it would require an inexpressibly complex and elaborate procedure to discern in the data of that scheme a Hayekian output function.

When he came to write *The Pure Theory of Capital* Hayek had come under suggestive influence from a number of writers whose relevant work had been published too late to affect *Prices and Production*. His attitude had noticeably softened towards Frank Knight, with whom he had earlier engaged in seemingly irresolvable debate. He refers several times to Keynes's *The General Theory of Employment, Interest and Money*,[11] especially to its view of the interest rate as reflecting the public's desire for liquidity in face of the policies of the banking system. That conception was not immediately relevant to Hayek's purpose because he had explicitly excluded money. But Hayek's most significant reference, perhaps, is to Gunnar Myrdal's suggestion of the need to distinguish between the *ex ante* and the *ex post* temporal viewpoints. Myrdal's theme appeared originally in Swedish in 1931. In 1933 it appeared as one of four long essays by different authors in a book edited by Hayek.[12] In *The Pure Theory of Capital* Hayek constantly emphasised the forward-looking view. In 1937, in his remarkable article called 'Economics and Knowledge',[13] Hayek had made explicit a conception of equilibrium far removed from the notions derived from physical mechanics. Equilibrium, he said, should be deemed to consist in the compatibility of plans. In *The Pure Theory of Capital* he made ingenious and effective use of this idea. He had recognised (though he did not fully adapt his text to the recognition) that time-lapse takes on its vital importance, not in a stationary society, but in a society attempting to make the transition to a superior technology by building-up (despite the existing full employment of its means of production) the necessary material apparatus. How, at the moment when the decision to make such an attempt was being taken, could the skein of time-lapses that it would involve be known? They could be known only if the plans of different individuals or firms were not only quite explicit in their minds and each of them single-tracked (that is, envisaging a path of action without variants) but if also they were seen to be mutually compatible and to form a coherent whole which contained no internal contradictions. The time-lapses could be known, that is to say, only in a Hayekian equilibrium, as the sole alternative to a stationary state whose presumed indefinite persistence would also make their measurement possible, but which in the nature of things was the negation of a process of investment in new equipment.

In speaking of the expectations and intentions which compose a Hayekian equilibrium as 'single tracked' I mean that their perfect mutual compatibility, which is the essence of the conception, has meaning only if the course of affairs in time-to-come, which any particular individual envisages, specifies for any randomly-chosen moment no more than one point in the space (of no matter how many dimensions) required for the description of that course. Such a conception has, perhaps, its greatest usefulness in compelling us to ask, in view of its evident utter unattainability, what in fact the process of history must be like. Individuals will not necessarily surrender the freedom of imagination, of enterprise, of attempted exploitation of the void of time-to-come, in order to try to reconcile their ambitions with those of all other individuals. The seething cauldron of history mocks such a notion. Even at a lesser level of generalness, the difficulties multiply. Different individuals will plan their respective courses of action in differently defined, differently conceived spaces. A dimension which appears in one such space will be absent from others. Two men cannot arrange to walk side by side when each is studying a map of a different country. We have to ask also up to what horizon the plans will be carried, and whether and why it should or can be the same for all. Hayek by no means presses things thus to extremes, but his classic article was one of the very few which called in question, in those days or since, the *accessibility* of equilibrium, either as an intellectual or a practical solution. Recontract and *tâtonnements* are merely gestures. Equilibrium is analytic, telling us how things would be if we ever got there.

I think the idea that a great work of the intellect can be created by starting with 'an open mind' must be misleading. The impulse must come from some question which has seized the thinker's curiosity and from some suggestion which has leapt from his long meditation on it, a spark from some chance conjunction of impressions. There must be some inspirational idea, some line to be followed, before a man can gather the moral and nervous force which such a task requires. He must be seized by a faith. The decision to pursue a particular suggestion, whether that the earth goes round the sun or that capital is time, must irresistibly *impose itself* in virtue of incisive beauty or immensity of potential revelation. The notion that problems of capital are problems of the necessity for time to elapse between effort and result in production is, at its first impact, arresting in its suggestion of simplicity and power. The advancement and secure founding of knowledge demanded imperiously that this conception should be examined by a powerful mind with dedicated zeal and stringent thoroughness. To have done this once and for all is Hayek's very great achievement.

'ECONOMICS AND KNOWLEDGE'[14]

The word *equilibrium* pervades economic theory. It names in turn the members of a plurality of ideas plainly distinct from each other. Yet this ascendancy arises from a deep common source. Equilibrium is the expression of a fundamental adoption of method, an assumption about the nature of the human individual and his essential predicament. Equilibrium is, in fact, the name of a view of the scheme of things. In that scheme, the user of this term supposes, human conduct and thus history itself are the manifestation and upshot of the successful employment of reason. Equilibrium characterises human affairs when, and because, the participants have responded wisely to their circumstances. Those circumstances evidently include, for each person, the existence and activity of other persons. Equilibrium thus means the wise response of individuals to each other. In one of the most brilliant and perceptive of all his works, the essay called 'Economics and Knowledge', Hayek set out the profound, subtle and intricate questions which flow from the making of the equilibrium assumption.

In 'Economics and Knowledge' Hayek takes what is often called the subjectivist standpoint, the view that for the human being the business of life is *thought*. For the individual in deciding his course, what he thinks is the case, *is* the case. The data, the description of his circumstances, the account of the universe with whose immediate posture and basic laws he has to reckon, is the account which he has himself extracted from his own experience and judgement. This experience, the things and events that have come under his notice, the modes of thought which instinct or education have implanted in him, the intuition which Nature gave him, are to some degree peculiar to each individual. Yet we are bound to assume that they have a basic likeness amongst different people. To be human is to have some insight into human nature and human responses. If it be true that equilibrium, the *best* for each individual that he can attain in face of the competition of all the other individuals, is a goal sometimes actually approached by society, what in detail is the process by which the different individual conceptions are reconciled with each other? That is to say, how do the data assumed by the different individuals come to be, so far as they need to be, the *same*.

A student of human affairs not already enmeshed in received economic theory might at first be inclined to question the basic premise. Do we try to guide our conduct by applying reason to a carefully built-up picture of the world's principles and its momentary state? Or is equilibrium no more than an intellectual obsession? Despite history's record of ferocity and evil, which seems so vividly to bear out Macbeth's assessment of life, there is a vast contrary evidence: the all-encompassing web of markets and diplomacy, the fabric of laws and contracts, the international basis of calendars and navigation. If humanity tries, however erratically, to organise itself, it tries for equilibrium. But there is still a danger in this word for the theoretician. He must not take equilibrium to be an account of the world's process. What would 'equilibrium' mean, if we had to use this term to describe a game of football? It could only mean that the final whistle had already blown.

'Economics and Knowledge' declares its Hayekian birth. All the caution, subtlety and rigour which a training in the law elicits from a first-rate mind is here brought to bear on problems of meaning. Sometimes in the course of it a new vista of theory is glimpsed, only to be left unexplored in favour of the clearing-up of an immediate semantic riddle. However, the vital and novel central theme rightly claims ascendancy. 'The only part [of economic theory] which is concerned with causes and effects, and leads to propositions capable of falsification,[15] consists of propositions about the acquisition of knowledge'. This carries us a long way, and places us on that ground where Hayek's meaning for equilibrium can be built. From that ground a far horizon will draw some readers' eyes to the notion, not just of the gathering of information but of the origination of new possibilities. But this is not the business of Hayek's essay and he does not turn that way.

Equilibrium, Hayek says, refers to relations amongst actions. Actions of an individual are in equilibrium so far as they can be understood as part of one plan; that is to say, 'only if all these actions have been decided on at one and the same moment and in consideration of the same set of circumstances'. By this last phrase we must understand, of course, the same body of subjective knowledge, the same set of circumstances supposed by the individual to be the case. There follows in the text, however, an enigmatic statement: 'Since the actions of one person must necessarily take place successively in time, it is obvious that the passage of time is essential to give the concept of equilibrium any meaning'. I think the distinction is needed here between the notion of time-to-come, which is plainly essential to the existence of any plan, and the notion of the actual lapse of time, that is, the enactment of an historical sequence of events. How can a thing *be*, save in a single (I would say, solitary) moment? This moment, however, can transform itself, as every moment does, into a successor. And provided the individual's relevant knowledge is unchanged by that transformation, the new equilibrium can be identical with its predecessor. (But can even a moment pass without change of knowledge?) So much for equilibrium as the state of a single mind at a single moment. But we are still at the threshold of the real problem. In what sense and by what steps can there be an approach to equilibrium amongst the actions of many persons?

If at some moment the body of subjective knowledge, the conception of the nature and the posture of things, including, so far as needed, the ideas in the minds of others, entertained by one member of a society, differs from that of another member; if, let us say, such differences prevail generally amongst the members of the society; then evidently the bodies of knowledge respectively entertained by some of them must change if there is to come about a unity of outlook amongst all the members. Change does involve more than a single moment, it involves, in some sense, a comparison of moments. Thus the lapse of historic time, which Hayek invoked as we noted earlier, is called for when we consider the *approach* to equilibrium. The perceptions and judgements, which cause some members of the society to change their subjective knowledge or beliefs, will 'take time'. Hayek insists many times that equilibrium is only of interest to us, and only serves for providing refutable propositions (in contrast with the tautologies of abstract and self-sufficient logic) when we consider how the unity of knowledge amongst the members of a society could *come about*. The unity itself is a state, and characterises a 'single moment'. The approach to this unity is a process, and occupies historic time. He renounces the task of describing the process of approach. That is an empirical task (perhaps, we might add, an endless one). His real concern in 'Economics and Knowledge' is to define the state of equilibrium when it embraces a number of individuals: 'For a society, then, we *can* speak of a state of equilibrium at a point of time – but it means only that the different plans which the individuals composing it have made for action in time are mutually compatible'. With this definition of the goal, the form of the question concerning the pursuit of it is also determined: How can the (subjective) knowledge of each individual, such as bears on his plan, become the same as the knowledge on which each other individual bases a plan of his own?

To have attained these questions and definitions, to have made knowledge, its subjective nature, its governance of individual action and the enigma of its formation, the central strand in the economic theoretician's skein of themes, shows Hayek as one of the great innovators. He himself in his book refers to other pioneers: to Ludwig von Mises, Frank Knight, Maynard Keynes and Gunnar Myrdal. His own achievement is to have brought all such suggestions to a focus and a verbal encapsulation.

There are still some points of semantics and internal logic to be cleared. In the course of its attempted execution a plan will encounter, besides the actions of other individuals, the events in the non-human universe. If these have been wrongly assessed, the plan will prove not to be realisable. Must we then deny it the standing of a component of an equilibrium? To do so would conflict with the principle that equilibrium characterises plans as such, existents at a single point of the calendar. At such a moment, no judgement is possible, and no judgement is meaningful, which refers to realised events of later moments. To do so would involve a contradiction in terms. A related question is the possible meaning of a *change* in the course of events in the non-human world. The question can best be answered by first asking what is its relevance. The non-human world can disrupt a plan. When will it do so? Evidently when its behaviour proves different from what the maker of the plan assumed. Change in the non-human world must be defined as a course of events different from what was expected. If the plans which are thus disrupted composed an equilibrium, what was expected, and is proved false, was the universal expectation of all the makers of the plans. Instead, the expectation could prove justified. Evidently, expectations and plans can envisage an evolution, a succession of states of the world differing from each other. Equilibrium, it follows, does not imply stationariness. 'Equilibrium analysis', Hayek says, 'becomes in principle applicable to a progressive society and to inter-temporal price-relationships'. Ought we not still to add 'in expectation'?

Let us finally ask whether the theme of the essay as a whole, that the concept of the equilibrium of a society is definable, and claims a central importance in economic theorising because there is a natural tendency for the subjective knowledge and opinions of different individuals to converge, can be accepted as an ascendant principle of general application? The kind of objection that suggests itself can be illustrated by the concept of a *speculative market*. All goods whose effectiveness in serving human needs can be conveyed through calendar time; all goods, that is, which are either durable or preservable, or are capable of embodiment in the successive stages of a productive process and emerging, in effect, at the end of it, are *necessarily* objects of speculation. But a speculative market is only brought into balance and temporary rest by the presence in it of camps holding *opposite* opinions about the impending movement of price.

SCIENTISM AND THE STUDY OF SOCIETY

Political economy stands in a peculiarly fruitful relation to intellects of a particular kind. The pursuit of this discipline calls for a mind whose natural motion is that of strict and critically exacting logic, yet which has powers and sensitivities of another sort from the algebraist's ingenious insight and surprising conjuration of truths. For political economy deals indeed in abstractions, but does so in the service of the study of mankind and its affairs. The political economist must not be colour-blind in the face of history's tides of colour and variegated light. He must be interested above all in what can flow from the thoughts of the human individual. If those thoughts themselves are, in their taking place, the very act of origination of history, *ex nihilo* so far as that origination is a mundane business, then the study of human affairs must seek in the individual mind the roots of its insight and its explanations. The nature of history, in that case, is the overt manifestation of the nature of human thought in the richest meaning of the word *thought*, the meaning which embraces perception, reason, emotion, imagination and decision. The political economist, seeking the essential nature and the ultimate sources of the engenderment of history, the transient being of 'the news', must be ready to acknowledge in his field a limitless potential for novelty and the unprecedented. The universe is open. The political economist needs the Renaissance mind.

Such a specification of total competence is, of course, beyond human compass. Dante, Michelangelo and Newton have not been rolled into one. But some men have shown that they could have turned in any one of many directions and carried that one path into new ground. Some claim of this sort can be made for Hayek.

The nature and source of history is one of the oldest of humanity's unappeasable enigmas. Some have believed the appearance of movement to be illusory. The Parmenidean stillness or Sir Karl Popper's orally expressed view that time is an illusion, would presumably change the form of the problem. Could we then meaningfully ask for a source or origin? Short of so radical a solution there is determinism. In some sense, in the determinist view, things happen, but only in the way they were necessitated from the beginning to happen. Why bother, then, with the fact that they seem to us to happen? Or in contrast with all this we can assume that humans have some responsibility for their own history. Among those who believe that the course of things is bound to follow one unique predestined path, which they can somehow describe, there is still a division between those who exhort us to strive to bring about that inevitable result, and those who enjoin us to prevent it. Does not each of these ironies reveal some instinct of belief in our freedom?

Such questions, the unsolvable riddles of existence, must hang in every scholar's consciousness with more or less insistence. But the practical scholarly arts, the writing of history, the making of theory in the moral sciences, perforce must let them ride. Hayek has answered the question of determinism or non-determinism only by implication. But no reader of *The Counter-Revolution of Science*[16] can doubt where he stands in his practice. History is made by human beings in their spontaneous exercise of human faculties.

Hayek as economist has not allowed these dilemmas to impede him. As a social philosopher he lightly brushes them in the course of an argument about the proper method of economic theory. This argument, though it occupied a whole book and invoked an immense erudition, is really concerned with one question only: Can economics be pursued in the manner of a natural science? His unequivocal *no* rests on the answer to another question: What kind of thing can we observe and study as a natural, self-delimiting whole, an essential and organic unity, a genuine thing-in-itself? He answers: In the affairs of men, only man himself satisfies this condition. Man is a product of nature. The social products of men's activity, the institutions, customs, constitutions, codes of law and morality, the forms of culture in a wide sense, and also, and especially, the episodes which compose history, are the largely undesigned and uncovenanted results of the efforts, enterprises and experiments made by individuals in a groping pursuit of private ends. These results cannot be understood by a direct inspection of their forms and processes, for their coherence is not something expressly designed by man or nature. It is in a sense accidental. These self-evolving phenomena can be understood only by considering the ends from whose pursuit they unforeseeably emerge, and the human needs and desires, the instinctive or intuitive responses and thought-processes of individuals which are their sources. These human characteristics are known to us direct. Each of us seeing them in himself infers them in others. By contrast with the entities which the natural scientist discerns or conceives as the solutions, mathematical or other, of nature's enigmas, the social artefacts are shaped by too variable a conflux of forces to have a necessary being of their own. Most especially of all it is to the episodes of history that Hayek ascribes this character and to them that he denies an inherent necessity which would make possible a *theory of history*. There is no necessary sequence in which definable stages, phases, systems or styles of events must in the nature of things follow each other, for this is not the nature of things.

The question of the nature of history is of course a profound and encompassing one. It gathers into itself the whole human or the whole cosmic riddle. It is the question of determinism, no less. Historical determinism takes forms differing widely in their degrees of clarity, consistency and incisiveness. Some of them seek to leave room for human initiative and scope for effective political action other than mere obedience to the pre-ordained development. Strict determinism would have none of that. But economists and other social theorists do not look in the face of the question what role and what meaning, in strict determinism, would be left for a notion of *choice*. Hayek leaves open the door for choice in some interesting sense, without offering a suggestion as to its nature.

HAYEK ON FREEDOM

A great part of Hayek's immense intellectual effort has been moved and directed by the single idea of *freedom*. As an economist he has argued with untiring passion for free competitive enterprise as against the total direction of all economic activity by a central authority. An economist as such will rest his case for freedom on its superior economic efficiency. Hayek is immeasurably more than an economist and in his massive later works, *The Constitution of Liberty* and *Law, Legislation and Liberty* he has examined the indispensable foundations of freedom itself in its essence. Compared with the ultimate nature and meaning of freedom for the free and for the unfree, economic efficiency is perhaps a lamp of minor brilliance. Even the notion of economic efficiency is itself elusive and hard to define. But more arresting than that question is the argument, surely invincible at the first impact, that authoritarian central control of business is a huge and all-encompassing waste of the original powers of the human mind. Every instance of an individual's having a practical improvement of his own invention which he is *not allowed* to put into practice is the destruction of possibilities, the closing of some vista which might lead beyond any horizon. Even this is a lesser aspect of a far greater whole. To be free is breath itself. But would life be a keen invigorating air if it did not release the poet's splendour of words and the painter's tide of colour, and encourage the mathematician's web of gossamer entailment and even the businessman's enterprise and ambition? Hayek as economist has perhaps been eclipsed by Hayek the apostle of freedom. On any reckoning he must be accorded by friend or foe his unquestioned place amongst the giants.

14 Keynes the Meeting-point of History and Thought

Whatever theory of history we may hold, surely we must agree that Keynes was the instrument of profound effects on the events and the ideas of our century. But equally, it was the vast upheavals of our century that gave him opportunity and inspiration. A man of immense psychic energy and versatile, inventive mind found himself called on to help politicians take vengeance upon history for the appalling tragedy of war. He saw impractical demands for reparations instead of a sober effort at oblivion and co-operative reconstruction. Yet these demands, made by men who had not thought out what the effects would be of trying to impose them, brought him face-to-face with economic drama on a great scale. Here, suddenly, was a problem of 'macroeconomics'. This was something different from questions of the self-adjustment of prices in orderly markets, of the web of mutual benefits achieved by specialism and exchange. Macroeconomics, the study of business in its aspect of large aggregates and their mutual relations and influences, could only be conducted in terms of money values. Keynes had already been concerned with 'currency and finance'. The man of brilliant gifts, of mathematical training, of high intellectual background, of familiarity with the monetary field, saw his life work awaiting him. In him there was conjoined the need and opportunity, the capacity and the zest for an intellectual enterprise of unsurpassed importance. In him, events and thoughts shaped each other on an Olympian scale.

Keynes was the re-inventor of the notion of economic *policy*. In the Victorian age the ideal to be pursued was that of *letting things alone*. Free trade and the gold standard ensured the self-balancing of economic forces at an optimum. Freedom and stability seemed to ensure each other. No wonder, after 1918, statesmen hoped that this ideal, this *idyll*, might be restored. No wonder it seemed the only form of economic health. But the war had broken up the passive and pacific world. No doubt the war was a symptom, a bursting-out of gathering forces, but what it released gave Keynes's genius its chance.

His spell-binding rhetorician's prose gave him his power of persuasion. His personal charisma, even his damaging wit, gave him ascendancy over his colleagues or at least gained him attention. In face of massive general unemployment, Keynes urged deficit spending by the government, a throwing-aside of the idea that governments ought to bind themselves by the same rules that prudent private households observed. To think otherwise was the 'fallacy of composition'. The individual who saves gets richer, but when we all save more in each week or year than previously, we impoverish each other. The advocacy of public works to fill a gap between aggregate earning and aggregate spending, at their full-employment levels, must find a place in economic theory. Besides the theory of individual action (by householders and businessmen) we need a theory of aggregative action, we need macroeconomics.

The *Treatise on Money* contained one especial sparkling jewel, unrecognised by Keynes himself and discarded from the *General Theory*: an invention anticipated by a few years by Myrdal and by him given explicit form as the vital distinction between the expected and the realised content of an identified interval, the distinction between the view of that interval *ex ante* and *ex post*. It is this distinction, essential, momentous, liberating, which informs the 'fundamental equations' of the *Treatise on Money* and shows that it is intended, designed investment which (in a closed economy) can be *not* equal to the saving gap, the gap between aggregate income and aggregate consumption.

Had Keynes adhered to his fundamental equations, had he understood their secret, the *General Theory* would have avoided its unhappy appeal to the identical, definition-entailed, equality of realised, recorded investment and recorded saving as a *condition* determining the level of general output and employment. An identity cannot be a condition. It is to Gunnar Myrdal that we must accord the honour of having first encapsulated the vital difference of nature and meaning, the entirely possible difference of size, between what is supposed *ex ante* and what is seen *ex post*. Keynes unknowingly took a step which implied it. Illness, war and death thwarted his promise to re-write the *General Theory* in *ex ante* terms. I attempted in a short book[1] to express its central theme in *ex ante* language, and Keynes wrote of it, in a letter to me: 'I like your reliable logic'.

The question whether Keynes's work published in the 1930s was a 'revolution' in economic theory, the question what were his essential originations, are endlessly debated. Keynes changed economics beyond recognition. At the outset of the 1930s the 'theory of value and distribution' was a self-sufficient body of ideas, highly coherent, depending on a small nucleus of basic notions and clinched by a resort to Euler's theorem which showed that when, under perfect competition, the factors of production are virtually paid in kind and at the rate of their respective marginal products at equilibrium, the total of payments to all factors will exactly exhaust the total product. In all of this theory the assumption of perfect divisibility of factors and product, and the assumption of perfect competition, make it needless to refer to money except as a numéraire. The purpose of this theory of 'value and distribution' was to explain the ratios at which particular goods and services exchanged for each other, and thus to explain how means of production were allocated to the various lines of production and how the society's total income was shared amongst the suppliers of these means. Money was quite separately discussed in terms of its quantity and velocity, which together explained the general level of money prices. In the *Treatise on Money* Keynes greatly elaborated this theory by conceptually dividing the stock of money into the parts which circulated in exchange for other things, and the part which lay idle as reserves. But why is there need for *reserves*?

What is a *reserve*? It is something kept in hand in case of contingencies whose nature and time of occurrence cannot be foreknown, it is a means of coping with uncertainty, with that lack of knowledge about time-to-come which is not the mere result of inattention or avoidable failure in management, but is an inherent, irremediable reflection of the scheme of things, of our imprisonment in the present moment, from which we can escape only in thought. Money held in reserve is not a mere mechanism of account. It is a source of moral comfort, of ease of mind, it has *liquidity*, general versatile exchangeability. Bankers and businessmen, haunted by their balance-sheets, well know what liquid assets are, but to economic theorists this was an unfamiliar idea.

Keynes's great *technical* invention was *liquidity preference*. Liquidity preference, the desire and instinct to hold part of one's assets in the form of ready money, spendable without doubt, delay or loss on whatever an unforeknowable crisis or opportunity may require, is a reflection of the elemental humun condition, the need to decide action for a hidden (or, as I would say, a yet uncreated) time-to-come. The theme of the uncertainty of expectation, its entire dissolution beyond a brief stretch of years, flashes intermittently through the chapters of the *General Theory* and is expressed with uncompromising force in Keynes's counter-blast to his critics in the *Quarterly Journal of Economics* of February 1937. It is this theme and its implications which give to Keynes's work its character of a revolution.

Expected, deferred, receipts of money value are valued in the present at less than their nominal amount. They are discounted. Money in hand is valued for its liquidity, and will not be parted with except for a promise of a larger total of repayments. The bonds which represent such promises are saleable on a market, and it is the market price of such bonds, in relation to the deferred payments, of fixed date and amount, which they promise, that determines the *rate of interest* for the deferments in question. In the *Treatise on Money* Keynes vividly describes the bond market. It is a *speculative* market, and the bond prices from hour to hour move in response to the fluid opinions of the participants, staying only at some level where, for the moment, the Bulls, who expect a rise of price, and the Bears, who expect a fall, are content respectively to be holding bonds or money. Every rise in the price of a bond with a fixed coupon reduces the interest rate which this bond for the moment embodies, and every fall increases the rate, since the rate is an arithmetical relation between the coupon and the price.

Uncertainty in human affairs has been a theme of literature since the Book of Ecclesiastes. Its centrality has been recognised by economists, Philip Wicksteed and Frank Knight in especial. Keynes eventually brought to its expression a panache and vigour of language which, in the 1970s, it at last became fashionable to quote. The matter which he left as an unsolved enigma is the psychic process by which the businessman decides what form his enterprise shall take in face of profound, essential, irremoveable uncertainty. He insists on the vital role of 'confidence', but does not analyse or explain its nature or its source.

15 Sir John Hicks's 'IS-LM: an explanation': a Comment

In his dissection of Keynesianism, Alan Coddington (1976)[1] makes his deepest incision between 'Chapter 12 Keynesianism' and all other varieties. In this I think he goes to the heart of the matter. *The General Theory*, I would say, is a harp of many strings, not all of them well-tuned and some mutually most discordant. We may surely say that everything we hear from this instrument must be listened to attentively and critically. Something can be learned from Keynes even when we feel on surest ground in faulting him. He does not ask futile questions, though we may sometimes feel that he pursues his quarry into a deep thicket. Moreover, it will be wasteful and obtuse to carry to an extreme the idea that, in the terms borrowed by Sir Isaiah Berlin from Archilochus, Keynes's explanation of involuntary unemployment is a hedgehog, and not a fox: 'The fox knows many things, but the hedgehog knows one big thing.' The one big thing in Keynes's ultimate conception is our unknowledge of what will create itself in time-to-come. 'We simply do not know.' The author of *A Treatise on Probability* expressly rejects the notion that probability can turn this unknowledge into its opposite. When we accept this view, the possibility of involuntary unemployment becomes self-evident. In a money-using society which wishes to save some of the income it receives in payment for its productive efforts, it is not possible for the whole (daily or annual) product to be sold unless some of it is sold to investors and not to consumers. Investors are people who put their money on time-to-come. But they do not have to be investors. They can instead be liquidity-preferers; they can sweep up their chips from the table and withdraw. If they do, they will give no employment to those who (in face of society's propensity to save) can only be employed in making investment goods, things whose stream of usefulness will only come out over the years to come. If this tune which I have played for so many years irritates the hearer, I am sorry; but on the other side of the trench which Alan Coddington's article defines, there lies a body of doctrine utterly different in spirit and method from this theme of the unknowable (or I would say, not yet originated) future. Keynes's explanation of the nature of involuntary unemployment can be shown in a mask of entirely different appearance. It can be articulated as an effect of tendencies for economic variables to gravitate into equilibria. The question that must be asked is, how do they find their way to such equilibria, what happens to them on their way to such an equilibrium?

Keynes himself, in the *General Theory*, abandoned his luminous invention, the Fundamental Equations of the *Treatise on Money*, and allowed the shadow of professional orthodoxy to dim his bright inspiration, in which he was independently inventing what Myrdal in a Swedish doctoral dissertation had already coined into *ex ante* and *ex post*. Early in the *General Theory* Keynes explicitly subscribes to the neoclassical proposition that employers will always give employment to a man who offers himself for a wage not greater than the marginal product of the body of men similar in skill and zeal to himself who are already in employment. And what is this marginal product? How does the potential employer find out its size? It is the net sale proceeds of the goods which this would-be employed man would add to his employer's output. Those sale proceeds will not be known until the man has been engaged, until the goods have been produced, and until they have been sold. Until then the marginal product *is not and cannot be known*. The extra goods may actually diminish the value of a stock of existing goods facing inelastic demand. The employer is Cantillon's merchant, who buys at a known price, or a known wage, in order to have the prospect of eventually selling at a price which, when he buys, he cannot know. Keynes should have nailed his *Treatise* colours to the mast, not hauled them down.

* * *

In the literature of economics the word *equilibrium* covers a multitude of ideas and of vacuous substitutes for thought. Its pervasive presence and the ascendancy its serious meanings have exercised show plainly that it 'does something' for the economic theoretician. What does it do? It enables him to exhibit the economic world as determinate, explicable, calculable, and even predictable. Equilibrium is orderliness, harmony, the advancement of one's own interest by serving that of others. Equilibrium is interactive rationality, the recognition that society is an organism. Above all, it is the necessary condition, the basis and sanction of *proof*. Pride in proof is legitimate. Proof is certainty, an end to debate, and it is more, in the scale of values and sensibilities of many of us. Proof is beauty. If economic theory is to validate its claim to be a deductive system, a science, then the equilibrium idea is indispensable. But proof can exist only in a closed world. It depends upon 'givens'. If we are not supplied with 'givens', *and if we are not defended from things not given*, of which we were not told, things which can blow in on us in the cold draught from time-to-come, there is no proving things. Sir John Hicks has lined his road of life with splendid constructions of logic. But in these last unsettling years he has felt the need to examine how well these buildings can resist the climate of uncertainty; not an occasional rare storm, but the recognition of time in its bleak eternal implications.

At the meeting of the Econometric Society at Oxford in September 1936, seven months or so after the publication of the *General Theory* (which some however had seen in proof), three papers on the *General Theory* were presented respectively by James Meade, Sir Roy Harrod, and Sir John Hicks. Harrod had just published *The Trade Cycle*, a jewel-box of original ideas exploiting Keynesian elements. (I remember his saying in discussion, 'Suppose that output is growing . . .' Someone asked him, 'Do you mean that output *has been* growing or that it is *going to* grow?' But Harrod rejected this question. 'I mean that it *is* growing,' he said. Despite a conviction that '*ex ante–ex post*' released economic theory from crippling chains, I think what Harrod achieved by his dismissal of it was a full justification.) Sir John Hicks's paper was the first presentation of *IS-LM* and has been for forty and more years the most famous and the most influential interpretation of Keynes. Central and essential to its argument is a notion of equilibrium. In '*IS-LM*: An Explanation' Sir John asks himself with stringency and answers with candour the question whether the notion of 'a period' with given history behind it and an unknown future beyond it can be so defined and used that equilibrium can play its part and work its magic. He finds for his equilibrium-based entity a role shrunken and less confidently played, but still not to be hissed off the stage. In this 'explanation' Sir John still does not seem to me to acknowledge the essential point: the elemental core of Keynes's conception of economic society is uncertain expectation, and uncertain expectation is wholly incompatible and in conflict with the notion of equilibrium. His proposed evasion of this unwelcome idea is set out in a quotation from *Causality in Economics*:

> Suppose we make them expectations that the values that are expected, of the variables affecting decision, will fall within a

> particular range. This leaves room for liquidity, since there are no certain expectations of what is going to happen; but it also makes it possible for there to be an equilibrium in the sense that what happens falls within the expected range. . . . What happens (during the period) falls sufficiently within the range of what is expected for no revision of expectations to be necessary.

I do not think his suggestion in footnote 12 that 'Shackle . . . has been feeling in this direction' at all represents my course of thought. I am not sure what 'this direction' is; but the conception I described in Chapter 28 of *Decision, Order and Time* (1961), headed 'Profit and the Range of Non-Revision', was not meant to underpin any notion of equilibrium. My proposal (stated also on pages 218–20 of that book) was part of an attempt to elucidate the nature of uncertain expectation. Perhaps my repudiation of the equilibrium frame of analysis can best be summarised by saying *all markets are in some degree speculative*. There is hardly anything outside of perishable food or ephemeral entertainment whose price today is not influenced by ideas of what its price will be tomorrow, next week, next year. But those ideas are figments, suggested, not determined, by our observation of the present.

16 Controlling Industrial Economies:[1] A Review Article

The chapter with which this volume opens, rapidly swept me into a current of nostalgic happiness, deep professional admiration and a hope that administrators, policy-makers, City Editors and academic economists everywhere will read it.

Amongst people concerned with numerical records of business, there are two kinds of temperament and taste. The fact that the visible aspects of trade can be or must be described by numbers has, ever since the seventeenth century, suggested the idea that business could be a field for scientific study. Cournot in 1838 had shown that mathematics could attain a brilliant clarity of thought in this field with a startling ease and incisiveness. A hundred years later the mathematics of economic theory joined hands with the mathematics of statistical theory to form the new technology of econometrics. Why has it proved so difficult to fit the garment of fact on to the skeleton of theory? The endeavour to do so has fascinated a multitude of gifted people. Yet contrary to the early hopes of its practitioners econometrics has not swept the field clear of the other kind of factual researchers. Keynes himself, it is said, would run his eye down two columns of numbers and draw suggestions from a discernible pattern. Judgement, however, has also more basic tasks. If we wish to theorise about the affairs of an 'industry' we must define it in such a way that the firms composing it are really alike in the respects which bear on some problem in hand. The realistic and practical statistical wisdom of P. B. W. Rayment's chapter on *Intra-'Industry' Specialisation and the Foreign Trade of Industrial Countries* is developed from the question: How can we explain the large recorded volume of trade amongst firms nominally belonging to one and the same industry? Do they really sell to each other consumers' goods of virtually identical kinds? Of course, they do not. The misconception arises in the meaning given to 'an industry'. If we treat as an industry all the activities necessary to the emergence of some kind of consumption good, this 'industry' will be a collection of collaborating firms variously specialising in partly-processed or component intermediate products. Trade amongst such firms is part of the team-work essential to the 'division of labour'. The industry, we might say, is something abstracted from the Leontief input-output table as a whole. An 'industry' consisting of firms really alike in product and method would need a refined definition. As Rayment says, few people are so myopic as to be indifferent between an electric razor and an electric refrigerator for the purpose of shaving, yet both are products of the 'electrical goods' industry.

Firms at any time belong to one or several patterns of coherence. But they are at all times part of the stream of history, they must evolve or be eclipsed. The definitions and classifying systems we use must keep pace with the swift transformations of technology, or they will mis-lead us.

More than a century ago, Jevons was urgently warning British statesmen of an impending exhaustion of our coal resources. These are now reckoned at the present rate of consumption to last for three hundred years. It seems obvious that mineral resources of all sorts must eventually be exhausted if we continue to exploit them. Yet G. F. Ray's chapter on *Industrial Materials: Past, Present and Future* illustrates the astonishing 'perversity' of the behaviour of many prices of industrial materials during the present century to 1970. Instead of rising with growth of consumption and the resort to leaner sources, prices have largely fallen, in comparison with wage rates in manufacturing industry. Does this record of the fate of forecasts render less alarming the figures in Ray's table (pp. 70–1) of the life expectancy of world reserves of a number of minerals at various supposed rates of growth of consumption? The seeming fallibility of all such forecasts is, perhaps, a tenuous paradoxical consolation for one or two coming generations.

S. F. Frowen and P. Arestis have brought the new tool of computer simulation to bear on the problems of dynamic multipliers in their paper on the *Impacts of Fiscal Actions on Aggregate Income and the Monetarist Controversy*. Lord Kahn's original multiplier construction was in comparative-static terms and did not go deeply into the effects of variant methods of financing an extra stream of net investment. Frowen and Arestis have considered possible changes of response of consumers and producers subsequent to the first impulse, and have shown that there is a vital difference in the pattern of events, according as the extra stream of net investment is financed by tax revenues or by money creation. This is a new and subtler insight than that of the financing of a supposedly 'stationary' state of affairs. To dynamise the Multiplier theorem is a first-rate contribution to the theory of employment. Without claiming universal applicability or high sophistication, they have illustrated most effectively the kind of insight to be gained from the computer.

In a chapter of classic distinction, F. Blackaby has set out the overt sources of Britain's dramatic relative decline in real income per head during the years 1960 to 1976 with convincing simplicity and detachment. An essay where no wasted word or unclear proposition is to be found cannot be summarised. I will merely add two questions to Blackaby's opening list. Ought we not to distinguish two kinds of purpose which policy might hope to serve? In medical practice, small doses of a drug are sometimes injected to overcome a patient's immediate critical condition, some such drugs being poisonous in larger or repeated doses. Some economic policies may work analogously. In the early 1930s, Keynes's advocacy of deficit spending was a dramatic remedy for a desperate disease. Continuing 'demand management' is an altogether different thing. In a so-called 'free-enterprise economy' it is almost a contradiction in terms. Intervention by government ought, perhaps, to be seen as medicine, not as diet. More basically still, we may ask whether economic disease is, so to speak, psychosomatic. Can its ultimate source be a failure of spirit and morale? Whence can a nation draw imaginative inspiration, the idea of things beyond the near horizon? A silent, self-disciplined and altruistic change of outlook, not a crusade or 'movement'? This is not a task for politicians but for individual example. In his last paragraphs Blackaby foreshadows an evolution in which 'incomes policy' becomes 'social contract' and social contract becomes a consensus where restraint is seen by all to be the interest of all.

The administrator, journalist or politician who wishes to have the real terrain in which economic policy must work brought in some aspects before his eyes will gain a salutary vision from the widely various contents of this book.

Statistical investigation is a *creative art*. Schemes of classification can be invented in endless variety. Their design must be judged with subtle ingenuity to serve possibly conflicting purposes or criteria. Principles of aggregation can sometimes only achieve simplicity at the cost of obliterating vital but unknown distinctions. The preparation of statistical materials is as delicate a task as that of the painter's colours or the procedures of the chef. Like the cook, the statistician can be tempted to pound up his materials beyond recognition and distinct meaning. In the fresh, stimulating essays to be found in this volume, Frowen has gathered illustrations of the range and width that statistical investigation can encompass, and also of the difficulties and dangers of that art and the caution and detachment with which its results must be employed.

17 Markets, Entrepreneurs and Liberty:[1] A Review Article

Since its beginnings in the early 1870s, Austrian economics has been shaped successively by a number of brilliant minds, each seized by a highly individual conception differing from those of the others. At first Menger, Wieser and Böhm-Bawerk explained that in order to have value in exchange a thing must not only require labour to produce it, but must also be the object of need and desire. Individuals according to temperament and circumstance are *subject* to feelings of need and desire: The need for a specific extra daily quantity of a thing is less acute, the larger in given circumstances, the daily quantity to which it will be added. At some level of daily supply, what must be given up for a small additional supply will be as much desired as that extra supply. There will be a subjective balance at the *margin*. This explanation of how value in exchange finds its level was not new to the Austrians of the 1870s. Cournot's application of the differential calculus essentially and automatically involved the marginal idea, and there were other pioneers of the subjective marginal explanation.

An explanation of value in exchange unifies the whole business world of producing, selling, buying and consuming things. It explains how the whole available quantity of some productive means comes to be devoted in this proportion and that to various industries; the prices that are paid for each such means and thus the incomes of those who supply them; and the quantities of this good and that which can be daily or yearly sold at prices which will cover their cost of production.

Subjective marginal equivalence will be sought by each individual in all his exchanges. But unless the price of any good in terms of another is the same for all individuals, there will be something to be gained for some of them by a change in quantities given and received. If a self-consistent pattern of all exchanges can be supposed to be found, we have a theory of exchange value for the circumstances of some one historical epoch. Such a theory explains the quantities exchanged of all goods, including means of production, and their prices in terms of each other. It rests upon suppositions about *individual* action, so that its method came to be called methodological individualism. It explained a pattern of activities that could persist unchanged so long as people and their tastes, resources and ideas remained unchanging. Such constancy is, of course, utterly unreal.

Action springs from the thoughts of individuals. But some individuals are endowed with exceptional powers of imaginative conception and the urge to exploit the possibilities they see. Joseph Schumpeter showed that economic change has been largely the work of such entrepreneurs. This theme, entirely different from that of the market generation of prices, was a second Austrian contribution to the understanding of business. In our own time the conception of entrepreneurship has been given a somewhat different form by Israel Kirzner, who regards the entrepreneur as alert rather than himself creative.

Some economists have conceived economics as a geometry, a system derived as the logical reflection of a small number of propositions regarded as self-evident truths, or taken for granted as a basis for reasoning. Ludwig von Mises gave this view an elaborate expression in his *Human Action*, but he insisted that all action is taken in essential uncertainty of its outcome: 'Action is always speculation'.

The term 'research programme', though cumbersome, fits perfectly one of the main pre-occupations of the Austrian school from one of its earliest to some of its living members. They have sought to answer the questions: What meanings is it useful to give to the word 'capital'; what is the incentive to bring capital into being; how is its creation rewarded; how can its quantity be measured? Böhm-Bawerk's great insight was the existence of a relation between the use of 'capital' and the fact that production takes time. There are stages in the production of any material object, at each of which we can regard the partly-processed good as having accumulated into itself a larger quantity of productive services than at the preceding stage, until it arrives at its final usable form. This time-consuming process entails that the useful or consumable product of work must be waited for, and it also seems to offer a measurable dimension, namely, the total lapse of time from the input of every unit of work to the finish of the process. There was thus a powerful temptation to argue that 'capital is time', to measure its quantity in any instance by the total 'waiting' involved in arriving at the finished object, and to formulate a law: The total of waiting endured by a given force of workers in making a particular kind of product will be pushed to the point where further extension would be more irksome than the resulting extra product could compensate.

This Austrian, or Böhm-Bawerkian, theory of capital seems to combine elegance, ingenuity and simplifying power. It explained why an income could actually, and legitimately, be drawn from the possession of a stock of capital, and it showed how this 'rate of interest' was determined.

To say that all this is wrong would be unjust and wasteful of insight and understanding. Nonetheless it suffers from grave theoretical and practical difficulties. The chief of these are, first, that in a modern industrial society, the making of any product is not simply a linear process: mining, smelting, steel-making and locomotive building. It involves the entire Leontief input-output table. Every telephone call or truck load of coal can help to make a thousand various things. To determine the total waiting time for any finished object would be a statistical task of scarcely-conceivable intricacy, utterly beyond practicability and tolerable cost. Secondly, even if all the products were made each by its own linear process, waiting would only be involved when the echelonned processes for one kind of product were first being built up. As soon as one such process had produced a finished good, that good could be consumed by the workers at other stages. Hayek and Lachmann worked intensively to refine the Austrian theory of capital. Hayek's world-fame rests not on this, but on his service to the cause of liberty. Lachmann's deep insights are into problems of subjectivism.

What have we in mind when we speak today of an Austrian school? The foundation idea on which all is built is that of freedom. This is a greater thing than any tool of thought, however brilliantly simple and powerfully unifying, however surprising in its revelations. Without freedom, the individual is a dumb creature, without dignity or power of origination. Austrian theoreticians know and emphasise (who more so than Hayek?) that liberty is not licence. We must assure to every fellow-human the rights and safeguards we desire for ourselves. But on this canvas a rich and various scene is painted.

The elemental thing we study is *choice*. If choice means anything, it means *origination*. The making of history (on however small a scale) is the making possible one path of affairs rather than another. By origination, I would say (and here take a decisive step outside all orthodoxy, even the Austrian) we ought to mean an act of thought which is a *first cause*, so that choice in its essential nature is unpredictable in its effects, its sequel. Many 'choices' are of course mere response or obedience to habit or simple reckoning. By choice we ought to mean a *momentous* act of thought. If such an act is truly originative, it cannot be foreknown in character or timing, and thus we are essentially and basically denied the power to specify the sequel of any present choice as a singular path even up to a new time-horizon. Austrians, in common with all other schools, appear unwilling to avow themselves non-determinists. Yet they insist, as a theme central to their thought, on the unpredictability of human affairs.

Words that occur in the titles of several books by members of the Austrian school are *market* and *process*. The two words are closely linked in their thought. The market is the place where the exchange value of one good for another is agreed amongst free transactors. It is the place where, in abstract ideal conditions, such a price at one moment prevails universally. But how can this be? There is another view of the market. It is the place where knowledge (namely, of prices) is generated and diffused. It is the place where transactors pool the ingredients of knowledge: their individual tastes, resources and (though undeclared) their expectations. But, with scores of thousands of distinguishable goods and millions of transactors, how are all these ingredients reduced to the limpid distillate of universal price? And this, not for one pair of commodities or services, but, in principle, for all formally possible pairs. How are prices in a common numéraire resolved? This is the problem of market *process*. The reality of 'the market' as a conception is as a means of search. Even this view of it, however, rests on an implicit assumption.

Search implies the supposition that there is some question, the answer to which can be stalked step-by-step and ultimately found. But markets can be quite differently used. Far from desiring to find a price which will be stable through satisfying all parties, the *speculator* desires price movement. In recent years the financial world has catered more and more for the gambler. A speculative market needs at all times two opinions about how the price will move next, otherwise the Bull can find no seller from whom to buy the commodity or the asset, and the Bear can find no buyer to whom he can sell. Schemes are offered in abundance for successfully guessing the next price movement. The persistence of speculative markets suggests that all such schemes are delusive. There could no doubt be a theory of how a Bull market or a Bear market comes into being and comes to an end but this field seems not to have been tilled by Austrian economists as such.

In undertaking to give an account of the whole history, the philosophy, the ethical attitude, and the analytical tool box of the Austrian school of economists, Professor Reekie has set himself to cover an enormous field. In fewer than two hundred pages he has given a zestful, stylish and highly engaging swift survey. His book is no narrow, purely partisan tract. The Austrian school today is a formidable band of first-rate minds, many of them contributors to the recent volume of the proceedings of the Ludwig von Mises symposium edited by Israel Kirzner under the title *Method, Process, and Austrian Economics*.

Professor Reekie's book will show academics and other students that there is a well-led, close-knit Opposition party to the General Equilibrium theme which, in one guise or another, still shows an impregnable vitality.

18 Method in Economic Theory

Choice of method must be guided by purpose. What is our purpose in conceiving economic theory? Our field of study is encompassed by the word Business. In business, something is all the time going on. This going on, this unceasing and ever-present transience, is part of our perception of *time*. The notions of time and of business, when this latter word is used in the abstract, are intimately conjoined. If we make *business* embrace the whole of the natural and the human world, business and time are identified. For us, business refers to what humans do. But this limitation does not exempt it from its nature, its essence, as something which, without time, would not exist, would not be there for us to observe, and would be nothing. This time-ness of business, this impregnation with part of the ultimate, elemental mystery, must overwhelmingly provide its character, make it what it is. Method in economic theory must start by considering time.

This surely is the first principle in economic theory. What do we directly know? Our thoughts. A thought is a transient, and the sense of its transience is the experience of time. A thought in being, a taking place, is *present*, and the time it tells us of is the present moment. That moment is solitary. Its being consists in its passage into a different moment, but the actual present is ever alone. An economic theory which requires us to suppose ourselves to be experiencing two separate moments, in equal actuality and validity, *together*, is a self-contradiction. Thought and feeling take place in a solitary present moment. Can we escape from the imprisoning present? Yes, for one kind of thought is imagination. The very transience of experienced thought, the transience of the present, suggests that other moments will in turn become actual in succession to it, and to each other. Where are these imagined moments, able to be referred to as individuals though merging continuously, to be located? The calendar-axis, the invented and imagined artefact, allows us to conceive extended time-to-come.

Business in a broad sense comprises all human activities of making things more useful and using them for survival and enjoyment. Determinism is the supposition that all such actions are exactly prescribed for us and that our part in them is mere passive enactment. Instead, we can suppose that human thought: perceptive, intellective, imaginative, decisive, can in the strictest sense bring into being some elements of these actions, by making *choices* whose detailed character and effects are not implicit in their antecedents. Scholars appear to have hesitated between these two kinds of supposition. They feel that choice is a momentous act worthy of study, but their mode of studying it is to seek to explain every act of choice in its entirety. An act of thought which can be shown to be wholly and precisely prescribed is not momentous. It is part of the course of affairs, but is powerless to affect that course. It is passive and sterile. The determinist view and the non-determinist view are as mutually remote and alien as can be conceived. Surely the first step in regard to method must be the election of one or other of these views. To speak thus is evidently paradoxical. If we elect the determinist view we have not elected it but suffered its imposition upon us. To elect the view that an act of choice can start a train of takings-place that was not implicit in what went before is already to impose fundamental tasks on economic theory, and precludes some kinds of answers to our questions.

To suppose that choices can be originative in an absolute sense (not traceable in all respects to antecedents however subtle and elusive) already restricts the powers of reason. Such choices are *first causes*. The acts which flow from them will be causal, either through the laws of nature or by suggestion. These choices will be *decisions* in a literal sense, they will *cut off* emergent history in some respects from its immediately preceding stages. In this respect such a choice of action will be an *uncaused cause*, something which cannot be inferred from any knowledge of the present.

Economic theory rests on the idea that we pursue our interest by applying reason to our circumstances. But the circumstances which matter for the success of our courses of action are those of time-to-come, and these will not be shaped until that time, as Lachmann has vividly insisted. What can we do?

How to answer this question is the central theme of economic methodology. Its becoming so is something of a paradox. For this question, which concerns the operations of the individual psyche, has come to the fore because the nature and working of the inducement to invest is the heart of the theory of general output; the theory of output as a whole or of employment.

Resources – material, psychic, exchangeable – are things seen in a light shed by a human mind. For that mind they are a source of endlessly suggested possibilities. Their presence answers the question: What can we do? We can imagine and invent; we can apply knowledge of nature and of affairs to a critical examination of the schemes of deployment that we conceive, to test in thought their possibly attainable results. The sequels imagined and deemed possible for any one scheme will be many and widely diverse, and will be a skein endlessly augmentable. The business of choice of action can be thought of in three stages: the creative, the critical and the comparative. But this business must be carried through with urgency and decisively consummated in action at some external deadline or some sense of excellence. Each scheme will have its best and its worst seeming possible outcomes, and exposure to the worst is the price of envisaging the best. Thus the individual mind, alone or by influence on others, can make its choice.

Thus conceived the decision-process suggests a change of terms. The act itself of choice is only the third phase of the process, able to take place only when the rival choosables have been brought into being in the decision-maker's thought. He is more aptly described as the action-conceiver.

The psychic process as a whole which this sketch suggests, even if we acknowledge that the action-conceiver will practise radical simplifying and abbreviating ploys, is plainly quite inaccessible to the theoretician and the observer. The decision-maker himself must consult knowledge that he is not aware of possessing, his imaginative powers are, we suppose, in part *non-existent* until called upon. The decision process is ignited in the individual mind, but we cannot discern the spark nor follow the burning of the powder-train. But this does not mean defeat. Aggregation is made meaningful in some degree by the fact that businessmen share many types of resources, they share 'the news' (as Keynes called the advancing tide-edge of recorded emergent history), they have in common the desire to achieve prosperity in various forms, and they are subject in some sense to similar or even identical constraints. Not only so. The questions we wish to answer concerning the inducement to invest, its engendering or inhibiting factors, will all have the same underlying answers.

The paradox of economic method is, that it is aggregative studies, macro-economics, which in some degree give us insight into the individual psychics of decision-making. How far can large-scale phenomena give clues to the nature of that most arcane operation of the mind, the business of choice? Such a clue could hardly arise from the steady maintenance by businessmen in general of a constant level of production and of prices. This constancy would suggest adherence to an unchanging policy, that is to say, an unchanging scheme of responses to the conditions which they have come to regard as settled and reliable.

If these conditions abruptly changed in a few conspicuous respects, would the businessmen act in a manner common to all of them? If they did, several different explanations might be mooted. Perhaps the businessmen, observing one or more of the changes, each adopted the same new expectations of a further course of events. If we could then somehow find out what these expectations are, and some notion of how they came to suggest themselves to the businessmen, there would at least be an enrichment of the store of material for debate. But the uniformity of action might have come about quite differently. It might be due to mere imitation of a few self-reliant spirits by a baffled and unseeing majority. Keynes suggested that when people are at a loss they try to 'follow the crowd'. The resulting concert of action he called conventional. The real difficulty of sorting out all such possibilities to arrive at economic theory is, that the object of study, the society in its business aspect, does not stay the same. In order to follow the course of the game, you must understand that the players can change the rules as they play, as Stephen Littlechild said in the second of his remarkable Professorial inaugural lectures. The elemental difficulty of economic theorising is that the process of inventing the object of study outpaces the study of it.

That object of study, society in its business aspect, has two antithetical characters. Whatever it does is, in the end, done by individuals, and the seeds of its action germinate in individual minds. But society consists of *interacting* individuals, and in fact it is their interactions that we can observe. Their motives, good or evil, are hidden, but their acts are not. Their interactions have become canalised in institutions, a word which seems to embrace almost every formal system of society. One of these, the market, is the one universal web of inter-dependence and communication, and its nature and effects are a question which divides economic theoreticians. Does 'the market' successfully and efficiently co-ordinate business activities, or does it merely provide a gambling casino? Differences of view amongst economists on the question whether 'the market' does or does not bring about a new approach to universal consistency amongst the quantities of this good and that good which exchange for each other may spring from differences of temperament and of moral attitude as well as from differences in formal assumptions and trains of reasoning. The analyst who believes in the co-ordinating power of the market mechanism is, perhaps, a man concerned for the welfare of the 'random individual', the welfare of all members of the society impartially viewed. The analyst who dismisses that co-ordinating power may be one who sees the exceptional mind, the man of daring imagination and enterprise, as the ultimate benefactor of society, gaining a transient profit for himself while shifting a whole sector of production on to a new technological plane.

How does the idea of the self-co-ordinating market come to exert so great an ascendancy over the thought of so many economists? It is, firstly, an extreme abstract ideal. It is the supposedly unique pattern of exchanges to which the consent of all market participants could be obtained if every one of them, with his given endowment of resources, had a complete conception of the entire array of possible patterns of exchange. Some of these patterns would benefit him more than others, but would not be agreed to by some members of the market. The essence of this ideal, its crucial condition, is a universal *knowledge* of all abstractly possible patterns of exchange. The purpose of thus stating the matter is to give a definition. What contact can there be between this definition and any approach to practical realisation?

The self-co-ordination of the market would require each participant to make known to every other member the complete array of his offers, each consisting of a list of quantities of specified goods he would supply on condition of a particular set of such quantities being offered to him by the other participants. His own list would be different for each set of quantities obtainable in return. Such a universal exchange of offers would be an idealised form of the process of competition. *Competition* is one of the half-score of words which together contain the whole economic theme. In this idealised form of a pure pooling of technically objective information, competition would be a mere shadow of the scene we actually observe, the torrent of endlessly inventive and proliferating activities of suggestion and persuasion called *marketing*.

What marketing does is not the mere diffusion of technically objective information about a fixed list of goods available. It *creates* in large measure the enjoyments and satisfactions of the consumer, by playing on the keyboard of his own imagination. What can such a dynamic, super-evolutionary process have to do with market co-ordination? And yet, part of the marketing organisation is the display of goods of standardised, easily assessed quality in supermarkets which keenly compete on quality and price.

Secondly, the self-co-ordinating market exemplifies the notion of *systems as an art-form*. In perfection, perhaps, a system should be the application of a single principle to phenomena which are in some respect universal. That principle should be surprising in its ingenious simplicity and its power to show diverse phenomena as a unity. If capable of mathematical manipulation, that principle will confer upon the system an affinity with a large part of modern science as a whole. To affirm the status of science for economics in this way has been an irresistible ambition for most of its originative scholars. But there is more. The scientist and the engineer have their art-forms equally with the sculptor, the poet and the symphonist. What makes one theory seize our minds more decisively than another? Partly of course because of its claims to be a truer model of reality. But even that claim to truth is judged partly, and most immediately, by the indefinable presence of beauty. The theoretician is an architect, building his subtle Parthenon or his intricate Belvedere.

There was one economist who sought to combine two visions, that of the analysable, intelligible structure and that of the flux of history, the world of improving technology and increasing scale. It was the latter vision that Alfred Marshall's Prefaces pointedly insist on, and that his 'long-period supply-curve' embodies. Yet Marshall also provides many items for what I would call the *toolbox conception* of economic theory.

The toolbox is not a machine that can be programmed to do the entire job of understanding a situation or segment of history. The workman can use one tool at a time, in the sequence that seems most illuminating and easiest to expound. We can use mathematical tools, suggestive metaphors or historical examples with eclectic freedom, eluding the stiff protocol or unreal, and sometimes unrecognised, implications of a completely self-contained model. Differentiable functions, perfect divisibility, and perfect competition give us indispensable insights. These three all taken together, with the implication they have of constant returns to scale, enable us to put in place the final voussoir, the keystone of the arch of neo-classical value theory, by applying Euler's theorem to solve the 'adding-up problem', the question whether the total of the factor-bills exactly exhaust the product. This is a result we can stand upon with justified satisfaction. All of its assumptions are unrealistic. By successively relaxing them, we can discern the answers to a number of questions. We can see just how the cranky world of reality raises difficulties for the systematiser, the apologist and the policy-maker. Theories of the business cycle of the kind where the interest rate endogenously governed is the key variable are likely to involve those 'long chains of reasoning' against which Marshall warned us. The most vital service Keynes rendered us in *The General Theory of Employment, Interest and Money* was to release the interest rate, and thus the inducement to invest, from endogenous dependence and make them subject to *liquidity preference*. The *General Theory* made centrally explicit what was already plain in the *Treatise on Money*, namely the governance, to a not negligible degree, of the long-term interest rate by the speculative market in gilt-edged securities. Behind liquidity preference looms the most elemental of all problems for economics; the paradox of decision: decisions are history-to-come in the making. If all plans could be co-ordinated in the process of their construction, some suggestions might emerge from this process concerning the effect of their beginning to be implemented. But this would tell nothing of the plans that would be made next month or next year, plans which would help to shape the outcome of present plans. The desire for liquidity is the response to an upsurge of awareness of unknowledge of time-to-come. To elect liquidity is to reject investment, to withdraw from investment is to fail to give employment and to put the Multiplier into action in reverse.

The prime embodiment of liquidity is money, and the notion of liquidity embraces almost the whole nature of money. There is an irony in these terms, for 'liquidity' suggests that it is in flowing that money serves its purpose, acting as a temporary proxy for goods which have specific physical and technical properties, goods which can be eaten, burnt, or worn as clothing, or used as tools. Why is money accepted in exchange for such goods useful in themselves? Money is the extreme example of a convention, of tacit universal assent to the adoption of a pure artifice. What is the motive of such adoption? Money enables a supplier to part with goods without having at the same time to decide what technically specified things he wishes to receive in exchange. He can defer that choice until he knows better what he is going to need.

Money belongs to a world of unknown to-morrows and the need to wait for each threshold to give its glimpse of emerging history. The need for money is bound up with time. Money is the means of borrowing and lending resources, but to lend money in exchange for a borrower's promise to pay stated sums at stated future dates is hazardous, for the lender cannot know when he may need his money, nor what price he will get for his bond if he sells it before all his loan has been repaid, nor what such money as he gets back will then buy for him. To lend is to give a known sum of money in exchange for an unknown sum. For this reason alone, quite apart from loss of purchasing power in an inflationary time, the total of promised repayments must be greater than the loan, there must be a rate of interest incorporated in the terms of the loan. Money is needed to cope with lack of knowledge of one kind, but brings unknowledge of its own. In the study of money we have again two aspects, each holding the main attention of one or the other of two kinds of economists. Some think of money as a system of flows in which money exchanges for goods or assets, the 'general price-level' of which will be higher, the larger the quantity of money changing hands per unit of time. These are the hydraulicists. The others think of money as something whose effects are the consequence of human decisions, and who seek the sources of those decisions in the events which engender expectations, events which are suggestive causes or, to use my own technical term, *impellants*. The theme of the endlessly variant nature of impellants and of their ineffably subtle and elusive immediate effects and of their secondary expanding concentric rings of rippling consequences is, perhaps, daunting enough to repel the most ardent and audacious scholar.

Economists seem always divided between those who start by studying records of the course that affairs have taken in fact, and those who start by trying to discern the kind of course that, in the nature of things (and especially human and social nature) affairs must take. Each of the two methods can be variously presented. The former, the historical method, invites the scholar to abstract patterns of circumstance with earlier and later phases, and to see in them the principles of a recurrent alchemy. Such a process of induction is at the opposite extreme from being rigorous, exact or closed. It feeds upon suggestion and pre-judges nothing, places no bar against candidate-ideas from any quarter, has no fixed list of elements or operative factors. It is historical not only in its sources but in the texture of its use of them. It would of course be absurd to suppose that it does not employ reasoned argument.

If the needs and capacities of mankind are always and everywhere elementally the same, will not their conduct in any given entire set of apparent circumstances be the same? Then, cannot the economist, by studying his own thoughts and feelings, tell what that conduct in essentials will be? To provide oneself thus introspectively with the means of interpreting observed circumstance in terms of the conduct that will flow from it, before beginning the observation of circumstance, is the *a priorist* method. To call it the deductive method is perhaps misleading, since any effort to understand the world involves reasoning.

The *a priorist* may find it difficult to keep separate the account he gives himself of what he does, from his recognition of the principles of action that a more incisive or more imaginative process of thought would lead him to. Critical judgement may show accepted guidance to be ill-founded and thus might set the spark to invention.

In the disciplines concerned with human affairs it is peculiarly true that form and content are one. Language is the mould and not the mere vessel of thought. Whatever aid it may get from mathematical notation and Cartesian geometry, economics must rely for the expression of its ideas ultimately on words. A few such words have hypnotised their users and led them to reify the various meanings which any one such word can suggest, so that argument and controversy have debated the properties and powers of invented entities. To separate out such words from the indispendable body of economic terms is a task for delicate discrimination. We surely need the word income, but the word capital stands for a ghostly impersonator. Capital is said to be self-perpetuating, to have a permanence which transcends the mortality of buildings, vehicles and complex tools that actually serve our purposes. The preservation of the capital that these objects represent depends on human decisions to re-invest part of the fruits of their use. The successful administration of this process rests on imaginative foresight and good fortune. The word 'capital' belongs to the field of finance and accountancy. It is an arithmetic not an economic term. Words are powerfully and ungovernably suggestive, calling up in one person's mind, from his individual store of experience or study, ideas not intended or foreseen by the writer of those words. A word can carry with it an entire theoretical structure, imposing upon its reader or hearer a body of assumptions on which its writer's or speaker's argument unavowedly depends. One word above all in economic discussion has this question-begging quality: claiming rights of intellectual law-giving which only a long history of subservience of the profession can legitimate. 'Equilibrium' needs to have its luggage examined by the customs-officer.

Equilibrium of course means literally a state of things where the two arms of the balance are equally loaded. In economics it is a more complex idea, where two opposing pressures on a third variable are made respectively weaker and stronger by their combined effect upon this variable until their eventual equality brings its movement and their own variation to a halt. When the two pressures are offers to buy and offers to sell some commodity, and the third variable is its price, we have the market where individual motives determine the aggregate effect. The many-layered notion of price thus begins to appear in its subtle and elusive nature.

General equilibrium names the state of affairs where the activities of all participants in all markets are adjusted to each other so that none can gain an advantage for himself without disadvantaging another. But there are maverick participants who see gain for themselves in causing or encouraging large and swift price-movements which are unrelated to a maintainable orderliness. The general adjustment must in any case give way to technological innovation. A market system is not a failure by definition if it is not always visibly and vigorously striving for general universal price consistency.

In a book of endless excellence, Professor Ludwig Lachmann has sought to solve the dilemma of knowledge derived from the first principles of the mind versus knowledge derived from examining the world 'outside' the mind, by resort to exact distinctions of ideas and thus to the ultimate, indispensable method of classification. His proposal in essence is that we should gather and classify historical instances, patterns and sequences of takings-place, of actions and their sequels, and then by two methods try to discern what kinds of sequel each such type of instance *can have*. Lachmann bans 'empirical generalisations', attempts to devise 'laws' of what must follow what. There is no 'must' of this kind of economics, because action springs from personal, unique interpretations of each presented situation. We can, I think, attribute this uniqueness to either of two sources. Lachmann refers to 'spontaneity', but he does not take the ultimate step of supposing that a thought can be in some respects untraceable to antecedents, no matter how perfect the observer's knowledge of those antecedents might be. If elements of thought can be strictly and entirely *ex nihilo*, it is plain that predictive 'laws' are excluded. Short of this acceptance of absolute origination, which to many people of philosophic or scientific background will seem incongruous, there is still inevitable difference of one person's experience from another's. No two people's effective knowledge or body of accepted suppositions can be the same. Close to the notion of a 'law' is that of a 'model'. A 'model' might embody several laws, but still have built into it a predictable response to this or that occurring numerical value or assessable quality of an external variable. Lachmann therefore distinguishes 'type' of historical instance from the artefact, abstract, 'model'. The model, in its pure form, says what will follow a presented situation. The taxonomy of historical and imagined 'types' suggests what, in great variety and diversity, *can* follow.

Economics in special degree evokes the tension between detailed realism and essential simplicity. The endless variety of form and colouring in the plant world disguises a unity in their bio-chemical mechanism of life. It is tempting to ask whether in the business world the surface complexity of procedures may not result from differences of opportunity offered to one and the same body of underlying principles. This unity in the essential processes of business is the indispensable condition for economic theory. To say this, however, leaves the question open, whether it is an account in detail of the surface phenomena, or a conviction that all can be understood by tracing these phenomena to their unified source, which will best serve scholarly and practical purposes. A brief explanation that all printed books consist of groups of printed symbols selected from a fixed alphabet, such groups being endowed with conventional meanings, would be no substitute for a library catalogue. Yet if, despite Marshall's necessary warnings, we cannot rest without some ultimate core of permanence and truth, only theory will do.

19 News from Sweden

Luck is hardly a respectable word for the economist. The conduct which he studies is claimed to be understandable, accountable and predictable because it flows from reason applied to a complete relevant knowledge of circumstance. But luck is a circumstance only known *ex post*. It is something which we cannot secure by forethought or endeavour which we cannot legislate for, except by maintaining liquidity as a means of coping with the uncovenanted and the unknown. Yet the writer of this memoir, having long since averred that luck is a factor of production, can support that view by his own unforgettable experience. For as a research student newly come to L.S.E. in the first days of 1935 I heard Brinley Thomas, just returned from Sweden, lecture on the momentous ideas which he had learnt there from the heirs of Wicksell, from Lindahl, Myrdal and Ohlin. For me these lectures were a torch lighting up my world of thought and setting fire to my imagination, and the fact of my being there to hear them, at the one moment, in the one place, from the one man who could convey them, was in retrospect a piece of luck incomparable and scarcely believeable. But this was the mere temporal and spatial frame of things. For Brinley himself, the runner from Marathon, the interpreter of the oracle, the bringer of still-Delphic words, was of all teachers of economics of my time the one most charged with celestial fire, the one who swept the brain of at least one hearer with a rustling wind of inspiration.

Are investment and saving two ways of reckoning one and the same thing, so that these words name two measurements which by their nature are in any given instance necessarily equal? If so, what becomes of Wicksell's second condition of monetary equilibrium, the equality of the demand for saving, namely, investment, and the supply of saving? Necessary equality, the equality of something seen under one aspect or measured by one operation, with itself seen under another aspect or operation, is the equality of two things which are identical. Identical equality cannot fail to be true, it is true by the meanings we give our terms. It cannot, therefore, be a *condition* which, in any instance, may or may not be fulfilled. If investment and saving are necessarily and always equal by definition, what becomes of the *Treatise on Money*, where Keynes's Fundamental Equations depend absolutely, for their meaning and effective illumination of affairs, on the possible inequality of saving and investment, an inequality which appears, perhaps, more likely and more 'normal' than the special, co-incidental case of equality? What becomes of the theme of Hayek's *Prices and Production*, where the creation of equipment over and above the making good of wear and tear, could outstrip for a time the willing non-consumption of the producing society? Monetary equilibrium for Wicksell means the absence of any tendency for prices in general to rise or fall. In framing the conditions whose fulfilment will ensure this absence, Wicksell speaks of *demand for* and *supply of* saving. In the theory of relative prices, quantity demanded of some good is thought of as a variable quantity depending on other variables, such as price and incomes. Demand in that frame of thought is a schedule. So likewise is supply. Variation of the price will affect demand and supply differently. If demand and supply were looked on as identically equal, the whole theory of an equilibrium of demand and supply would fall to the ground and be meaningless. When a transaction of buying and selling has been completed, or when a market day is over and all books have been balanced, the value of sales and the value of purchases are necessarily equal. There appears to be a contradiction. Are demand and supply necessarily equal or not? What can resolve this dilemma? Demand, as a schedule, expresses *conditional intentions*. So does supply, when thought of as a schedule. An intention is something which looks to a time to come. A recorded transaction, an account balanced and closed, looks to a time past. An intention envisages an action before it takes place, and a record sees it after it has taken place. Whether or not they involve a schedule, whether or not they are thought of as conditional, intentions envisage action *ex ante facto*, before the deed. A record sees it after the deed, *ex post*. The terms *ex ante* and *ex post* generalise and make explicit an aspect which is implicit in the notion of schedule of demand and supply. The treatment of investment and saving as necessarily equal, the notion that their inequality is excluded by their meaning, is a strange aberration, an extraordinary forgetfulness of what is implied by schedules of offer and demand. The aberration is explained by the notion and nature of a market. A market selects from the two schedules of *conditional* intentions, those members of the sets of quantities offered and demanded at a particular price, one from each set, whose totals are equal to each other. As soon as the market has performed its duty, we are no longer concerned with intentions, and the fact that we had to start with intentions is easily forgotten. In the context of the idea of a market, the distinction of *ex ante* from *ex post* is easily lost. Gunnar Myrdal in three works, or versions, the first of them published in Swedish in 1931, the second in German in 1933, and the third in English in 1939, pointed out to economists the universal relevance to their thought which the distinction of *ex ante* from *ex post* fundamentally claims. He directed them to look, not at a single date as the dividing mark between an historical interval which is already past and another, a different interval, which is to come: (not, we might add, as a point in a continuously differentiable function where the derivative has always a meaning and a value) but at a single historical interval looked at from *two* points, its threshold and its end: and he pointed to the difference of nature between the contents of such an interval which conjecture (or figment) ascribes to it from its threshold and what we may read about it as fact in the bookkeeping record at its end. This was the resolution of the impasse about investment and saving, an impasse which never occurred to Wicksell, nor to the Keynes of the *Treatise*, but which entangled the argument of the *General Theory* and, most fatally of all, allowed its mechanical, arithmetical and hydraulic aspects to appear dominant and alone interesting, instead of inviting attention to the whole landscape of ideas implicit in *ex ante*: the freedom of conjecture, the presence of a void requiring to be filled, the sources and manifold rivalries and conflicts of suggestion concerning the filling, the whole matter of uncertain expectation. Let us go further than the writers we are discussing and say: the whole matter of imaginative, originative choice and decision, the interplay of decisions not all envisaging mutually compatible sequels, the cauldron of influences from which history distils itself.

The transmutation of thought implicit in the words: *ex ante*, *ex post*: was already independently at work in the *Treatise on Money*. Keynes seized it in his practice in the same years as Myrdal seized it in a formulated thought. The definitions of income and profit in Chapter 9, the Fundamental Equations which employed those definitions in Chapter 10, contain and depend precisely on this distinction. Keynes did not use these expressions, they did not appear in published form even in Swedish, it seems, until the year following the publication of the *Treatise* in 1930. But Myrdal had of course written them down several years before their publication. Myrdal and Keynes hit upon the essential notion simultaneously in ignorance of each other's thought. But it was Myrdal who understood the fundamental subversion of theory he was effecting. In *Monetary Equilibrium*, the belated

English version of his essay, he says that 'probably the chief contribution of this essay, if any, is to have originated the concepts of *ex ante* and *ex post*'.[1] The claim is just. Myrdal perceived vividly what he was doing. Keynes did not explain that in his Fundamental Equations he was enacting a revolution of theory. The coin of *ex ante*, *ex post* thus bears Myrdal's stamp and is his coinage, though Keynes engraved the same pattern on his work concurrently. Inexplicably, Keynes immediately abandoned his new tool. He thought that orthodox constructions could do what was required. They could not, and the *General Theory of Employment, Interest and Money* mistestifies its theme.

Brinley Thomas, of course, was not concerned with Keynes and did not, I think, make any comparison of the Stockholm School with the *Treatise*. The other great originator belonging to the Stockholm School was Erik Lindahl. I cannot now recall what was Brinley's exposition of him in his lecture course of 1935. Lindahl went in for 'accounting' equations where given totals, as of expenditure, *et cetera*, were shown dissected in different ways. His work, like Myrdal's, was meant as an 'immanent criticism' of Wicksell's, an attempt to clarify and deepen it without going outside its essential implicit frame. It was, however, on a somewhat different track that Lindahl made his most inspired suggestion. In his article 'The concept of income' in *Economic Essays in Honour of Gustav Cassel*, Lindahl proposes to regard income as the appreciation, which takes place as the present moment moves on through the calendar, of sums of money expected to be received at stated deferred dates. Such sums, being discounted over shorter and shorter deferments, gain thereby in value, and this flow of gain, arising from the advance of the 'present' date to which they are discounted, is the meaning which Lindahl gives to income. This is a suggestion which has much of the elusive, arresting and fascinating quality of Böhm-Bawerk's concept of capital. It is so brilliantly incisive a simplification. Like a conceptual scythe it mows a great swath of difficulties and piles their solutions up in one vehicle ready for use. Yet it imports extraordinary difficulties of its own. What is the nature and source, what is the foundation and guarantee, of those receivable sums which are looked forward to and whose growth in apparent size (that is, in discounted value) as they draw nearer constitutes income? They are, of course, expectations, some of them visibly well-founded, as one's salary cheque at the end of the month. Others are, perhaps, transient gleams on a far horizon. But above all, what of the *disposal* of those sums which, arriving at the present, fall into the destined recipient's lap and can be used by him either to consume or to create new, additional sources of such payments for the future? The size of income today appears thus to depend on today's disposal of resources. This seems incontrovertible in Lindahl's terms, and intuitively, though surprisingly, convincing, but it is quite different from the orthodox notion of income.[2]

The news from Sweden of which I have been trying to give some brief account, and which, for me, was first brought by word of mouth by Brinley Thomas, was injected into a particular phase in the history of economic thought, against a background which it helped to render obsolete. I shall venture in what now follows to try to paint in a few lines my own conception of the state of economic theory in the nineteen twenties (a legacy from the pre-1914 world of relative tranquility) and to state the theme which for me sprang from such seeds as Myrdal's, Lindahl's Hayek's and Maynard Keynes's work of the late twenties and thirties. In giving to this rather personal theme the shape and expression it has taken in my own thought, I am merely trying to show one aspect of that luck to which I referred at the beginning.

'There is a tide in the affairs of men . . .' Assuredly in the history of any one discipline, and in that of any one academic corporation, there are times of surging, zestful and inspired activity, when there is a pulse in the veins of thought and a shared excitement in every conversation. Compared with the brilliant episodes of mathematics and natural science, new thoughts in political economy are not widely deemed to be glamorous. Is not political economy about administration, about constraint and scarcity, about making-do in the narrow frame of life, is it not the dismal science? It is, on the contrary, the human intellect and spirit at work in the virgin field of time. Above all, it is about the filling of the void by imagination and ambitious daring, it is about the nature of enterprise, the originative basis of choice, the conflict with unknowledge. It is about the business adventure. Political economy in the Victorian age had believed itself able to become a natural science on the model of Newtonian mechanics, spare, shapely and unified. Men's needs and tastes on the one hand, their circumstances on the other, determined the essential forms of their conduct. Their individual choices were reconciled in the market, where each was a free response to the system of relative prices determined by all of the tastes and circumstances taken together. Thus by means of the market, with its process of trial and error somewhat less systematic than the computer, its problem posed with somewhat less visible explicitness than in algebra's language of simultaneous equations, conduct, paradoxically, could be free, inter-active and yet rational, all at once. This conception, so all-encompassing, so essentially simple, so unarguably beautiful, so prestigiously illustrating the solvent power of mathematics, so gratifyingly endorsing men's rational control of their affairs, seemed to exhibit those affairs as a worthy constituent of the Order of Nature. The war of 1914–18 and what followed it destroyed the appearances to which that conception could be supposed relevant and sufficient.

Victorian value theory was a closed, self-sufficient system with no loose ends. Its closed completeness was finally clinched and proved by the great triumph of its theory of the distribution of income. This depended at two points on the assumption of perfect competition. For in the first place, it depended on Euler's theorem which provides the proof that if the production function relating output to employed quantities of factors of production is of that kind which gives constant returns to scale, then output will be precisely accounted for by multiplying each employed factor quantity by the derivative of output with respect to the factor, and summing the resulting terms over the whole list of factors. But secondly, provided the actual production function, even if not of that type, has a point of tangency with such a surface at the point where production is taking place, the effect will be just as if the production function were of the required type. And under perfect competition, production *will* take place at such a point of tangency, since that point will give minimum unit cost. One last step completes the theory of distribution. If factors are paid *in product*, or if not in product, then in value of product at the prices, *independent of output*, which perfect competition ensures, and if each is paid at the rate of the marginal product of its employed quantity, that is, the derivative of output with respect to that quantity, then the whole output will be just and only just equal to the total factor bill. It is not surprising that perfect competition was held sacred and inviolable by economists defending the central citadel of theory, long after monopolies and oligopolies began to loom over the land. It was, literally, indispensable to value theory in making its chief implicit claim: to be beautiful, therefore to be true.

But value theory embraced an assumption more deadly by far than perfect competition, that of perfect knowledge. The method of value theory is to suppose men rational, to suppose that each pursues his interests by applying reason to his circumstances. What are those circumstances? They are not the visible facts of the present except in so far as these will persist into time to come (however soon) when present choices will have their effects. They include for each man the effects that will flow from the choices now being made, at the same time as he is making his, by other men. And how can each man know what are the simultaneous choices of other men? But this is the least part of the paradox of rational inter-active choice. What of those choices which not only will have their effects in time-to-come, but which will be made in that time? What of *choices to come*? Is choice foreknowable? Does choice, in the discourse of economists, mean something different from what it means on the lips of men in their lives from hour to hour, where choice (if they give the matter thought at all) appears to them inceptive, nonimplicit, the start of something not foreordained but created then and there by them? How does value theory claim to cope with these dilemmas?

Economics has as its centre two notions, each of which is at once an idea, an institution and a mechanism. These are *the market* and *money*. It is the market which provides a starting point, mundane, familiar and 'visual', for value theory's account of the paradox of simultaneous fully-informed choices. The ideal solution of the paradox is pre-reconciliation. Each member of the market must be ready with his own list of conditional intentions, his ultimate selection amongst them depending on what ultimate selection is made by each other man out of *his* list. Somehow these lists must be pooled and compared, so that a general solution, if it exists, can find for each man that one of his conditional intentions which he prefers, given the commitment of each other man to the one indicated for him. This solution is a General Equilibrium. If it exists in the logical sense, and if there is some way of finding it, then it solves the problem of how inter-active choices can be rational. It does so by stipulating that the set of pre-reconciled choices must embrace all choices which at all affect each other, and that all these choices must be effectively made at one and the same moment. It does not confine the *reference* of these choices to that same moment in which they are made. They can refer to action to be taken in time to come, they can be transactions on a futures market. But the commitment to every action, whether that action is to be immediate or not, must be made simultaneously with all other such commitments, else it cannot be part of an all-embracing pre-reconciliation. The choices can compose a Hayekian equilibrium of mutually consistent *plans*. What they cannot do is to allow for *choices to come*. Nor, needless to say, can they allow for new knowledge in science and technology, new insights into the nature of things and the *potentiae* of things, novelty in a profounder sense than news of particular actions and utterances. General equilibrium, universal fully informed demonstrably optimal inter-active choice, is a notion belonging to a timeless world.

What is money? It is a store of purchasing power. But in a timeless world one cannot store things. In a world of time, why do not people spend all the money that comes in as soon as they get it on things useful in themselves? 'All the money that comes in' would then include all the equally unhesitant and immediate spending of others. Money would circulate with unlimited rapidity and money prices would rise beyond all bounds. Why does this not happen all the time? It is, for one thing at least, because people do not know what they are going to need or to desire. Money enables them to receive their income without, by the same act, spending it: without having to decide, at the moment when they give something in exchange, what precisely specified particular thing they shall receive in exchange. By the same token, it compels those who make goods to make them and pay for the necessary factors of production without instantly selling the whole of the products to the owners of those factors: without, in fact, paying for the factors in products. Money enables choices to be *deferred* in the face of uncertainty.

In the middle 1920s political economy was still equipped with a body of central doctrine which depended essentially on assuming perfect competition: which treated money as a wholly separate department from the mutual exchange values of things wanted for their own sake: and which, despite its claim to be a subjective theory, treated choice as governed by immediate and visible circumstance and, within the psychic make-up and activities of individuals, by their tastes alone. It was this political economy which from the middle 1920s until the Second World War, came under assault from the side of ideas and from the side of events.

From the side of ideas, one theme may be said to have ultimately challenged orthodoxy far more radically than any other. Let me give it an edge of my own. Time is not a contingent circumstance which can be assumed away, and elided from the accounts we give ourselves of the nature of things. Such elision is a nonsense. Time and experience, time and consciousness, time and thought are one. Can a man have any thought, except he has time for its occurrence? What is 'the present' except the presence to us of *thoughts*? If we have thoughts that do not refer to 'the present', they must be provided with a locus by our own invention, the calendar axis. The content of that axis, the things that fill it, where it represents time-to-come, will also be our own inventions, suggested, tested and constrained by our knowledge of how things are in our world, in fact and principle. Expectation is invention, imagination, a light thrown into a void yet reflected back to give colour and meaning to 'the present'. Choice of immediate action is choice of a step in an intended chain of steps, leading to states of affairs and successions of such states in time to come. Immediate action is chosen in view of an imagined sequel, a portion of history envisaged as able to follow this immediate step and unable, in a desired form, to follow rival available immediate steps. The present constrains the future, but the envisaged remote future influences and shapes the immediate future.

Do economists, then, concern themselves with such speculations or express themselves in such terms? I have tried, above, to give warning that these passages express a personal vision. Yet the work of the Stockholm School in the late 1920s and early 1930s of which Brinley Thomas brought news to L.S.E. in 1935 after his year in Sweden, and the work of Maynard Keynes in his *Treatise on Money*, where he independently invented and used what is in effect an *ex ante ex post* distinction and method, give some warrant for pursuing the *matter of time* with temerity, rather than reject it as no concern of economists, as seems the agreed posture of many of the most eminent theoreticians in these latter days.

On his return from Sweden, Brinley Thomas in the Spring Term of 1935 at L.S.E. gave a course of lectures on the new adventures of thought of Wicksell's successors, most especially Erik Lindahl and Gunnar Myrdal. His class was small (half-a-dozen or so). I know the name of only one other member of it besides myself. He and I sat together close to Brinley's lectern, scribbling madly to keep pace with an utterance thrilling but Delphic, which required the utmost concentrated attention to grasp and to write down. Once my companion, glancing at my notes, saw there a gap deliberately left, corresponding to a similar gap in his own notes, and ventured to ask the lecturer to clarify the point. This minute incident is a measure of our engagement in the theme and of its difficulty. (The particular subject was, at that moment, Myrdal's discussion of the incentive to invest.) There was a magic, not only in the ideas but in the vessel of speech which conveyed them. Brinley Thomas's ascendancy flows not from mere lucidity and clever dissection of his matter. Many lecturers have such a gift. Far beyond this, there is something unanalysable, something vatic and inspired, in his presentation of a subject which in his mouth is at the opposite pole from its traditional dismalness:

Favete linguis. Carmina non prius audita
Musarum sacerdos virginibus puerisque canto.

he could have said with every authentic tone and ring of truth.

20 A Student's Pilgrimage

The Editor of this journal* long since invited me to give some account of my scholarly experience. At his renewed desire I shall try to trace the evolution of my thoughts over the exact half-century since my first article was published. But this will be the brief story of ideas, not, in the main, of personal events.

We read sometimes of *general ideas*, such as belong to no one compartment of knowledge or culture but underlie them all. In that perspective, I think that all creative endeavours, of the poet, the painter, the symphonist, the mathematician, and even of the far-scanning business man, are informed by a single elusive but powerful urge, which we must call the desire to achieve beauty. All these various types of human individual are *dreamers*. 'Behold, this dreamer cometh'. The man thus spoken of is the hero of the greatest success-story in human annals, the rescued waif in his coat 'of many colours', who became the Prime Minister of his adopted land. History as it condenses from the void of time-to-come is the mutual entangling of individual dreams. Since business life lies near the heart of general history, it too must share this character of a textile fabric of imagined things, changing as they are actualised. This, then, is the phenomenon that economists undertake to study. Is my suggestion here a paradox and a Quixotry? It is the view of things that long thoughts have brought me to.

Elizabeth Bowen in one of her novels has a sentence which can be a wonderful solvent of regret: 'Chance is better than choice, it is more lordly. Chance is God, choice is man.' It was no deliberate choice of mine which led to my becoming a humble clerk (at first, a mere office-boy) in a bank at the age of seventeen. It was then, however, that I started to read economics as a likely path to lead sometime to a university degree; a path suggested by the nature of the bank's business. As a child I had at first only one playmate, my father, a mathematician. Thus early I breathed a little mathematical ozone. I told the manager of the bank of my ambition, and this kindly and enlightened man allowed me an hour in the middle of each day for study. (It would have been otherwise impossible: my work seldom

* The *Banca Nazionale del Lavoro Quarterly Review*. – Ed.

ended before seven in the evening: this was before the days of xerox copiers.)

The next piece of good furtune, somewhat disguised, was a period of ten years when low vitality was improved by a largely outdoor life as a schoolmaster. I took up again my solitary studies. A book by J. A. Hobson had the excitement of a detective story, the tracking down of the cause of unemployment. Then, in 1931, I received the 'sealed orders' for my career, in two momentous books: *A Treatise on Money* by John Maynard Keynes (whom my father had coached in mathematics for the scholarship which took Keynes to Eton) and *Prices and Production* by Friedrich A. von Hayek. In these books I embarked on a thrilling voyage. The genial, brilliant and at times paradoxical *Treatise* gave me the feel and vision of a world of scholar discourse and debate, relaxed, Olympian, intoxicating. *Prices and Production*, which I read next, brought an extra, astonishing excitement. A diagram which I had invented for myself, to illustrate Keynes's rudimentary account of the Austrian theory of capital (in the *Treatise*, volume two) suddenly appeared before my eyes in print, in Hayek's book, the rising columnar representation of the time-structure of production. At this moment there began, in various journals, the debate between the two writers, with Frank Knight as a third contender. The torrent of ideas swirled and swept around me. My voyage had begun.

* * *

If it was Chance, whatever that may be, that steered me to economics, Chance was kind to me. For it is a field of study which gives scope for many kinds of aptitude, and even distinctly favours versatility rather than high exclusive proficiency in one. If mathematical conceptions are exciting and congenial, so will economic theory be. There is nowadays a movement of thought which would like to persuade itself that mathematics, the apotheosis of reason and certainty, can discover a new language or notation for describing the process of original thought, the business of exploiting the unknown by untrammelled invention. I cannot doubt that a peculiarly felicitous notation has sometimes exhibited suggestive powers amounting almost to being able to 'think for itself'. Who shall say what paradoxical powers mathematics may bring forth? Yet it is difficult to banish the suspicion that system and freedom have an ultimate mutual intolerance. Few creative mathematicians until recently have concerned themselves with economics, though some have given indispensable, if posthumous, help. Where would the 'adding-up problem' of factor-shares be, without Euler? or where, the ingenious beauty of Leontief's *Tableau Economique*, without Arthur Cayley? But economics is about human affairs, about history-in-the-making, and to understand emergent history we turn to history already made. The nature of history is the nature of humanity. And economics, like every other scholarly involvement, is an art-form. 'Polymath' is not always a polite appellation. But the economist needs to be a great enjoyer of ideas and a connoisseur of their means of expression, a daring sculptor of argument, an eclectic and sometimes an heresiarch.

Agatha Christie has told us that she made up her plots while standing at the kitchen sink. I am in good company, for it was amongst the vapours which there envelop one that I came to the decisive conviction that probability cannot serve the ultimate business of choice. Uncertainty, I thought, is surely not a pyramid of clustering hypotheses each 'partly' believed in, but a wide-spreading plain where things widely unlike each other all claim to be *possible*. What gives an hypothesis the entrée to the counsels of the mind is not the being believed in, but the *not being disbelieved in*. A 'mathematical expectation', it seems to me, is an adding together of mutual exclusives. Does that make sense? Only if every one of those mutual exclusives is going to make its appearance, more or less *often*, in a far-stretching series of trials of some system capable of only restricted variation. When such a series of trials is in contemplation, and when an extensive series has already been performed with that same system, the recorded frequencies of that past series may legitimately be looked upon as *knowledge*, in some practical sense, about the outcome of the contemplated series *as a whole*. But where there is knowledge there is not uncertainty. Uncertainty, *unknowledge*, is what confronts the chooser of action when his act of choice is going to be *once-for-all*, when it is going to be crucial, when it is going to be an experiment the making of which will *destroy the possibility* of ever making that experiment again. In such a case we cannot say what *will* happen, even if we only claim to say it half-heartedly, as a 'probability'. We can only attain some notion of the kinds of thing that *can* happen.

It was, I think, Jacobi who pointed out that in mathematics a problem can sometimes be solved by inverting it. In urging that the meaningful question about rival, mutually exclusive, suggested answers to some enigma is not whether each of these answers is probable, but whether it is possible, I am in some sense proposing to invert the orthodox conception. For we can treat *perfect adjudged possibility* as entire *absence of disbelief*. The zero of our scale of epistemic standing will represent zero disbelief. Increasing distances along this scale from this zero point will stand for higher and higher degrees of disbelief. Disbelief will reach an absolute maximum at a level standing for *non-possibility*.

These ideas are exploited in the notion of focus-points. A sequel imagined for some feasible action must be assessed by the action-chooser in two respects, its *desiredness* (or counter-desiredness) and its *possibleness*. If he confines himself to imagined sequels to whose actualisation he can discern no obstacle (that is to say, sequels which seem perfectly, and therefore *equally*, possible) it is only the most and the least desired of these sequels imagined for a particular action, that need concern him. For it is these which, by themselves, constitute the adjudged potential of the action in question. (I draw attention to this last sentence, and to its dependence on the stipulation of equality of possibleness of the rival imagined sequels.) In order to compare two feasible actions and decide upon one of them, the chooser need only ask himself whether the extra desiredness of one of them is or is not sufficient to outweigh the lesser counter-desiredness of the other.

If, rather than confine himself to hypothetical sequels which he judges to be perfectly possible (ones, that is, to which he can discern no obstacle) he looks to sequels whose extra desiredness or counter-desiredness is made accessible by the acceptance of a less-than-perfect adjudged possibility, the effective 'best' and 'worst' results of the action in question will be located where increasing disbelief just cancels increasing desiredness or counter-desiredness. I have been accustomed to speak of the combined moral effect of *desiredness* and *disbelief*, when their respective degrees are functions of each other, as *ascendancy*. Then we can say that the potential of any feasible action will be represented, in the thought of the action-chooser, by the two constrained maxima of ascendancy.

A span of forty years divides a day in 1937 when the notion of *potential surprise* presented itself to me as a means of graduating the epistemic interval between acceptance and rejection of an hypothesis, from a day in April 1977 when I finished writing *Imagination and the Nature of Choice*. In that span my scheme of thought was enriched but not essentially changed.

To invert the graduation of the epistemic interval by conceiving the interval in terms of *disbelief*, and in especial by expressing the highest degree of acceptance of an hypothesis as zero disbelief or perfect adjudged possibility is to attain a vital end: it is to liberate the business of assigning degrees of epistemic standing from being a *distribution* of a fixed quantity. When a list of hypothetical answers to some question is taken to be complete and exhaustive, we are thereby taking it as *certain* that the truth lies with one or other of these answers. To assign numerical probabilities to the answers in the list is to *distribute* amongst them shares of certainty. It is convenient to represent certainty by the numeral *one*, and numerical probabilities are consequently represented by proper fractions. If now some revision of knowledge leads to an augmentation of the list of hypotheses, it will be necessary to transfer some probability away from members of the initial list to the new members. But why should the acceptability of an hypothesis be a function of the number of its rivals?

What, indeed, is a *sharing of certainty*? What does the assigning of a share of certainty tell us? Can it tell us, in reference to some unique, crucial and self-destructive experiment, about to be made at a proper-named point of the calendar, that this experiment *will* have such-and-such a result? No. Can it tell us that the experiment will *not* have such-and-such a result? No. Then what does it tell us? There is a more deadly matter to be confronted. If the list of plural rival hypotheses is admitted to be liable to extension, to augmentation by the formulation of extra hypotheses, probabilities cannot meaningfully be assigned to the extant members of the list. For it will be obligatory to make the list of hypotheses formally comprehensive by including a *residual hypothesis*, a Pandora's box of contents unknown in character and number. Finally we must ask, why should the epistemic standing of any one hypothesis depend upon, and vary with, the number of its discerned rivals?

The need and the nature of a non-distributional uncertainty-variable was proposed in an article called 'Expectations and Employment' in the *Economic Journal* of September 1939. Other articles followed, and in 1949 the construction which emerged from them was presented, with some of its implications and suggestions, in my *Expectation in Economics*, published by the Cambridge University Press. The referee who recommended the publication of my manuscript was Sir Austin Robinson, to whom I am thus eternally indebted.

Amongst the articles referred to above was one called 'A Theory of Investment Decisions'. It appeared in the original series of *Oxford Economic Papers* (number 6) in April 1942. A few days after its publication I received from Sir Roy Harrod a letter which gave me an immense surge of encouragement and happiness. That article in its opening sentence introduced a word which has become the central term of my conception of the business of choice, a business which, as I have become profoundly convinced, is in the first place a work of *imagination*. The choosables must be imagined, originated, created, by the chooser himself. They are thoughts, figments. Their nature of invented and *endlessly inventable* things profoundly affects the required character of a means of graduating the epistemic interval which we may conceive to distance from each other the acceptance and the rejection of an hypothesis. For their endless potential proliferation implies that a distributional variable must be wholly inappropriate.

For if choosable courses of action are inventable *ad libitum* by every individual possessor of resources, the sequel of any individual's inceptive use of his resources will be affected, in ways that are *logically* unforeknowable, by the choices that others will make in time-to-come. To use, as I have, the word *logically* in this connection is to give to the word *invent* the meaning of autonomous creation. It is to assume that some thoughts can be in some respects exempt from governance by antecedents, that they can in these respects be uncaused. Such an assumption seems to me indispensable, if we are to claim to be, in a fundamental sense, makers of our own history.

Chance (Elisabeth Bowen saves us so much argument) brought me into a live university *milieu* for the first time on the first day of 1935. Economic theory was in those years being swept by a tidal wave of innovation. Seeds sown long since by Cournot and Marshall had suddenly sprung up into the harvest of imperfect, or monopolistic, competition. A glamorous (I use the word responsibly) theory of money had come into view in Keynes's *Treatise*, and the great pit of business depression into which the world had plunged was the occasion for Hayek's seductively enigmatic *Prices and Production*. Gunnar Myrdal by the dramatic use of a legal term had compelled economists to recognise *explicitly* that action is the fruit of expectation. Keynes's 'Fundamental Equations' of the *Treatise on Money* depended, in some sense unwittingly, on just such recognition. In 1935 the economic air was vibrant with these ideas.

Chance brought me to the London School of Economics at the moment when Hayek was reforming and reformulating Böhm-Bawerk's theory of capital; when Hicks was (in that very term) going to propound the production plan and the role played in it by the rate of interest; when Brinley Thomas (in that very term) was going to tell a minute class how the seeds sown by Wicksell were blossoming in the work of Lindahl and Myrdal; and when rumours about the book that Keynes was writing were drifting up from Cambridge. Thus by a blessing of chance I entered the LSE to begin my PhD dissertation at an electric moment of charged and tingling intellectual excitement.

The wheel which began to turn in 1931, when I read *Prices and Production* for the first of many times, seemed to come full circle in 1976, when I had the honour and astonished happiness of accompanying Professor Hayek on a lecture tour in Spain. Did surging inflation at that time vindicate the theme of *Prices and Production*?

The Austrian theory of capital supposes that *lapse of time* is in itself a factor of production which, if its quantity is increased, allows a more far-reaching division of labour and thus secures a greater output from given efforts of nature and men. Thus it earns its reward in the form of an interest rate. Such a reward, it was thought (mistakenly, in my view, except in regard to the *building-up* of a process of production) was called for because lapse of time in production would engender impatience in those engaged in production, who were waiting to enjoy the fruits of their work. Lapse of time would accordingly be maintained at that extent where a small increase would secure extra output only just sufficient to compensate for the extra delay. (My objection here is that no delay is involved once the process is on stream, for then yesterday's output is ready to be consumed today.) In thus accounting for an interest rate during a process of building-up of production, the Austrian theory appealed to a *balance at the margin* between the cost and reward of a flow of saving and investment. If so, how could there be, as supposed in the *Treatise on Money*, and fleetingly also on page 21, lines 10–18, of the *General Theory*, a divergence between desired saving and desired investment?

The purpose of the Austrian theory of capital is to account for the existence and the level of a rate of interest. It does so by supposing that the desired flow of saving and the desired flow of investment (making of facilities for production) mutually determine each other. If so, how can desired saving and desired investment in productive facilities diverge from each other and account for unemployment? In order to account for the possibility of massive general unemployment, Keynes needed to invent a new theory of the interest rate. The new theory was Keynes's greatest technical innovation.

Liquidity preference is in itself almost an epitome of Keynes's theory of money and employment. Resources are liquid when they do not depend, for the retention of their value, on the presence and persistence of circumstances confined within a narrow range of variation. Resources are liquid when they are uncommitted to a highly specialised venture. But production is the activity of specialising materials and means to particular technical or aesthetic purposes. There is a conflict between the retention of liquidity and the giving of employment. The businessman desires liquidity, and refrains from giving employment, when he feels that he cannot exclude the possibility of disastrous losses as the sequel of any available venture. These ideas are the burden of chapter 17 of the *General Theory of Employment, Interest and Money*, a chapter where Keynes seeks the utmost concise simplicity in stating the ultimate foundations of the theory of employment. But this statement is too general and abstract. It becomes dramatic and vivid when expressed in the mundane business vocabulary of money, bonds, interest rates, equity shares and the tangible productive facilities of an enterprise. Bonds and shares are *durable*. Their market value today therefore depends on ideas of what will be their market value next week, next month, next year. They are *speculative* assets. The long-term rate of interest can be roughly expressed as the market price of a bond with a long time to maturity, divided into its fixed annual coupon. But its price is determined, from hour to hour, in a speculative market, by the shifting inter-active views and relative weight of the Bulls and Bears whose role was invoked by Keynes in the *Treatise on Money*.

It was the release of the interest rate from the servitude of its role in a general equilibrium which had for me the most powerful practical appeal. But this release was an aspect of something more encompassing and momentous, the acknowledgement that, as I would put it, business is the pursuit of possibilities. Possibilities are thoughts, and they are bound up in bundles each containing good and bad together. Such a bundle (I am here still describing my own scheme) has to be bought as a whole, you cannot have the good possibilities without the bad. Keynes explained massive general unemployment as the consequence of a self-reinforcing spasm of uncertainty, a sentiment which the nature of the human predicament renders from time to time inevitable. In thus explaining it, he explicitly and uncompromisingly rejected the expression, let alone the elimination, of uncertainty by means of objective 'probability'. The most striking thing of all about this abnegation is the absence, from Keynes's writing, of anything to fill the gap left by the rejection of probability. The 'inducement to invest' in chapter 12 of the *General Theory* is not the upshot of research and calculation, it is 'animal spirits'. It is a clear-cut mistake, as Keynes himself explicitly made clear, to identify the Keynes of the *Treatise on Probability* with the Keynes of the *General Theory*.

* * *

1935 for me was a seething cauldron of ideas. Its heady fumes inspired a thrilling plan. Keynes's *General Theory* cried out, it seemed to me, to be interpreted in Myrdal's terms. I still had a year of my Leverhulme scholarship to run. I had a supervisor, Professor Hayek, of extreme enlightened generosity. I embarked on my plan. My dissertation was completed in February 1937 and polished in the early morning hours of each day during that spring and early summer. It was shown to Sir Henry Phelps Brown (for whom I worked during the body of the day as his research assistant) and by him to James Meade, and was published by the Oxford University Press in May 1938 as *Expectations, Investment and Income*. It was published in a second edition, with a long additional prefatory chapter, just thirty years later, in 1968, this time by the Clarendon Press. When an author becomes an Oxford graduate (as I had by acquiring an Oxford D.Phil) the Oxford University Press undergoes in his regard a mysterious transformation, and while the dignified building in Walton Street remains unchanged in outward appearance, it is for him thereafter the Clarendon Press.

In this first book already, *expectation* was the informing notion and basic theme. For already it was overwhelmingly evident to me that if economics is the endeavour to understand one broad source and aspect of human conduct, it is concerned with *thoughts about time to come*.

In that book I was far from any full conception of the depth and reach of ideas, the involvement with the ultimate philosophical enigmas, which inhere in the term *expectation*. Expectation is imagination, the *originative* gift, the gift which burns, if with a more dazzling light, in the thoughts of the poet, the symphonist, the mathematician. Expectation is momentous. It is the source of human history.

Expectation is necessarily, in the first place, imagination. But plainly it is not unconstrained figment. It is *critical* imagination limiting its creation of hypothetical sequels of any specified course of action, rendered feasible by the individual's possessed resources, to what is free from discernible obstruction. It is only sequels *deemed possible* that can bear upon the business of choice. But though the sequels imagined, originated, for any feasible action must thus lie within bounds of possibility, they are not, in their nature, limited in number. Since such creation of a skein of rival hypotheses takes time, this process will be somewhere arrested by a deadline, and the skein will remain incomplete and uncompleteable. Expectation thus envisaged is inherently, essentially alien to the purpose of providing a single-number valuation of an investment project, a plan for constructing a specialised production facility looking to many years of useful life. Expectation thus envisaged insists on the mutual unlikeness, the width of qualitative difference, of sequels which are, to the best understanding and insight of the investor, equally possible. Such expectation must be quite differently exploited and employed from the mode of use of the 'mathematical expectation' or a single-number forecast. What I conceive to be its proper use has been the theme of many books, from *Expectation in Economics* of 1949 with its references to articles from 1939 onwards, through *Time in Economics* (North Holland) containing my Professor F. de Vries Lectures of 1957, *Expectation, Enterprise and Profit* of 1970 and others, to what I hope is a rounded statement in *Imagination and the Nature of Choice* published by the Edinburgh University Press in 1979.

* * *

I think there are two kinds of economics. One of them aims at precision, rigour, tidiness and the formulation of principles which will be permanently valid: an economic science. The other is, if you like, rhetorical. This word is often used disparagingly, but that is a modern unscholarly abuse. The rhetorician employs reason and appeals to logic, but he is a user of language at its full compass, where words are fingers touching the keyboard of a hearer's mind. I do not believe that human affairs can be exhibited as the infallible and invariable working of a closed and permanent system.

Notes and References

2 Means and Meaning in Economic Theory

1. N. Georgescu-Roegen, *Analytical Economics, Part I Some Orientation Issues in Economics* (Harvard University Press; London: Oxford University Press, 1966).
2. See *Decision, Order and Time*, 2nd edn, (Cambridge University Press, 1969) pp. 287–91; *Epistemics and Economics* (Cambridge University Press, 1972) pp. 181–4; *Expectation, Enterprise and Profit* (London: Allen & Unwin, 1970) pp. 149–51.

4 Cantillon Far Ahead of his Time

1. A. Coddington, *Varieties of Keynesianism*. Thames Papers in Political Economy, Spring 1976 (London: Thames Polytechnic).
2. J. R. Hicks, 'A Suggestion for Simplifying the Theory of Money' *Economica* new series, vol. 2, no. 5, February 1935, pp. 1–19.

6 Harrod as Economist

1. P. Sraffa, 'The Laws of Returns under Competitive Conditions' *Economic Journal* vol 36, December 1926, pp. 535–550.
2. This dilemma, so called by Marshall (*Principles*, eighth edition, footnote to p. 459), has been noted by Cournot in 1838.
3. R. F. Harrod, 'Notes on Supply', *Economic Journal*, vol 40, June 1930, pp. 232–41.
4. A. Cournot, *Recherches sur les principes mathématiques de la théorie des richesses* 1838.

7 Levels of Simplicity in Keynes's Theory of Money and Employment

1. G. L. S. Shackle, 'Interest Rates and the Pace of Investment' *Economic Journal*, vol 56, no. 221, March 1946, pp. 1–17, reprinted in G. L. S. Shackle, *Uncertainty in Economics and other Reflections* (Cambridge: Cambridge University Press, 1955), pp. 128–44.

8 On Hicks's *Causality in Economics*

1. Sir John Hicks, *Causality in Economics* (Oxford: Basil Blackwell, 1979).
2. G. L. S. Shackle, *A Scheme of Economic Theory* (Cambridge: Cambridge University Press, 1965) Preface and Introduction.

3. A. Marshall, *Principles of Economics* Preface to the 8th edition, reprinted in the 9th (variorum) edition edited by C. W. Guillebaud, p. 15, second paragraph (London: Macmillan, 1951).
4. G. L. S. Shackle, *The Years of High Theory*, p. 228, p. 247, and *Epistemics and Economics*, pp. 226–28.
5. I thought to redress, so far as one man might, the profession's lack of appreciation of Harrod's power and quality as a thinker, in my *The Years of High Theory* (Cambridge University Press, 1967) Chapter 16. He had a gift of dramatic and surprising confrontations of one concept with another, to produce remarkable theorems.
6. R. F. Kahn, 'The Relation of Home Investment to Unemployment', *Economic Journal*, vol. 41, no. 162, June 1931, pp. 173–198.
7. A review is not the place to enlarge on one's own ideas. It may be allowable for me to list some places where I have given an account of them:
   Expectation in Economics (Cambridge: Cambridge University Press, 1949, 1952).
   Time in Economics (Amsterdam: North-Holland Publ. Co., 1958).
   Decision, Order and Time in Human Affairs (Cambridge: Cambridge University Press, 1961, 1969).
   Expectation, Enterprise and Profit (London: George Allen & Unwin, 1970).
   Epistemics and Economics (Cambridge: Cambridge University Press, 1972).
   Imagination and the Nature of Choice (Edinburgh: Edinburgh University Press, 1979).
8. J. M. Keynes, *A Treatise on Probability* (London: Macmillan, 1921) p. 4.

11 Marginalism: the Harvest

1. J. R. Hicks, 'A Suggestion for Simplifying the Theory of Money', *Economica*, new series, vol. 2, no. 5, February 1935, pp. 1–19.
2. The precautionary motive could be satisfied by holding nonliquid assets, were it not for the danger of their depreciating in money terms in the meantime. But such a fear of capital loss is simply the speculative motive.

12 New Tracks for Economic Theory, 1926–1939

1. The title given by Professor Lord Kahn to his translation of Knut Wicksell's *Geldzins und Güterpreise*.
2. Hodge, 1939.

13 Hayek as Economist

1. *Prices and Production* (London: Routledge & Kegan Paul, 1931); 2nd edn., 1935).

2. K. Popper and J. Eccles, *The Self and Its Brain* (Berlin: Springer, 1977).
3. *The Constitution of Liberty* (London: Routledge & Kegan Paul, 1960).
4. *Law, Legislation and Liberty* (London: Routledge & Kegan Paul, Vol. I, 1973; Vol. II, 1976; Vol. III, 1979).
5. See note 1 above.
6. *Profits, Interest and Investment* (London: Routledge & Kegan Paul, 1939).
7. K. Wicksell, *Geldzins und Güterpreise* (Vienna: Fischer, 1898).
8. K. Wicksell, *Lectures on Political Economy* (London: Routledge & Kegan Paul, 1934).
9. 'Economics and Knowledge', *Economica*, new series, vol. 4, 1937, pp. 33–54 reprinted as Chapter 2 of *Individualism and Economic Order* (London: Routledge & Kegan Paul, 1949).
10. *The Pure Theory of Capital* (London: Routledge & Kegan Paul, 1941).
11. J. M. Keynes, *The General Theory of Employment, Interest, and Money* (London: Macmillan, 1936).
12. *Beiträge zur Geldtheorie* (Vienna: Fischer, 1933). Myrdal's essay was called 'Der Gleichgewichtsbegriff als Hilfsmittel in der geldtheoretischen Analyse'.
13. See note 9 above.
14. See note 9 above.
15. Hayek adopts this theme and expression of Sir Karl Popper's in a footnote, in place of 'verification' in the text.
16. *The Counter-Revolution of Science* (New York: The Free Press of Glencoe, 1955).

14 Keynes the Meeting-point of History and Thought

1. *Expectations, Investment and Income* (Oxford: Clarendon Press, 1938; Second Edition, 1968).

15 Sir John Hicks's 'IS–LM: an explanation': a Comment

1. A. Coddington, 'Keynesian Economics: The Search for First Principles', *Journal of Economic Literature*, vol. 14, no. 4, December 1976, pp. 1258–1273.

16 *Controlling Industrial Economies*: A Review Article

1. Stephen F. Frowen (ed.), *Controlling Industrial Economies* Essays in Honour of Christopher Thomas Saunders (London: Macmillan, 1983).

17 Markets, Entrepreneurs and Liberty: A Review Article

1. W. D. Reekie, *Markets, Entrepreneurs and Liberty: An Austrian View of Capitalism* (Brighton: Wheatsheaf Books, Harvester Press Publishing Group, 1984).

19 News from Sweden

1. G. Myrdal, *Monetary Equilibrium* (Hodge, 1939), p. 47.
2. My discussion of Lindahl's proposal is in G. L. S. Shackle, *Epistemics and Economics* (Cambridge: Cambridge University Press, 1972), pp. 66–68.

Index of Names

Index of Subjects